The Roots of Urba

Related Titles of Interest

BENYON, J.
Scarman and After: Essays Reflecting on Lord Scarman's Report, the Riots and their Aftermath

BENYON, J. & BOURN, C.
The Police: Powers, Procedures and Proprieties

BRYANT, B. & BRYANT, R.
Change and Conflict: A Study of Community Work in Glasgow

HERFUTH, M. & HOGEWEG DE HAART, H.
Social Integration of Migrant Workers and Other Ethnic Minorities

HOWITT, D.
The Mass Media and Social Problems

MILES, I. & IRVINE, J.
The Poverty of Progress: Changing Ways of Life in Industrial Societies

WHITE FRANKLIN, A.
Family Matters: Perspectives on the Family and Social Policy

The Roots of Urban Unrest

Edited by

JOHN BENYON

and

JOHN SOLOMOS

PERGAMON PRESS

OXFORD · NEW YORK · BEIJING · FRANKFURT
SAO PAULO · SYDNEY · TOKYO · TORONTO

U.K.	Pergamon Press, Headington Hill Hall, Oxford OX3 0BW, England
U.S.A	Pergamon Press, Maxwell House, Fairview Park, Elmsford, New York 10523, U.S.A.
PEOPLE'S REPUBLIC OF CHINA	Pergamon Press, Qianmen Hotel, Beijing, People's Republic of China
FEDERAL REPUBLIC OF GERMANY	Pergamon Press, Hammerweg 6, D–6242 Kronberg, Federal Republic of Germany
BRAZIL	Pergamon Editora, Rua Eça de Queiros, 346, CEP 04011 Paraiso, São Paulo, Brazil
AUSTRALIA	Pergamon Press Australia, P.O. Box 544, Potts Point, N.S.W. 2011, Australia
JAPAN	Pergamon Press, 8th Floor, Matsuoka Central Building, 1–7–1 Nishishinjuku, Shinjuku-ku, Tokyo 160, Japan
CANADA	Pergamon Press Canada, Suite, 271 No. 253 College Street, Toronto, Ontario Canada M5T 1R5

First edition 1987

Library of Congress Cataloging in Publication Data
The Roots of urban unrest.
Papers presented at a conference, organized by the Continuing Education Unit, Dept. of Adult Education, University of Leicester and the Centre for Research in Ethnic Relations, University of Warwick, held at the University of Warwick, 1986.
Bibliography: p.
Includes index.
1. Riots—Congresses. 2. Race relations—Congresses.
3. Police—Congresses. 4. Riots—Great Britain—Congresses.
5. Great Britain—Race relations—Congresses.
6. Police—Great Britain—Congresses. I. Benyon, John.
II. Solomos, John. III. University of Leicester.
Continuing Education Unit. IV. University of Warwick.
Centre for Research in Ethnic Relations.
HM281.R63 1987   303.6'23'0941   87–8269

British Library Cataloguing in Publication Data

The Roots of urban unrest.
1. Cities and towns—Great Britain
2. Social problems 3. Great Britain
Social conditions—1945–
I. Benyon, John II. Solomos, John
361.1'0941   HT133

ISBN 0-08-035840-3 (Hardcover)
ISBN 0-08-035839-X (Flexicover)

Printed in Great Britain by A. Wheaton & Co. Ltd., Exeter

For

LOUIE and **DON BENYON**

and

NICOLAS and **KYRIACOU SOLOMOU**

Civil dissension is a viperous worm
That gnaws the bowels of the commonwealth

WILLIAM SHAKESPEARE, *Henry VI*, Part I

It is not what a man outwardly has or wants that constitutes the happiness or misery of him. Nakedness, hunger, distress of all kinds, death itself have been cheerfully suffered when the heart was right. It is the feeling of injustice that is insupportable to all men . . . No man can bear it or ought to bear it.

THOMAS CARLYLE, *Chartism*

Contents

Part 3   Policing and Urban Unrest

Part 4   Unemployment, Racial Disadvantage and the Inner City

Part 5   The Quest for Social Justice

Preface

A principal function of the state is to regulate conflict and maintain order in society. The British state is widely regarded as having been successful in achieving these ends in the past: British historical development is frequently characterised as one of gradual evolution and relatively peaceful transition from one era to the next. However, even cursory examination shows that this rosy picture is wide of the mark, for British history reveals many instances of bloody civil tumult and disorder. Nevertheless, the years 1945–1980 were notable for the relative public tranquillity in British cities. As the editors point out in Chapter 1, there were of course many instances of violence but there were no riots in British cities to compare with those, for example, in the 1930s — or with those that have occurred in the 1980s.

It is little wonder, then, that people both in Britain and abroad were shocked by the urban unrest which occurred in 1980, 1981, 1985 and, on a much more limited scale, in 1986. What had gone wrong? Why were young people throwing petrol bombs on the streets of London, Birmingham, Liverpool and elsewhere? These were the sort of questions understandably being asked by members of the public. 'Is this really Britain?' asked many of the daily newspapers, which then proceeded to pontificate on the decline in respect for authority and the rule of law, and on the prevalence of agitators and conspirators — apparently, or perhaps wilfully, oblivious to the fundamental causes of civil disorder.

To the more discerning commentators the urban disorders in England highlighted the complex changes taking place in the economic, social, cultural and political institutions of the inner cities. Attention was focused on the changing nature of policing policies and dilemmas in these communities, and on police methods. However, much of the public discussion in the aftermath of the unrest tended to concentrate on immediate causes of events in particular localities, and on short-term remedies.

In an attempt to dig deeper into the causes of the urban unrest a conference was held at the University of Warwick in 1986. It was organised by the Continuing Education Unit in the Department of Adult Education at the University of Leicester and the Centre for Research in Ethnic Relations at the University of Warwick. The intention was to provide an opportunity to examine issues which underlie urban unrest, such as policing, unemployment, racial disadvantage and discrimination, and political powerlessness. These were the principal issues which Lord Scarman identified in *The Brixton Disorders* (Cmnd. 8427) published in

November 1981. Much of the conference was under his distinguished chairmanship, and his reflections on the day's proceedings form Chapter 15 in this volume.

The aim of the conference was thus to bring together people, with first-hand knowledge, to analyse the root causes which underlie urban unrest. In addition, and very importantly, the proceedings were intended to consider how the British disorders of the 1980s should be set in an historical and comparative framework; what action has been taken since the riots of 1981; what action needs to be taken to cure the current causes of unrest; and what the prospects are for the future. As well as the notable British practitioners and academics, the conference was fortunate to have present two eminent American visitors, who were able to provide a vital comparative dimension.

The conference was organised around four themes, and these constitute Parts 2, 3, 4 and 6 in this book. The first theme is concerned with the experiences and explanations of unrest in Britain and the United States, while the second focuses on policing methods and dilemmas, and disorder. The third theme concentrates on unemployment, racial disadvantage and unrest, while the final focus is on possible remedies and future prospects. The edited proceedings of the conference discussions have also been included in the volume (Chapters 8, 14 and 18), as many important contributions were made from the floor by people with first-hand experience of the key issues. Part 5 of the book consists of Lord Scarman's reflections on the conference, and Parts 1 and 7, contributed by the editors, seek to explore further some of the points raised in the conference.

Our deep thanks are due to all those who attended the conference, and who helped to make the discussions so lively and stimulating, and we are especially grateful to the authors of the chapters which follow. We would particularly like to thank Lord Scarman and Ann Dummett for chairing the proceedings, and also Devon Thomas and George Greaves for substituting for Paul Boateng, who was forced to withdraw from the conference at a very late stage because of illness. The Economic and Social Research Council helped to finance the conference, and we gratefully acknowledge this support, and we would like to thank Neil Price of the ESRC for his help.

It is a pleasure to pay tribute to all those at the University of Warwick who took part in the organisation of the conference. In particular we would like to thank Charlotte Wellington, the Administrative Officer in the Centre for Research in Ethnic Relations, and Professor Robin Cohen, Director of the Centre. We would also like to thank those in the Department of Adult Education at the University of Leicester, especially Colin Bourn, Director of the Continuing Education Unit, and John Cunningham, the Department's Secretary. Our appreciation is also due to Beryl Penny, Wyn Rutt and Maureen Cottrell, who transcribed the conference proceedings, and above all to Kerry York who typed the edited and revised chapters, offered perceptive comments about the book and produced the final typescript. We are also very grateful to Grace Belfiore, and to her colleagues at Pergamon Press, for support and valuable advice on the production of the book.

Finally, we would like to thank our respective families and friends for their support, advice and forbearance while we have been working on the manuscript.

14 February 1987

JOHN BENYON
Leicester

JOHN SOLOMOS
Birmingham

University of Warwick
Centre for Research in Ethnic Relations

Executive Director: PROFESSOR ROBIN COHEN
Research Professor and Associate Director: JOHN REX

The Centre for Research in Ethnic Relations was reconstituted as a Designated Research Centre, funded by the Economic and Social Research Council, at the University of Warwick in Coventry in October 1984. The Centre succeeds the Research Unit on Ethnic Relations at the University of Aston in Birmingham and will continue the work of the Unit in promoting advanced study and research in the field of race and ethnic relations. Its objects include:

- Undertaking long-term multi-disciplinary research in ethnic relations.
- Disseminating research results in academic and policy-making circles, and where relevant, to a wider audience including the media and community organisations.
- Providing training and teaching in the field of race and ethnic relations, through a Masters level course, seminars and public lectures, and short courses, as appropriate.
- Acting as a national and international focus for research in the field of race and ethnic relations by the provision of a research and information base for visitors, enquiries and conferences.

University of Leicester
Continuing Education Unit

Director: COLIN BOURN

The Continuing Education Unit was established in the Department of Adult Education at the University of Leicester to bring together the University and the wider community through the provision of conferences, courses and publications.

The Unit offers a wide range of courses and seminars, and has particularly specialised in legal and social policy issues, computing and management skills, information technology and biotechnology.

In the legal and social policy field, the Unit has recently organised highly successful conferences on the Police and Criminal Evidence Act 1984, and the Prosecution of Offences Act. Other major events have included conferences on the Data Protection Act, proposals to alter the law on shop hours, competition policy, and the deregulation of opticians.

In 1982, the Unit organised a national weekend conference on the 1981 disorders, which involved twenty-three speakers addressing the issues raised by Lord Scarman in **The Brixton Disorders** (Cmnd 8427). An edited collection of essays, based on the conference proceedings, entitled **Scarman and After** was published by Pergamon Books in 1984. Three major conferences on the Police and Criminal Evidence Act 1984 resulted in another volume, published in 1986 by Pergamon Books, entitled **The Police: Powers, Procedures and Proprieties.**

The Contributors

John Benyon is Lecturer in Politics and Public Administration in the Departments of Adult Education and Politics at the University of Leicester. He is editor of *Scarman and After* (Pergamon, 1984) and coeditor of *The Police: Powers, Procedures and Proprieties* (Pergamon, 1986). His publications include *A Tale of Failure: Race and Policing*, and articles in *Public Administration, New Scientist, Local Government Studies, Social Studies Review* and *Parliamentary Affairs*.

John Clare was appointed the British Broadcasting Corporation's first Community Affairs Correspondent in 1977, and he has earned widespread recognition as a journalist in this field. Before moving to the BBC he worked for ITN, *The Times*, the *Daily Mirror* and *The Observer*. He witnessed many of the disorders in 1981 and 1985 at first hand, and an account of the events in Brixton in 1981 appears in *Scarman and After* (Pergamon, 1984).

Ann Dummett was Director of the Runnymede Trust from 1984 to 1986. She has been active in the field of race relations since the 1960s, and has worked for the Joint Council for the Welfare of Immigrants. Her research includes studies of British nationality and immigration law, and among her publications are *A Portrait of English Racism* (Penguin Books, 1973) and *Citizenship and Nationality* (Runnymede Trust, 1976).

George Greaves is Principal Community Relations Officer of the Council for Community Relations in Lambeth, and is a member of the Community Police Consultative Group for Lambeth which was established in 1982. He gave oral evidence to phase two of Lord Scarman's Inquiry. He contributed chapters to *Scarman and After* and *The Police: Powers, Procedures and Proprieties*.

Professor Stuart Hall holds the chair of Sociology at the Open University, and has written extensively on inner-city problems, policing and racial disadvantages and discrimination. He coedited *Resistance through Rituals* (Hutchinson, 1976), he is coauthor of *Policing the Crisis* (Macmillan, 1978) and he is author of *Drifting into a Law and Order Society* (Macmillan, 1980).

Ivan Henry is Director of the Handsworth Employment Scheme. While at the University of Warwick he conducted research for his doctorate into community politics in Handsworth. The title of his thesis was *The Growth of Corporate Black Identity among Afro-Caribbean People in Birmingham*, and he has written a number of articles on this and related topics.

Professor Martin Kilson holds a chair in Government at Harvard University. He has conducted research into African history and politics, and has authored and edited a number of books in this field including *The African Diaspora* (Harvard University Press, 1976). He has also studied many aspects of race relations and political change in the United States, and he coedited *Key Issues in the Afro-American Experience* (Harcourt Brace Janovich, 1971).

Herman Ouseley is Equal Opportunities Policy Coordinator for the Inner London Education Authority. Until Spring 1986 he was Assistant Chief Executive of the London Borough of Lambeth. He previously worked as Race Relations Adviser first to Lambeth Council, and then to the Greater London Council, and he coauthored *The System* (Runnymede Trust, 1981).

Usha Prashar is Director of the National Council for Voluntary Organisations (NCVO). Until 1986 she was a Research Fellow at the Policy Studies Institute, and before this she was Director of the Runnymede Trust. Her research has included studies of various aspects of racial disadvantage and discrimination, and her publications include a chapter in *Scarman and After* (Pergamon, 1984).

Professor John Rex is Research Professor in Ethnic Relations at the University of Warwick, and he has conducted extensive research in the field of race relations, including studies of Handsworth. Among his many books and publications are *Race, Community and Conflict* (Oxford University Press, 1967, with R. Moore), *Race Relations in Sociological Theory* (Weidenfeld and Nicolson, 1970), *Race, Colonialism and the City* (Routledge and Kegan Paul, 1973) and *Colonial Immigrants in a British City* (Routledge and Kegan Paul, 1979, with S. Tomlinson).

The Rt. Hon. Lord Scarman, OBE, was a Lord of Appeal in Ordinary from 1977 until 1986. He was Chairman of the Law Commission, 1965–1973, and he chaired the Tribunal of Inquiry into the violence and civil disturbances in Northern Ireland in August 1969. He conducted the inquiry into the 1974 Red Lion Square disorders (Cmnd. 5919) and 3 years later he chaired the Court of Inquiry into the Grunwick dispute

(Cmnd. 6922). In 1981 he conducted the inquiry into the Brixton riots, the report of which, *The Brixton Disorders 10–12 April 1981* (Cmnd. 8427), has provided the basis for so much of the subsequent debate about urban unrest in Britain in the 1980s. His books include *Law Reform: the New Pattern* (Routledge and Kegan Paul, 1968) and *English Law — the New Dimension* (Stevens, 1974).

David Smith is a Senior Fellow at the Policy Studies Institute, and has carried out extensive research into policing methods and problems, including the acclaimed research commissioned by the Metropolitan Police, published as *Police and People in London* (Policy Studies Institute, 1983). He is also the author of studies on racial disadvantage and unemployment, including *Racial Disadvantage in Britain* (Penguin, 1977).

John Solomos is a Research Fellow at the Centre for Research in Ethnic Relations at the University of Warwick. He is editor of *Migrant Workers in Metropolitan Cities*, and a contributor to *The Empire Strikes Back* (Hutchinson, 1982). He has written papers on the politics of black youth unemployment, race relations policies and theories of racism, and these have appeared in journals such as *Political Studies* and in collections such as *Race, Government and Politics in Britain* (Macmillan, 1986).

Devon Thomas works in the South Bank Inner City Centre, London, which he helped to establish to focus on the employment and economic needs of inner-city communities. He has lived in Brixton since his family arrived from Jamaica in the 1950s, and he was a prominent figure in the Brixton Defence Campaign which was set up to give support to those who were arrested, and to their families, during the events of 1981, and thereafter. He contributed a chapter to *Scarman and After* (Pergamon, 1984).

Professor Richard Thomas is Associate Professor of History and Urban Affairs at Michigan State University. He has studied the history and development of race relations in Detroit, and in the United States generally, and he has published many articles in this field. He is currently studying the evolution of political alliances involving black people and other groups.

Richard Wells is a Deputy Assistant Commissioner in the Metropolitan Police, and in September 1986 took charge of 7 Area (North West London). He was previously Director of Public Affairs at New Scotland Yard and before this he was a Commander at the Police Training School at Hendon. He joined the police after graduating from Oxford in 1962 and most of his 25 years have been spent in operational duties in various parts of London.

PART 1

Interpretations of Urban Unrest

CHAPTER 1

British urban unrest in the 1980s

JOHN BENYON and JOHN SOLOMOS

With hindsight, the second of April 1980 appears to have been a watershed in postwar politics in Britain. This was the night when smouldering unrest erupted in the St. Paul's District of Bristol. To most people in Britain the riot came as a complete surprise, although it had been predicted a year before by Ken Pryce.[1] At the time many commentators and politicians seemed to regard the Bristol eruption as a one-off event — a strange aberration in social behaviour.

Almost exactly a year later these complacent interpretations were rudely shattered. During the weekend of 10–12 April 1981 serious disorder in Brixton resulted in many injuries and widespread damage. On Saturday 11 April, during nearly 6 hours of violence, arson and looting, 279 police officers and at least 45 members of the public were injured, 61 private vehicles and 56 police vehicles were damaged or destroyed and 145 premises were damaged, 28 of them by fire.[2] Television cameras brought pictures of the rioting into the houses of millions of people, who saw for themselves the fury that had been unleashed.

Shock and surprise in 1981

What were the reactions of the British public? In the *Sunday Telegraph* Peregrine Worsthorne claimed that people felt rage and frustration[3] but Lord Scarman was probably nearer the mark when he described how 'the British people watched with horror and incredulity',[4] for the commonest view seems to have been one of shock and bewilderment.

The widespread surprise at the explosion of unrest was in many respects understandable. British cities have a long history of disorder, but in the period from 1945 until 1980 they were characterised by relative public tranquillity. During these 35 years there were, of course, many instances of violent behaviour and a number of 'moral panics', such as those over teddy boys in the 1950s and the mods and rockers in the 1960s.[5] In August 1958, racial attacks and anti-black riots occurred in Nottingham and north Kensington. The 1970s experienced great public concern over 'mugging' and also over football hooliganism,[6] and furthermore it was a decade when considerable anxiety was expressed over violent picketing, such as that at Saltley Coke Depot in February 1972 and at Grunwick Photographic Laboratories between August 1976 and autumn 1977.[7] However, from the end of the Second World War until 1980 there were no riots in British cities — as distinct from those in Northern Ireland — to compare with the unrest which occurred subsequently.

The outbreak of disorder in Bristol in April 1980 can thus be seen as a turning point, for since then urban unrest has erupted in many British cities. In July 1981, 3 months after the Brixton disorders, disturbances took place in many parts of the country. On Friday 3 July a pitched battle occurred in Southall between hundreds of skinheads and local Asian people, and the police quickly became embroiled. This was the one incident in the series of urban disorders that can be described as a 'race riot'. On the same night in the Liverpool 8 district of Merseyside, an apparently minor incident sparked off rioting which lasted intermittently until 6 July. The next day disorder occurred in Moss Side, Manchester,[8] and in the following week disturbances were reported in places such as Handsworth in Birmingham, Sheffield, Nottingham, Hull, Slough, Leeds, Bradford, Leicester, Derby, High Wycombe and Cirencester.

Disorder again erupted in Brixton on 15 July 1981. At 2 a.m. eleven houses in Railton Road were raided by 176 police officers, with a further 391 held in reserve. The police had warrants to look for evidence of unlawful drinking, and to search five houses for petrol bombs, although no evidence of either was found. During the operation the houses sustained very considerable damage — windows, sinks, toilets, floorboards, furniture, television sets and personal possessions were smashed. Lord Scarman, who had just completed the first phase of his inquiry, visited the scene of the havoc and John Fraser, the local Member of Parliament, described what was found:

> I could come to no conclusion other than that a large number of policemen had deliberately set out to wreck the houses, to make them uninhabitable, by taking up floorboards, breaking water pipes, removing gas and electric meters, hand rails and bannisters and smashing almost every window.[9]

The resultant outcry led to an internal inquiry by Deputy Assistant Commissioner Dear (now Chief Constable of the West Midlands) which exonerated those involved, and stated that the police officers had been issued with sledgehammers and crowbars 'to effect speedy entry'. Compensation of £8500 for structural damage, and further sums for damage to personal property, were paid by the Metropolitan Police.

This raid, and the resultant violence on the streets of Brixton, convinced many people that the way policing is carried out is a vital factor in the context of urban unrest. An inquiry into the Railton Road raid by the Police Complaints Board discovered 'serious lapses from professional standards' and an 'institutional disregard for the niceties of the law'. The Board reported that 'the unprofessional conduct of officers engaged on that operation could be a reflection of their conduct on less sensitive occasions'.[10]

Urban unrest in 1985

Disorder was again evident in 1982, although on a much reduced scale. The attention of the news media was firmly focused on the South Atlantic, and so few accounts of disturbances in British cities were reported. It is clear that urban unrest continued to occur in parts of London and Liverpool, and similar disorder seems to have taken place in 1983. The next year the Metropolitan Police Commissioner reported that during 1984 'there were many mini-riots which had the potential to escalate to Brixton 1981 proportions', and he added: 'London is nowadays a very volatile city'.[11]

In September and October 1985 serious urban unrest again became the focus of popular attention.[12] The key events are chronicled in the Appendix at the end of this chapter, and from this it can be seen that the first major eruption occurred on Monday 9 September 1985 in the Lozells Road area of Handsworth, Birmingham. The riot resulted in the deaths of two Asian men, Kassamali and Amirali Moledina, who suffered asphyxiation in their burning post office. 122 other people, mainly police, were reported injured and the value of damaged property was put at £7.5 million. Further rioting occurred the next day when Mr. Douglas Hurd, the Home Secretary, visited the area. Other disturbances, widely regarded as 'copycat', were reported elsewhere in the West Midlands, for example in Moseley, Wolverhampton and Coventry, and in the St. Paul's District of Bristol.

The Handsworth/Soho/Lozells area, with a population of 56,300, is regarded by Birmingham City Council as the most deprived district in the city. Unemployment is a major affliction, and at the time of the riots 36 per cent of the workforce in Handsworth was out of work, while the figure for people under 24 was 50 per cent. It is an area in which it was claimed that in recent years there had been reasonably good relations between young blacks and police, as a result of the practice of community policing introduced by Superintendent David Webb in the late 1970s. However, at the end of 1981 Webb left the police service, and although his approach was continued by his successor he, too, moved from the area in April 1985. The new superintendent instituted changes which included moving a number of the area's community police officers to other duties, and clamping down on activities by local youths which had previously been tolerated. In particular police attention turned to the use of cannabis by black youths, and a number of raids took place during the summer of 1985. For example, on 10 July 150 officers raided the Acapulco cafe in Villa Road, and seven people were arrested.

These changes in officers and tactics resulted in an increase in tension between youths and the police. In July 1985 two serious disturbances occurred in Handsworth, but both were played down and went unreported by the media. In the first, about 70 youths rioted, attacking police vehicles and officers and looting a shop. It took over 2 hours to restore order. A few days later police officers who were questioning a youth were attacked by a large group of young people. The context within which the eruption on 9 September occurred was thus one of deteriorating relations between young people, especially blacks, and the police, as well as one of widespread unemployment and social disadvantage. The tinder merely required a spark, which was provided when a black youth became involved in an altercation with an officer over a parking ticket. It was alleged that during the incident, at which more police arrived, a black woman was assaulted. Three hours later some 45 buildings in Lozells Road were ablaze.

Brixton was the scene of the next outbreak of violent disorder, during the weekend 28–29 September 1985. Police reported 724 major crimes; 43 members of the public and ten police officers were injured, and 230 arrests were made. As in Handsworth, the event which led to the rioting involved police officers and a black person. At 7 a.m. on 28 September, armed police entered Mrs. Cherry Groce's house in Normandy Road, Brixton, looking for her son. Two shots were fired by an officer, and a bullet damaged Mrs. Groce's spine, causing permanent paralysis. At 6 p.m. the local police station was attacked with petrol bombs, and during the next 8 hours large numbers of black and white people took part in burning and looting which caused damage estimated at £3 million. During the riot a freelance photographer, David Hodge, sustained injuries from which he died 3 weeks later.

Two days after Mrs. Groce was shot, rioting occurred in Liverpool 8. In this instance the disturbances were precipitated when four black men were refused bail at Liverpool Magistrates' Court. They had been charged in connection with a fracas in August, but local youths claimed that they were being treated unfairly and picked upon by the police. During the summer there were reports of rising tension in the area, and on 30 August a crowd demonstrated outside Toxteth Police Station, and then attacked police cars and the station itself. A number of assaults on police officers were also reported. As in Brixton and Handsworth, police relations with youths, and especially young black people, was a significant factor in the explosive mixture, and in Toxteth, too, the disorder was precipitated by an incident involving police officers and black people. Quite why rioting occurred in

Peckham in London, on the same night, is not clear. The context seems to be similar to the other instances, that is one of rising tension between young people and the police, and at about 10 p.m. on 30 September the centre of Peckham was effectively sealed off for at least 4 hours. Police reported 'various sporadic acts of lawlessness', and it seems evident that many people, especially blacks, were prevented from returning to their own homes.

The disturbances at Broadwater Farm Estate

The most serious of the disorders occurred at Broadwater Farm Estate, in Tottenham, London. The rioting began at about 7 p.m. on Sunday 6 October 1985, and during a night of extraordinary violence PC Keith Blakelock was stabbed to death, 20 members of the public and 223 police officers were injured and 47 cars and some buildings were burned. Guns were fired at the police, causing injuries to several officers and reporters, and the police deployed CS gas and plastic bullets, although these were not used. A first-hand account of the events was given by Steve Platt in *New Society*:

> 'The flames scorched the front of our house', Pantelis Georgiou told me when I took refuge there at the height of the trouble . . . 'All we could see was a sheet of flame. The next thing I knew the street was full of 250 or 300 people, throwing whatever they could find at the police . . .'
>
> Evdokia, his wife — shaking and scared, as the battle raged outside — peered into her back garden while we talked. Rioters had torn down and burnt the fence. There was no longer anything between us and the Broadwater Farm Estate's Willan Road, where the worst of the fighting was under way and — unbeknown to us — a policeman was being knifed to death . . .
>
> A black couple trying to leave the area via Willan Road were turned back at the police lines, to a chorus of the monkey noises used to abuse black footballers by racists at soccer matches. 'Fuck off niggers', yelled one of the policemen. 'Go back and live in the zoo. You can burn that down'. 'Go back in your rat hole, vermin', echoed another. 'We'll be in to get you soon enough . . .'
>
> Whatever the underlying causes of the riot, there was no denying the intoxicating thrill it offered as relief from everyday life on the dole. All over the estate, crowds of bystanders and onlookers were gathered. 'It's better than the telly, isn't it?' said one old lady, who appeared to be taking her dog for a walk in the midst of this curious mixture of madness, mayhem and the oddly mundane . . .[13]

The next day, the Metropolitan Police Commissioner, Sir Kenneth Newman, stated:

> Yesterday evening the ferocity of the attack on the Metropolitan Police was senseless and beyond belief. . . . To write off such acts as directly attributable to a lack of jobs, or facilities or past unfairness is to indict all those who are unable to work or who are black, white or poor, but do not sink to such depths.

> Petrol bombing, arson and looting are alien to our streets. They must not go on. Last night I deployed members of my Tactical Firearms Unit in readiness to use plastic bullets. They were not used, because the containment operation, though grave in its economic and human costs, was successful.

> But, I wish to put all people of London on notice that I will not shrink from such a decision should I believe it a practical option for restoring peace and preventing crime and injury. I would have hoped not to have had to express that thought, but yesterday evening's events have made it a regrettable possibility.

The Home Secretary said that he fully supported Newman, and so with the ferocious events at Tottenham the use of plastic bullets on the streets of Britain became a real possibility.

As in Handsworth, Brixton and Toxteth, the context within which the disturbances occurred in Tottenham was one of deteriorating relations between the police and young people, especially blacks, and the trigger event involved police officers and black people. The chief superintendent for the area, Colin Couch, was a strong believer in community policing, and he put as his first priority the prevention of public disorder. However, it is clear that many of his police constables and sergeants did not agree with this approach.

During the summer of 1985 there was evidence of increasing tension, and a prominent member of the Hornsey Police Federation was quoted as saying that rank-and-file officers 'desperately wanted to go in hard and sort out the criminals'. Some serious incidents occurred during this period on the Broadwater Farm Estate, such as an attack on police by youths which resulted in one officer sustaining a bad head wound, and there was also a series of attacks on an Asian-owned supermarket. Senior police officers appeared to play these incidents down, but black youths complained that off the estate they were increasingly harassed by the police. During the week before the riots a stop-and-search operation was conducted at the entrance to the estate, and young blacks said that they were unfairly picked on and subjected to abuse and rough treatment. On 9 January 1986 a report prepared by Michael Richards, a Deputy Assistant Commissioner at

Scotland Yard, was presented to the Haringey Police–Community Consultative Group. The report confirmed that tension between the police and youths in the area had been increasing for some time before the riot was triggered. It concluded that the disorder was planned, rather than a spontaneous reaction, but the account given was clearly partial in that the views of non-police eyewitnesses were excluded. On 13 January 1986 Mr. Bernie Grant, leader of Haringey Council, again called for an independent public inquiry into the disorder, but this was promptly dismissed once more by the Home Office Minister, Mr. Giles Shaw. It does seem incredible that rioting as serious as that which occurred was not investigated by an official inquiry, and one can only wonder at the Government's stance on this.

The incident which triggered the riots began when police officers stopped a car driven by Floyd Jarrett, a 23-year-old black man well-known in the area as a worker at the Broadwater Farm Youth Association. The police officers stopped him because his tax disc was out of date, and he explained that this was because he had only just returned from a youth exchange trip in Jamaica. One of the officers decided to arrest Jarrett for suspected theft of the car, but after an alleged altercation Jarrett was in fact charged with assaulting a police officer. On 13 December 1985 Jarrett was not only acquitted of this charge, but was also awarded £350 costs against the police.

What happened after Jarrett arrived at the police station on 5 October is subject to dispute. The arrested man claimed that he was assaulted, detained for over 5 hours without being allowed to make a phone call, and then released. The police stated that he was treated correctly. The Jarrett family claimed that five police officers used Floyd's key to enter his mother's home, whereas the police stated that they found the door open. Some weeks later, at the inquest into the death of Mrs. Jarrett, police officers admitted that this story was untrue. During the police search of the house Mrs. Cynthia Jarrett collapsed and died. The family alleged that her death was caused by a police officer who pushed her over; the police denied that this had occurred. On 4 December 1985 the inquest returned a verdict of accidental death. Mrs. Jarrett was certified dead at 6.35 p.m. on Saturday 5 October, and news of the tragedy spread quickly around the estate during the evening. The next day, after sporadic incidents, violent disorder erupted at about 7 p.m.

Expectations of further riots

Disorder occurred again in 1986. During the spring there were renewed reports of increasing tension in some areas. In Notting Hill, for example, there were allegations of assaults by the police, and the planting of drugs, while in Nottingham a number of forced entries into black people's homes, and a series of street searches, caused widespread anger. On the

Broadwater Farm Estate virtually every black male under 30 was interrogated — over 350 people were arrested and held, often for long periods, and yet the majority were released without charge. In July 1986 the Metropolitan Police mounted a huge raid in Brixton which involved nearly 2000 police. 'Operation Condor' was aimed at a few selected premises in which cannabis offences were allegedly being committed. The raid entailed a large number of officers being brought into Brixton in a special train, from which they clambered down the embankment to surround the targeted buildings.

In early September 1986 serious disorder occurred on the streets of the North Prospect Estate in the Devonport constituency of Plymouth. A large crowd of white youths set up burning barricades, and smashed windows, doors and fences on the estate. A few days later the Avon and Somerset Police organised a large raid in the St. Paul's District of Bristol. Almost exactly 1 year after the Handsworth riots, 600 police moved into the area to search several premises in connection with drugs and drinking offences. 'Operation Delivery' entailed simultaneous raids on 12 houses in Bristol, but the centrepiece was 'Operation St. Paul's' which took place on 11–13 September 1986. The reaction was serious rioting and attacks on the police involving petrol bombs, bricks and stones. More than 100 people were arrested, and injuries were sustained by a number of police officers and members of the public.

The 1986 disorders were reported in the newspapers and on television and radio. However, in much of the media they were not regarded as the most important news, and the coverage lasted only a few days. Of course, the events were not as serious as those in 1985 and 1981, but even so one might have expected more sustained coverage of disturbances which 10 years earlier would have been greeted with incredulity. But this was 1986, and in a great deal of the brief media coverage there was a barely hidden undercurrent of boredom and resignation at yet more urban unrest. The shock and bewilderment evident in 1981 seemed to be absent by 1986 — instead there was a general expectation of further disturbances.

Moving beyond predictable explanations

The explanations which have been put forward for the recent riots are considered in Chapter 2, and in other contributions in this book. Like the predominant reactions in 1980 and 1981, those in 1985 were unfortunately all too predictable, and simplistic views abounded. Much of the press seemed particularly attracted by the conspiracy theory and the *Daily Express*, in its 'Tottenham Riot Special' edition of 8 October 1985, managed to reach new depths of fantasy. Under its headline *Moscow-trained hit squad gave orders as mob hacked PC Blakelock to death* KILL! KILL! KILL!, the *Express* explained:

The thugs who murdered policeman Keith Blakelock in the
Tottenham riots acted on orders of crazed Left-wing extremists.

Street-fighting experts trained in Moscow and Libya were behind
Britain's worst violence.

The chilling plot emerged last night as detectives hunted a hand-
picked death squad believed to have been sent into North London
hell-bent on bloodshed.

Many police officers, while not going as far as the press, suggested that
agitators had fostered the disorder. Mr. Norman Tebbit ascribed the riots
to 'wickedness', but, as a correspondent to *The Guardian* commented, if
riots are caused by wickedness the stock of human wickedness must have
risen alarmingly since the election of Mr. Tebbit's Conservative Party to
government.

In the aftermath of Handsworth, some Labour Party politicians such as
Roy Hattersley and Jeff Rooker seemed to agree with the predominant law
and order explanations. More generally, though, the response from
Labour Party speakers, and from those in community groups, local government, the churches, trade unions and from some police officers, was to
stress social deprivation, racial discrimination and disadvantage, and unemployment as causes of the disorders. Mr. Neil Kinnock attacked the
Government's complacency, and the cuts in support for councils running
the inner-city areas; it was, he said, government by 'lethargy and conflict'.

One of the purposes of this book is to try to go beyond the rather
superficial discussions which were fostered by most of the media, and by
some pundits and politicians. The speakers at the Warwick Conference, on
which much of the book is based, were asked to examine the *root* causes of
unrest rather than the immediate triggers of riots in particular localities,
and the short-term remedies. The proceedings of the Conference are
reproduced in Parts 2–6 of the collection, and the debate and dialogue
which followed the contributions are also included.

The broad historical canvas covered in Chapters 3 and 4, by Stuart Hall
and Martin Kilson, highlights the ways in which the recent disorders should
be set in an historical, social and comparative framework. This is one of the
central threads unifying the proceedings, in contrast to accounts of the
recent events which look at them in isolation from their wider context. This
is not to say that one can ignore the more specific issues and problems that
prevail in certain localities, and a number of the presentations by
practitioners reflect their perceptions of what is happening in many of the
inner-city areas. However, as John Benyon points out in Chapter 2, an
inherent difficulty in the search for 'causes' at the local level is the tendency
to ignore the wider context in which disorder emerges. A guiding theme
that runs throughout the volume is the need to strengthen our under-

standing of the post-1980 urban protests and of the ways in which we can go beyond short-term remedies by tackling the root causes rather than the symptoms of disorder.

The book is organised around the themes which shaped the Conference. Additionally, two papers by John Benyon attempt to contextualise some broader aspects of the politics of urban unrest. The first of these, Chapter 2, outlines and contrasts various explanations and interpretations of urban unrest and civil disorder. Touching upon a number of themes which are taken up in more detail in subsequent chapters, Benyon suggests that the debate on the causes of urban unrest needs to be broadened to look at the complex economic, social, political and cultural context in which it occurs.

The chapters in Part 2 take up the question of urban unrest from three different angles. Stuart Hall looks at the experience of urban unrest in contemporary Britain and stresses that its roots have to be understood before we can attempt to do something about it. In particular he suggests three contextual variables that need to be examined: social deprivation and disadvantage, the political climate, and the experience of racism. Martin Kilson takes a longer time-span as his reference point when looking at the history of urban unrest in the United States, emphasising the various stages through which the management of race and urban crisis has gone over the past 40 years. In looking at this longer experience of urban unrest in the United States this chapter provides a useful contrast with the more recent United Kingdom experience, and suggests some important parallels. Taking as his vantage point his practical experience of reporting race and urban issues for the BBC, in Chapter 5 John Clare provides some powerful and sobering reflections on the events he has reported, and on the failure to tackle the problems which the riots have highlighted.

The chapters in Part 2 lay the groundwork for analysing urban unrest in its broader historical and social context, and those in Part 3 exemplify the political sensitivity of analysing the role played by the police in relation to urban unrest. Chapter 6, by David Smith, provides a critical and timely analysis of the interrelationship between police roles and the outbreak of violent confrontations between sections of the community and the police. Exploring the rationale of recent policy changes in relation to the police, Smith argues that within the context of growing unrest and disorder the political dilemmas of policing are becoming more acute and need to be confronted at a national policy level.

Richard Wells sketches in the complexities of policing urban localities from the point of view of the police themselves. Linking his model of the causes of unrest to an account of the dilemmas which confront the police in many inner-city areas he argues that the police need to win trust and support from local communities if they are to succeed in reducing the chances of further urban unrest. Short, contrasting views of the role of policing in the inner cities are offered by Devon Thomas and George

Greaves, who both have long experience of the problems which confront black people in the London Borough of Lambeth.

Part 4 consists of three chapters which look at the reality of unemployment, racial disadvantage and inner-city decline, and the failure to tackle the problems which have been evident in many urban localities for some time. John Rex's chapter opens with a reminder that as early as 1979 he had warned of impending violence and disorder if nothing was done to remedy the problems faced by the black community in Handsworth.[14] Looking at this diagnosis from the perspective of 1986 Rex sees little room for a more optimistic forecast, unless a radical programme of social reform is instituted. A similar analysis is provided by Ivan Henry, who analyses the events in Handsworth as a form of protest against social disadvantage and racism. Chapter 13, by Usha Prashar, reflects on the lack of positive action in the period since 1981. She contrasts this lack of response with what happened in the United States during the 1960s.

The central factor: social injustice

Some of the themes which preoccupied the first three sessions of the Conference are taken up by Lord Scarman, whose reflections form Part 5 of this book. Taking up the arguments developed by Hall and Kilson in the first session he argues that the core issue which underlies the unrest is the lack of justice for sections of British society, particularly the ethnic minority communities.

The concluding session of the Conference consisted of two papers which attempted to look at the options in the aftermath of the riots, and these form Part 6 of this book. Chapter 16 by Herman Ouseley looks critically and uncompromisingly at the key factors which have to be confronted in developing a way forward out of the current impasse in Britain. Richard Thomas, by contrast, looks at the history of unrest and racial disadvantage in the United States, particularly in the City of Detroit. Both chapters, however, address the question of how to move forward from a situation of violent unrest and racial inequality to one where there is greater equality, and peaceful racial and cultural diversity.

The final part of the collection seeks to draw together some of the points raised by contributors. In Chapter 19 John Benyon considers the impact which urban unrest may have on the operation of the political agenda. Many of the chapters comment on the lack of action since 1981, and on other aspects of the political agenda. Benyon suggests that issues raised and put on the agenda by outsider processes of initiation — of which riots and violent protest are examples — are unlikely to invoke effective political solutions, unless they become sponsored by insider groups and political parties.

The final chapter by the editors briefly reviews some of the central themes which emerge from the contributions to the book. The critical issues include racial discrimination and disadvantage, social deprivation, unemployment, police policies and practices, and political exclusion. These aspects of the context of urban unrest are raised in many chapters, and they are linked with the vital notion of justice. Indeed, the fundamental root of urban unrest appears to be unjust treatment.

There is a long history of violent protest and disorder in Britain, and the common factor in many of these events seems to have been a perception by the participants of injustice. In Chapter 20 the editors tentatively suggest six key factors which may be associated with urban unrest, the most crucial of which is a sense of injustice. The five other factors are ineffectiveness of government policies, low levels of identity with the polity, low opportunities for participation, a decline in perceptions of legitimacy and falling levels of voluntary consent.

Each of these factors may lead to discontent amongst sections of the population; together they may cause withdrawal from the institutions and organisations of mainstream society, or may generate deeply felt anger and hostility. As Huntingdon has pointed out,[15] apathy and indignation may succeed each other: disillusionment on occasions explodes into anger, when one further example of injustice is experienced. Layton-Henry describes this as:

> smouldering apathy where an apparent quiescent acceptance . . . con-
> ceals pent-up resentments, bitterness and anger which occasionally break
> out into outbursts of sporadic violence.[16]

Such an explosion may be cathartic, but the pressures will begin to build up again if the root causes are not tackled. Unless British society and above all the Government and state institutions act to ameliorate unemployment, racism, social deprivation, police malpractices and political exclusion it is difficult to disagree with so many of the authors in this book, who see further urban unrest as only a matter of time.

Notes

1. K. Pryce, *Endless Pressure*, Harmondsworth: Penguin, 1979.
2. *The Brixton Disorders 10–12 April 1981: Report of an Inquiry by the Rt. Hon. the Lord Scarman, OBE*, London: HMSO, November 1981 (Cmnd. 8427).
3. *Sunday Telegraph*, 29 November 1981.
4. *The Brixton Disorders*, para. 1.2.
5. See for example, S. Cohen, *Folk Devils and Moral Panics*, St. Albans: Paladin, 1973; S. Hall and T. Jefferson (eds), *Resistance Through Rituals*, London: Hutchinson, 1976.
6. On 'mugging' see S. Hall, C. Critcher, T. Jefferson, J. Clarke and B. Roberts, *Policing the Crisis: Mugging, the State and Law and Order*, London: Macmillan, 1978; J. Benyon, 'Spiral of decline: race and policing', in Z. Layton-Henry and P. Rich (eds), *Race, Government and Politics in Britain*, London: Macmillan, 1986, pp. 227–77. On football hooliganism see E. Dunning, P. Murphy and J. Williams, *The Social Roots of Football Hooligan Violence*, London: Routledge and Kegan Paul, 1987; R. Ingham (ed.), *Football Hooliganism: the Wider Context*, London: Inter-Action Imprint, 1978.
7. See for example, R. Clutterbuck, *Britain in Agony*, Harmondsworth: Penguin, 1980.

8. For a first-hand account see M. Nally, 'Eyewitness in Moss Side' in J. Benyon (ed.), *Scarman and After*, Oxford: Pergamon Press, 1984, pp. 54–62.
9. House of Commons Official Report, Parliamentary Debates (*Hansard*), Session 1980–81, Sixth Series, Vol. 8, 16 July 1981, col. 1425.
10. House of Commons Official Report, Parliamentary Debates (*Hansard*), Session 1980–81, Sixth Series, Vol. 10, 29 October 1981, cols 991–8; House of Commons Official Report, Parliamentary Debates (*Hansard*), Session 1982–83, Sixth Series, Vol. 41, 28 April 1983, col. 372; *Policing London*, No. 8, June/July 1983, pp. 6–7; *New Law Journal*, Vol. 133, No. 6100, 22 April 1983, p. 363; *Report of the Police Complaints Board 1982*, HC 278, London: HMSO, 12 April 1983, p. 1.
11. Quoted in *The Guardian*, 17 October 1984, p. 3; see also, N. Lyndon, 'Inside the ghetto', *The Sunday Times*, 4 July 1982, p. 17; J. Benyon (ed.), *Scarman and After*, Oxford: Pergamon Press, 1984, pp. 53, 61 and 241; *Scarman Returns*, Channel 4, 9 September 1984.
12. This account is based on that given in J. Benyon, *A Tale of Failure: Race and Policing*, Warwick: Centre for Research in Ethnic Relations, March 1986 (Policy Paper in Ethnic Relations no. 3) which was derived from: newspaper and television reports; personal accounts; interviews with local people; *Hansard* for 21 October and 23 October 1985; Scotland Yard releases and reports; *A Different Reality: Report of the Review Panel*, Birmingham: West Midlands County Council, February 1986; *The Handsworth/Lozells Riots, 9–11 September 1985: Report of an Inquiry by Mr Julius Silverman*, Birmingham: City Council, February 1986; *The Broadwater Farm Inquiry Report*, London: Broadwater Farm Inquiry, 1986.
13. S. Platt, 'The innocents of Broadwater Estate', *New Society*, Vol. 74, No. 1189, 11 October 1985, pp. 48–9.
14. J. Rex and S. Tomlinson, *Colonial Immigrants in a British City*, London: Routledge and Kegan Paul, 1979.
15. S. Huntingdon, *Political Order in Changing Societies*, New Haven: Yale University Press, 1968, p. 88.
16. Z. Layton-Henry, *The Politics of Race in Britain*, London: Allen and Unwin, 1984, p. 169.

Appendix: A chronicle of civil commotion in 1985

Summer 1985 Reports of clashes between youths and police in Birmingham, London, Liverpool and elsewhere; armed raids by police in Brixton and West Midlands; increase in tension reported in areas such as Handsworth and Tottenham, as police seek to clamp down on minor offences.

24 August John Shorthouse, aged 5, shot dead during an armed raid in Birmingham; later uniformed police are attacked and a WPC is badly beaten.

30 August Toxteth Police Station attacked by demonstrators protesting at the arrest of four black youths; in Brixton it is alleged that armed police searching for drugs break down the front door of Paula Belsham's house, and hold a gun to her head, and subject her to an intimate examination [reported in the press, and in the House of Commons, see *Hansard*, 23 October 1985, col. 352].

1 September A new organisation called Anti-Fascist Action is formed to resist by force the growing wave of racist attacks.

2 September In the Cabinet reshuffle, Douglas Hurd replaces Leon Brittan as Home Secretary, and Kenneth Baker steps into Patrick Jenkin's place at the Department of the Environment.

3 September Kenneth Oxford, Chief Constable of Merseyside, threatens to end community foot patrol policing in Liverpool 8 (Toxteth) if attacks on officers persist.

5 September	Liverpool City Council announces that its 31,000 employees are to receive redundancy notices, as its funds will run out by Christmas.
7–8 September	Handsworth Festival takes place: little trouble reported as carnival revellers and local police dance in the streets.
9 September* 4.45–5.15 p.m.	At about 11.30 on this Monday morning an Asian shop-keeper is stabbed in the arm outside the bank in Villa Road. In the late afternoon, a police officer issues a parking ticket to a black driver; the vehicle is untaxed, and the driver is arrested on suspicion of being disqualified and giving a false address; there are allegations of racial abuse; further police arrive, and there are accusations that a young woman is assaulted by an officer; during the ensuing fight between bystanders and the police, 11 officers are reported injured and seven police vehicles damaged; two arrests are made.
7.40 p.m.	Villa Cross Hall is reported to be on fire, and fire officers who arrive are warned by youths not to tackle the blaze.
7.50 p.m.	Police officers who try to help the fire brigade are attacked by youths throwing bricks and petrol bombs.
8.05–8.30 p.m.	Some other buildings are burning, and shops are being looted. More police arrive and chase youths in the vicinity of Villa Cross pub.
8.45 p.m.	Several premises in Lozells Road, including garage, are blazing; rioters control area: sealed off by burning cars; SOS phone call by Asian brothers in post office.
9.00–11.00 p.m.	Further looting and attacks on the police; 45 properties on fire, including the post office; 470 police officers are unable to regain control.
11.30 p.m.	Police gradually succeed in fighting their way into the area, negotiating burning barricades in Lozells Road and other streets; water from fire hoses short circuits electricity.
Midnight	Although the police still sustain some attacks the rioting winds down, and fire officers deluge buildings with water; 848 police officers are in the area.
10 September* 3.00 a.m.	Still chaotic with fires burning, as looters return to retrieve goods hidden in gardens.
4.00 a.m.	Order is restored.
7.00 a.m.	The bodies of Amirali and Kassamali Moledina are discovered in the smouldering wreckage of the post office; [a 21-year-old white man was subsequently charged with their murder].
Morning	Groups of bewildered people congregate, surveying the devastation, surrounded by cohorts of reporters.
1.15 p.m.	The Home Secretary arrives in a convoy of cars; as he tries to talk to people shouts of abuse are followed by bricks, and he is forced to make a speedy exit in a police van.
1.40 p.m.	Further burning, stoning and looting occurs; vehicles, including a police van and ITN car, are overturned and set on fire.
2.30 p.m.	Sporadic incidents continue for some hours, and despite a heavy police presence there are accounts of people being robbed in shops by gangs, and of general lawlessness.
Evening	Over 900 police officers flood the area; some attacks are made on them, but their policy of keeping crowds moving succeeds in avoiding further serious disorder.

The police report that the 291 arrested people [which later rises to 437] are drawn from every racial and religious group, and the vast majority live in Handsworth; 124 casualties are reported, including 2 dead, and 79 police, 8 fire officers and 35 members of the public injured; 83 premises and 23 vehicles had been damaged, worth an estimated £7.5 million.

Outbreaks of disorder are reported elsewhere in the West Midlands, in places such as Dudley, West Bromwich and Moseley.

11 September	Mrs. Thatcher describes those who complain about unemployment as 'moaning minnies'; at Birmingham Law Courts, where 75 people are facing charges arising out of the disturbances, there are demonstrations and fights; at the SDP conference at Torquay, Dr. Owen says that 'none of us' have taken Lord Scarman's report seriously enough; disorders are reported in Coventry and Wolverhampton.
12 September	Cabinet decides that there should be no judicial public inquiry into the disorder; Home Secretary says the riots were 'not a cry for help, but a cry for loot'; Shadow Home Secretary asks why they occurred in an inner-city area with high unemployment, and not in the Home Secretary's constituency of Witney, where unemployment is low. Two white teenagers are sentenced to 3 years in custody for abusing and fire-bombing an Asian family in Stockwell Park Estate, London.
13 September	A series of crimes occur in St. Paul's District of Bristol, which was the scene of serious disorder in April 1980; unrest is reported in the area; at the ACPO conference in Preston, the chief constables tell the Home Secretary of the need for an increase in police numbers.
14 September	The Asian members of Birmingham Community Relations Council resign, protesting that there has been insufficient condemnation of the violence in Handsworth.
16 September	Ex-Labour MP Julius Silverman is chosen to chair the inquiry by Birmingham City Council into the disturbances.
20 September	Mr. Enoch Powell makes a widely condemned speech which seems to call for a policy of repatriation.
28 September* **7.00 a.m.**	At 7 o'clock on this Saturday morning a posse of police, some armed and others with dogs, raid a house in Normandy Road, Brixton. It is later reported to be the 51st armed raid in Brixton in 1985. After the front door is broken down, two shots are fired by the police, who are searching for Mr. Michael Groce, a man wanted for questioning for possession of a shotgun. His mother, a 38-year-old black woman, Mrs. Cherry Groce, is hit by a bullet which causes her permanent paralysis.
Morning	Rumours spread throughout Brixton that Mrs. Groce is dead; tension grows as crowd gathers outside her house.
2.00 p.m.	Bottle thrown at police superintendent in car; deputation goes to police station to protest about the shooting; crowd gathers outside.
3.15 p.m.	Youths rampage down Normandy Road, attacking reporters and camera crew.
5.15 p.m.	A group marches in protest to Brixton Police Station on the corner of Gresham Road and Brixton Road.
5.50 p.m.	About 300 youths attack police station with bricks and petrol bombs; station is under siege until riot police disperse crowd at about 6.15 p.m.
6.35 p.m.	In Brixton Road, motorists are stopped and their cars are set alight; some looting occurs.
7.15 p.m.	The police are unable to contain the disorder, and the rioting spreads.
8.30 p.m.	Extensive looting takes place; a number of robberies ocur; running battles in various streets; more cars set on fire.
9.30 p.m.	The police advance from Coldharbour Lane into Brixton Road, beating riot shields; a large crowd of spectators contains some people who taunt the police, who now appear to be on the defensive.
11.00 p.m.	Still extensive disorder; some buildings on fire.
Midnight	Police tactics suddenly change, and without warning officers charge into spectators, hitting out with their truncheons; a number of people are hurt and/ or arrested.

29 September*
2.30 a.m.
Afternoon

6.30 p.m.

Rioting has ended.
Crowds of youths gather and are moved on; serious allegations are later made that some police officers attacked residences on the Angell Estate; others allege abuse and assault; police report prolonged provocation.
Sporadic clashes occur between youths and police, and these continue into the night. The Metropolitan Police report that 43 members of the public and 10 police officers had been injured; 55 vehicles and a number of properties had been burned. Nearly a half of the 230 people arrested were white; a staggering 724 serious crimes were recorded, including 2 rapes, a number of assaults and robberies, and over 90 burglaries. During the disorder a freelance photographer, Mr. David Hodge, sustained injuries from which he died 3 weeks later.

30 September

Commander Alex Marnoch says police are investigating the role of political extremists in the disorder; at the Labour Party Conference the behaviour of some police officers is bitterly criticised.

1 October*

Afternoon

5.00 p.m.

5.30 p.m.

7.15 p.m.
7.55 p.m.

Officers from the District Support Unit mount a stop-and-search operation, in a search for drugs, on all cars entering the Broadwater Farm Estate in Tottenham. In Liverpool, four black men are remanded in custody on charges arising from disturbances on 10 August; scuffles occur between people supporting them and police officers.
Tension grows in Liverpool 8 (Toxteth); crowds gather and barricades are erected.
Officers from the Operational Support Division (OSD) seek to disperse youths by driving police Land Rovers, on the pavements as well as in the road, into the crowds.
Two motorists are pulled from their cars, which are set on fire in Upper Parliament Street; other vehicles are set alight, and a TV crew is forced to hand over a £20,000 camera.
The disorder appears to have died down.
Rioting begins again, with the violence primarily directed against the police; Archbishop Derek Worlock says the behaviour earlier of the OSD caused great anger; police report 14 public and 4 police injuries, 13 arrests and a number of properties and vehicles damaged by fire.

Disorder also occurs in Peckham, in south London; some shops are damaged, and clashes take place between youths and the police; a large area is effectively sealed off from 10.00 p.m. until 2.30 a.m., and some people trying to re-enter Peckham to return to their homes complain that police turned them away, and were abusive to black people. In north London, police are put on the alert for riots at Broadwater Farm, after a series of hoax phone calls which, it is believed, are intended to lure police into a trap.

2 October

Criminal Statistics (Cmnd. 9621) reveals that during 1984 in England and Wales the police recorded nearly 3.5 million notifiable crimes, an increase of 8 per cent on the preceding year.

3 October

The Home Secretary reports to the Cabinet on the riots, but a public inquiry is firmly ruled out. The unemployment figures for September are announced, and these reveal that 3,346,198 are registered as jobless (13.8 per cent); this is the highest total ever recorded.

4 October

Douglas Hurd tours Brixton; the funeral of John Shorthouse (5) who was shot on 24 August takes place.

5 October

Nine Anglican clergymen in Brixton issue a statement which strongly deplores the behaviour of some police in the area, the actions of the rioters, and social and economic conditions.

1.00 p.m.	Police stop Floyd Jarrett, a 23-year-old black man, as the tax disc on his BMW car is out of date. Jarrett, who is well-known in the area as a worker at the Broadwater Farm Youth Association, explains that he has not had a chance to renew the tax as he has only just returned from a youth exchange trip to Jamaica. PC Casey decided to arrest Jarrett for suspected theft of the car; after the ensuing altercation he is charged with assaulting PC Casey. [On 13 December 1985 Jarrett was acquitted of the charge of assault and an award of £350 costs was made against the police.] He is taken to Tottenham Police Station.
Afternoon	The arrested man claims that he is assaulted, and detained for over 5 hours without being allowed to make a phone call. The police claim that he is treated correctly.
5.45 p.m.	Four police officers enter the home of Mrs. Cynthia Jarrett, in Thorpe Street, Tottenham, about a mile from Broadwater Farm Estate. The police claim that the front door was open, the Jarrett family claim that officers used a key taken from Floyd Jarrett, who is still in custody. Police search the house for stolen goods, of which none are found, and at 5.55 p.m. Mrs Jarrett (49) collapses. The family allege that a police officer assaulted her; the police deny this.
6.35 p.m.	Mrs. Jarrett is certified dead on arrival at North Middlesex Hospital.
Evening	News of Mrs Jarrett's death spreads round the area.
6 October* 12.00 noon	As rumours abound about police involvement in the death, a meeting is held at Tottenham Police Station between officers and community leaders, including Floyd Jarrett. DAC Richards refuses to suspend the four officers involved in the incident.
2.00 p.m.	A crowd of about 100 gathers outside the police station; abuse is exchanged with officers but the demonstration, which lasts for 90 minutes, is policed by 10 officers and passes off without violence.
3.15 p.m.	Two home beat officers are attacked, and one suffers serious injury to his spleen.
6.00 p.m.	A meeting is held at the Broadwater Farm Community Centre, to which the police are not invited; the mood of the meeting is one of anger, and Councillor Bernie Grant is not allowed to speak.
6.30 p.m.	The windscreen of a police car, called to Broadwater Farm Estate by a hoax call, is shattered; one officer is injured in the eye by glass and is taken to hospital.
6.50 p.m.	People make their way from the Community Centre meeting towards Tottenham Police Station where it is intended to hold a protest rally; police transits arrive and officers in riot uniforms block the road.
7.05 p.m.	Police District Support Units (DSUs) are attacked in The Avenue; two cars are set on fire; exits to the estate are blocked by the police.
7.45 p.m.	Crowd of youths run down The Avenue towards police, overturning vehicles and setting fire to them; cars are driven at police lines.
7.55 p.m.	A gun is fired in Griffin Road, and a bullet is later removed from a police officer's stomach.
8.55 p.m.	A major fire is burning, and police try to advance.
9.30 p.m.	Supermarket in Willan Road on fire; police beaten back by missiles and attacks from rioters.
9.44 p.m.	Man with sawn-off shotgun fires at police in Griffin Road, injuring two journalists and a BBC sound man.
9.49 p.m.	A police constable is hit in the leg by the blast from a shotgun, which causes bad injuries.
10.10 p.m.	Flats in Moira Close are on fire; newsagents in Tangmere precinct ablaze; 7 firemen and 10 police who go to tackle the fire are attacked by a gang of youths.
10.15 p.m.	While retreating from the attack, PC Keith Blakelock slips and is fatally stabbed by several assailants.
10.17 p.m.	PC Blakelock is dragged clear by fire officer.

10.20 p.m.	Gas explosion in Adams Road; D11 squad arrive at Broadwater Farm Estate with CS gas and plastic bullets; other officers cheer their arrival, but they are not used.
10.30 p.m.	It is reported that a gun is fired in Griffin Road, and that the bullet grazes a police officer's head.
10.55 p.m.	Helicopter hovers above the riot, picking out participants in powerful searchlight.
11.00 p.m.	Keith Blakelock is certified dead at North Middlesex Hospital.
11.45 p.m.	Disorder peters out as rioters drift away.
7 October*	Commissioner of Police for the Metropolis, Sir Kenneth Newman,
1.10 a.m.	inspects scene and assesses the position.
4.30 a.m.	Large numbers of police move cautiously into the estate.
Morning	Local residents and hordes of reporters survey the wreckage; 47 wrecked vehicles are on the estate. Tension remains high, but large contingents of police prevent any recurrence of serious disorder.

Police report that casualties were: one police officer killed, 223 police and 20 public injured, and extensive damage to cars and premises by fire. It is believed that three separate firearms were used during the disorders. Subsequently, a number of arrests are made, including five for the murder of PC Blakelock. Police do not discover guns on the estate.

Sir Kenneth Newman 'puts all people of London on notice' that he will not shrink from using plastic bullets if necessary; the Home Secretary supports use of CS gas or other implements to suppress disorder.

10 October	After Leicester versus Derby football match, serious disorder occurs in Highfields district of the city; fighting and looting occurs; petrol bombs are thrown and several hundred police are needed to quell the youths.
	At the Conservative Party Conference, Douglas Hurd calls council leaders such as Ted Knight (Lambeth) and Bernie Grant (Haringey) 'the high priests of race conflict' and he announces a new offence of disorderly conduct [which is one of the measures in the Public Order Act 1986].
11 October	TGWU and NUPE members of Haringey Council workforce call a 24-hour strike in protest at Mr. Grant's remarks that 'the police got a bloody good hiding' at Broadwater Farm; they demand that all forms of violence should be condemned; Grant's supporters stage a counter demonstration.
	In her conference speech at Blackpool, Mrs. Thatcher states that there can never be any justification for rioting, and she pledges that there will be more men and equipment for the police if necessary.
18 October	Funeral of Mrs. Jarrett; ILEA NUT votes to refuse cooperation with the police, because of their alleged racist attitudes.
21 October	Home Secretary makes statement to the House of Commons.
23 October	Opposition motion for an independent judicial inquiry is defeated by 292 votes to 191.

Note:*   All times are approximate, as accounts vary; the times given are those upon which there appears to be the most agreement.

Sources: Compiled by John Benyon from: newspaper and television reports; personal accounts; Scotland Yard releases and reports; Birmingham City Council inquiry hearings; *Hansard*, 21 October and 23 October 1985; interviews with local people; J. Benyon, *A Tale of Failure: Race and Policing*, Warwick: Centre for Research in Ethnic Relations, March 1986 (Policy paper in Ethnic Relations No. 3); *A Different Reality: Report of the Review Panel*, Birmingham: West Midlands County Council, February 1986; *The Handsworth/Lozells Riots, 9–11 September 1985: Report of an Inquiry by Mr Julius Silverman*, Birmingham: City Council, February 1986; *The Broadwater Farm Inquiry Report*, London: Broadwater Farm Inquiry, 1986.

CHAPTER 2

Interpretations of civil disorder

JOHN BENYON

Shortly after the riots in England in July 1981 Sir Edmund Leach, President of the Royal Anthropological Institute and former Provost of King's College Cambridge, said that unless Mrs. Thatcher's 'brutal monetarist policies' were reversed 'we shall be plunged into an irreversible social disaster in which we will witness the social collapse of our country'.[1] Newspapers and television proclaimed similarly dire warnings of impending catastrophe (although not necessarily the same views of Mrs. Thatcher's policies), from politicians, police officers, church leaders, community spokesmen — indeed from anyone and everyone, it seemed, but the rioters themselves.[2] In November 1981, in his report into the Brixton disorders, Lord Scarman warned of the danger that: 'disorder will become a disease endemic in our society'.[3] On racial disadvantage he stated: 'Urgent action is needed if it is not to become an endemic ineradicable disease threatening the very survival of our society.'[4]

It is noticeable how frequently pathological language is used in discussions of law and order. There are 'outbreaks' of disorder, and 'epidemics' of crime, and a 'crisis' can occur if the 'contagion' spreads too far. In the House of Commons on 23 October 1985 the Shadow Home Secretary, Mr. Gerald Kaufman, described how 'society is suffering from a sickness of violence and from a deep failure to understand and accept the origins of the sickness'.[5] Disorder is seen as a disease of the body politic but, like so many ailments, it may be rather easier to recognise than to cure. To continue the medical metaphor, diagnosis determines treatment, but if the condition is not fully understood there is a danger that the prescribed remedies merely treat the symptoms of the disorder, rather than curing its causes. In the aftermath of each incident of urban unrest in the 1980s a rash of instant diagnoses appeared, and this chapter will examine some of the more common explanations which were put forward.

23

'On the road to urban anarchy'?

As discussed in Chapter 1, the widespread surprise at the 1980 and 1981 riots was perhaps understandable. Many people expressed fears similar to those of Sir Edmund Leach, quoted above, that there was a danger of imminent social collapse. However, the vision of Britain teetering on the brink of social and political disintegration is not a recent one. In 1730, Daniel Defoe addressed a pamphlet to the Lord Mayor of London in the following terms:

> The Whole City, My Lord, is alarm'd and uneasy . . . The Citizens are no longer secure within their own Walls, or safe even in passing their Streets, but are robbed, insulted and abused . . . and such mischiefs are done within the Bounds of your Government as never were practised here before (at least not to such a degree) and which, if suffered to go on, will call for Armies, not Magistrates, to suppress it.[6]

In 1812 Robert Southey was not even sure that the army could be relied upon:

> At this time nothing but the Army preserves us from the most dreadful of all calamities, an insurrection of the poor against the rich, and how long the Army may be depended upon is a question which I scarcely dare ask myself.[7]

One hundred and seventy years later, Lord Scarman, too, spoke of the role of the army in curbing disorder. During the Brixton riots, he said, there was an occasion when a few officers:

> Stood between us, the inner city of London, and a total collapse . . . of law and order . . . if that thin blue line had been overwhelmed — and it nearly was on the Saturday night — there was no other way of dealing with it except the awful requirement of calling in the army.[8]

The use of the army to quell civil disorder in Britain would indeed be a dramatic development, although of course soldiers have been involved in Northern Ireland's bloody conflict for nearly two decades. The army has been used on many occasions of disorder in the past, such as during the turbulent years of Victorian Britain. In 1908 a parliamentary select committee reported that since 1869 troops had been ordered to intervene in 24 separate disturbances, and twice they had been ordered to fire.[9]

An opinion poll in February 1985 found that 64 per cent of those surveyed expected further riots to occur in British cities.[10] Seven months later they were proved right, and they were described as 'sobering —

indeed shocking — events' by the Home Secretary in the House of Commons on 23 October 1985. 'Strenuous and imaginative' action was required to tackle the riots, declared Mr. Hurd in his speech against an Opposition motion which called for the establishment of an independent judicial inquiry. 'It is no good responding to them simply by the wringing of hands.'[11]

Despite Mr. Hurd's injunction, the predominant response to the riots did seem to be a wringing of hands, although this was often accompanied by a gnashing of teeth. This was evident in much of the media comment and in views expressed by many politicians. For example, Sir Ian Percival, MP for Southport, considered that society was being assailed by:

> a combination of sheer villainy on an unprecedented scale, exploiting every grievance, real or supposed, and a deliberate, skilled, organised and dedicated attack on our very way of life . . .[12]

Sir Ian's remedy was 'to give total support to the police', and this view was widely shared by media commentators and other MPs. Unless it was forthcoming, warned Sir Eldon Griffiths, who is parliamentary adviser to the Police Federation, 'our country will find itself on the road to urban anarchy'.[13]

The disorders in 1985 were indeed horrifying. Four people died as a result of the riots, and many others were seriously hurt. Moreover, under the cover of the disturbances many serious crimes took place, including rape, assault and robbery. The violence at Broadwater Farm Estate was particularly appalling. An unarmed police constable was stabbed to death, and up to three guns were fired at the police. The spectre of Northern Ireland's troubled years hovered over much of the subsequent discussion, and it is perhaps worthy of note that two of the principal figures involved in dealing with recent urban unrest — Douglas Hurd and Sir Kenneth Newman — have both served in Northern Ireland, one as Secretary of State, the other as Chief Constable of the Royal Ulster Constabulary.

A disordered past

Sir Kenneth Newman was one of many who described the rioting as 'alien to our streets', and many people thought that this was an unfortunate expression to choose. Sir Peter Emery, MP for Honiton, made his views clear:

> The vast majority of people expect the precepts of Anglo-Saxon behaviour and of law and order to be maintained. These standards must be maintained, despite what other ethnic minorities want.[14]

However, both Sir Kenneth and Sir Peter are wrong to suggest that Britain's towns and cities have in the past been characterised by order and tranquillity. Indeed, in many respects this country's history appears remarkably turbulent, with frequent outbursts of disorder.[15] In the eigtheenth century, civil commotion occurred over various grievances, such as the price of flour and bread, wages and conditions, political reform, the Militia Act, enclosures and turnpikes, and excise duties. The most notable disorders were the Gordon Riots in June 1780, as a result of which 285 people died, and a further 25 were hanged for taking part in them.

In the last century, violent disorders included Luddism, the post-Napoleonic Wars disturbances, rural riots such as the Captain Swing outbreak in 1830–31 and the Rebecca disorders in Wales between 1839 and 1844, and the Sunday Trading riots of 1855. A significant cause of disorder in the nineteenth century was the demand for political reform, and many serious riots occurred in cities such as Bristol, Manchester, Birmingham, Nottingham and Derby, as well as in the capital. In 1820, expressing fears similar to those which Sir Ian Percival had 165 years later, Lord Grenville said 'we are daily assailed with undisguised menace, and are little removed from the expectation of open violence'.[16]

Many of the violent disorders during the past 100 years have been associated with social grievances, unemployment or lack of political representation. In the disturbance in Trafalgar Square on 'Bloody Sunday', 13 November 1887, police clashed with unemployed people, leaving three dead and 200 injured. The periods before and after the First World War were characterised by extensive disorder, over issues such as votes for women, home rule for Ireland, and industrial disputes. In 1910 troops were called in to handle disorder at Tonypandy, in the Rhondda, and the next year during violent clashes in Liverpool and Llanelli, four people were shot.[17] In 1919, disorders took place in areas such as Luton, Wolverhampton, Coventry and Swindon. Race riots occurred in Cardiff, where three people were shot dead, Plymouth, Newport, the East End of London and Liverpool, where Charles Wootton was killed. A strike by the police in Liverpool in August 1919 resulted in widespread disorder and tanks on the streets. Despite frequent assertions to the contrary, the 1930s were years of considerable disorder. Violent clashes were a feature of the period, as outlined in the Appendix at the end of this chapter.

Perspectives on collective violence

It has been argued by a number of analysts that three broad perspectives on riots can be identified.[18] The *conservative* view regards collective violence as 'rare, needless, without purpose and irrational'.[19] It assumes that existing structures are adequate, and there can therefore be no justification or necessity for violent agitation. Disorder is seen as an aberration perpetrated by irresponsible and criminal elements, who may be motivated by greed and excitement, who may be the dupes of political extremists, or who may merely be imitating the behaviour of others.

The *liberal* perspective sees violent outbursts as inevitable under certain conditions, such as high unemployment and widespread social disadvantage. This approach identifies a number of possible sources of grievances, including racial discrimination, police misconduct and lack of political representation, but it tends to view riots as at best only moderately helpful in bringing improvements.

The *radical* view, however, interprets collective violence as purposeful, structured and politically meaningful. It is seen as a normal, legitimate and effective means of protest by groups who have no other opportunities and who are experiencing real deprivations and injustices.[20] According to this view, riots may be seen as a dramatic warning signal, a strident demand for a redistribution of power and resources, or even as the first stirrings of revolution.

In the aftermath of the riots in 1980 and 1981, and the recent disorders in 1985 and 1986, the three perspectives were espoused. The conservative evaluation was the most frequently seen, articulated by politicians, police officers and certain sections of the mass media. However, the liberal perspective was also often evident, from groups such as the Labour and Alliance parties, church and community organisations and some of the quality media. The radical interpretation was offered by some in the Labour Party, and by various community leaders, and was evident in the reports of two of the inquiries carried out into the 1985 urban unrest.[21] The official inquiry into the Brixton disorders in 1981, like that conducted in the United States after the disorders in 1967, while acknowledging the conservative interpretation, tended to adopt the liberal perspective.[22]

Lord Scarman's interpretation

Lord Scarman reported that the disorder occurred in the context of political, social and economic disadvantage, including high levels of unemployment, poor housing, and widespread racial discrimination. Black people, he found, suffered from the same deprivations as whites 'but much more acutely'.[23] The despair of many young blacks led them to feel rejected by British society, a perception that was strengthened by the low level of black political representation and by the freedom British law gives to those who demonstrate in favour of racist measures.

Lord Scarman accepted some of the points made by exponents of the conservative perspective, specifically the inexcusability of the disorder and the possibility of excitement and gain as motives, but he tended to stress the liberal approach.[24] He reported that crime was a problem, but implied that a significant cause of this was unemployment and social disadvantage.

A crucial factor was the hostility between young people in Brixton and the police, who they see as pursuing, abusing and harassing them and as representing a regime which is 'insensitive to their plight'. Taken together, said Lord Scarman, these factors:

> Provide a set of social *conditions* which create a predisposition towards violent protest. Where deprivation and frustration exist on the scale to be found among the young black people of Brixton, the probability of disorder must, therefore, be strong. Moreover, many of them, it is obvious, believe with justification that violence, though wrong, is a very effective means of protest: for, by attracting the attention of the mass media of communication, they get their message across to the people as a whole.[25]

In these remarks there is even a hint of the radical perspective on disorder, seeing riots as an effective means of drawing attention to grievances. However, the interpretation in *The Brixton Disorders* is generally that, though perhaps understandable, the disorders were inexcusable.

The liberal and radical views: social and political flaws

For the purpose of examining the various explanations that have been put forward, the liberal and radical perspectives can be grouped together. Both interpretations focus on 'basic flaws' in society and its political arrangements, though the liberal viewpoint considers that these can be ameliorated by reforms and redistribution while the radical approach requires a more fundamental restructuring. Interpretations which highlight various social and political flaws as causes of riots are sometimes called 'deprivation theories', but this label is not satisfactory as it does not cover all the causes suggested within this category.

The basic flaws theories tend to focus on social injustice, inadequate institutions and the maldistribution of resources and political power as causes of disorder. Riots are seen as a result of the failure of structures to accommodate demands and to satisfy the grievances and expectations of certain groups, and as the result of unfair treatment. Some theorists have drawn attention to *poverty and hardship* as causes of collective violence, but the relationship does not seem to be that straightforward. A number of studies have shown that participants in disorder are often not the most deprived people.[26]

A more plausible theory is that which emphasises *relative deprivation*, where people feel that in comparison with a reference group they do not have that which they need or deserve. This notion is associated with the idea of *unrealised expectations* as a cause of discontent, and Davies introduced the concept of a 'J-curve' to show how a crisis occurs when rising expectations are thwarted by a downturn in their satisfaction.[27] Both the proponents of the *frustration–aggression* model of behaviour, and those who employ the concept of *cognitive dissonance*, see the gap between expectations and performance as giving rise to a tendency to behave violently.[28] According to these theories, a person who is unable to achieve goals which he or she believes should be attainable experiences a build-up in tension which eventually explodes in an uncontrollable outburst of anger. This is cathartic, and after the violence the tension is dissipated, although it may begin to build up again.

These theories pinpoint deprivation as the fundamental cause of rioting, but the violence itself is seen as blind fury. Others have argued that, while deprivation is an underlying problem, the violent protest should be seen as rational and purposeful action by those who have been systematically excluded from full participation in the processes and benefits of society. Thus, the explanation for disorder is *political exclusion*, as well as disadvantage. Bachrach and Baratz suggested that riots are the ballot boxes of the poor, and as such are the means of forcing demands onto the political agenda, which otherwise would be ignored. Hirschman also argued that *lack of political voice* is a key factor. He stressed the importance of political voice for the healthy functioning of the political system, and he suggested that many of the most active, able and articulate residents have migrated from the inner-city areas. These are the people who, had they remained, would have complained, organised and agitated for improvements and extra resources, and the result of their exit has been to leave a voiceless and frustrated population. Riots can be seen as an especially forceful case of political voice.[29]

The term *political marginalisation* has been used to describe the position of those who are powerless and deprived, and the notion of *alienation* is also applied by some theorists to characterise the demoralisation and estrangement from society and its values of those who suffer social rejection and disadvantage.[30] Some theorists have suggested that *weak social integration* is a cause of disorder.[31] This results, it is claimed, from poverty, poor housing and unemployment, and concomitant high levels of crime, which leads to a demoralised population in the area. Accompanied by a high turnover of local residents, these factors cause a decline in consensus on values and weakened social ties. Thus disadvantage leads to a social disintegration with a high potential for outbreaks of violent disturbances.

Another explanation of riots highlights *perceptions of injustice* as the central factor. According to this view, if people believe that the outcomes of decisions, or the behaviour of those in authority, are unjust they may become increasingly resentful and angry. In line with the theories of cognitive dissonance and frustration–aggression, the tension builds until one further, seemingly small, incident of unjust behaviour results in a violent reaction. Perceived injustice, rather than actual deprivation, may thus be the key factor in mobilising protest. Its significance was stressed by Thomas Carlyle in 1839:

> It is not what a man outwardly has or wants that constitutes the happiness or misery of him. Nakedness, hunger, distress of all kinds, death itself have been cheerfully suffered when the heart was right. It is the feeling of injustice that is insupportable to all men. . . . No man can bear it or ought to bear it.[32]

Racial discrimination is likely to cause feelings of injustice, as is *improper police conduct*. Indeed, *repressive measures* and *coercion* have been shown to decrease the legitimacy of the political system and to provoke feelings of injustice, and thereby cause violent disorders, though if the level of repression becomes sufficiently high riots then tend to cease.[33]

The conservative views: law and order and 'riff-raff' explanations

Explanations which are associated with the conservative perspective on riots tend to focus on law and order issues, rather than on social injustice and disadvantage and political power. In the United States they were termed the 'riff-raff' theories of riots, since they see riots as being perpetrated by the most worthless and disreputable people — the riff-raff society. If the liberal and radical perspectives focus on the basic flaws in social and political arrangements, the conservative interpretation stresses the basic flaws in human nature. This point was made by the Home Secretary in the debate in the House of Commons on 23 October 1985. He said the liberal perspective leaves out:

> The excitement of forming and belonging to a mob, the evident excitement of violence leading to the fearsome crimes that we have seen reported and the greed that leads to looting . . . to explain all those things in terms of deprivation and suffering is to ignore some basic and ugly facts about human nature.[34]

Riff-raff explanations tend to focus on individuals' wilful behaviour, or on their weakness and gullibilty. Rioters are seen as people indulging in *criminal activity*, motivated by a desire to loot and rob, and rationally choosing to do this having calculated the costs and benefits.[35] *Excitement* is seen as a reason for disorders, and young people in particular are said to derive 'fun value' from them. Rioting is seen as another manifestation of the football hooliganism syndrome.[36] Another view, advanced by Le Bon, suggests that *crowd behaviour* explains disorder. He argued:

> By the mere fact that he forms part of a crowd, a man descends several rungs in the ladder of civilisation. Isolated, he may be a cultivated

individual; in a crowd, he is a barbarian — that is, a creature acting by instinct.[37]

According to this approach, if a group of people gather together, their behaviour may degenerate into mob or 'mindless' violence. This is most likely to happen, suggests another theory, if there is *social disorganisation* as a result of community disruption, perhaps brought about by redevelopment or an influx of newcomers to an area. This introduces the impact of immigration, and the effects of 'alien' cultures, and these arguments can be seen in the remarks of a number of MPs and media commentators. An associated explanation pinpoints *moral degeneration* and a *decline in respect for the rule of law* as causes of riots and crime in general.[38] This view holds that values and modes of behaviour have deteriorated and traditional social controls are no longer effective in preventing violence. The moral degeneration is considered to be the result of inadequate socialisation; blame is apportioned to institutions such as the family and schools. Hence remarks such as those made by Mr. Giles Shaw, Minister of State at the Home Office:

> In Britain today discipline is a dirty word. It has long since ebbed from millions of homes and it has been dragged from thousands of schools. The police stand as the main bastion of discipline and responsibility in our society.[39]

The media may also be held responsible for the perceived erosion of values and traditional restraints on anti-social behaviour, and television in particular may be blamed for the *legitimation* of *violence* as a form of protest. This links with a further explanation of rioting, which suggests that it is *contagious behaviour*, which may be transmitted from one area to others in the form of 'copycat' disorders.[40] In 1985, for example, a number of people suggested that the riots in Britain were a result of the television broadcasts of disorders in South Africa.

A final, and very common, theory of rioting is that it is engineered by extremists and subversives. The *conspiracy theory*, that agitators are fostering discontent, appears to have been advanced to explain almost all the disorders that have occurred in Britain since the Gordon Riots of 1780.[41] For example, after the riots in Liverpool in August 1919, *The Times* carried a story that 'the authorities' believed the disturbances were 'part of a definite conspiracy, which had its roots abroad, to subvert the present system of government in this country'. The main shortcoming of this theory, which seems to be particularly attractive to the media, police and politicians, is that there is rarely, if ever, any plausible evidence to support it. Both the Kerner Commission in the United States in 1967, and Lord Scarman in 1981, specifically investigated the suggestion that the disorders were the result of a plan or conspiracy, and both inquiries dismissed the theory. Lord Scarman was emphatic: 'They originated spontaneously. There was no premeditation or plan'.[42]

Reactions to the 1985 disorders

The reactions to the disorders in 1985, as in 1980 and 1981, were broadly in accordance with the perspectives outlined above. Conservative politicians, newspapers and police officers adopted riff-raff explanations and ascribed the riots to criminality and greed, hooliganism and 'mindless violence', extremists and subversives, imitation, base impulses in human nature and general evil, or to a failure in education and a breakdown in family life and proper values. Douglas Hurd said after the Handsworth disorder that it was 'not a social phenomemon but crimes': it was 'not a cry for help but a cry for loot'. Mr. Norman Tebbit, Conservative Party Chairman, said after the Tottenham riots that they were the result of 'wickedness', and he later suggested that the moral degeneration was a legacy of the permissive society of the 1960s. Mr. Giles Shaw, the Home Office Minister, was uncompromising in the House of Commons' debate on 23 October 1985:

> It is no use trying to find some excuse for criminal behaviour. Excuses must not be found. Mitigating circumstances do not exist. We cannot condone or qualify culpability.[43]

A number of senior police officers said that the riots were planned, either by political extremists (or 'militant insurrectionaries' as Sir Eldon Griffiths put it[44]) or by drug dealers. The media seized on both these propositions and, to take the example quoted in full in Chapter 1, on 8 October 1985 in its 'Tottenham Riot Special' edition, the *Daily Express* led with a story of how 'a hand-picked death squad' which had been 'trained in Moscow and Libya', 'acted on the orders of crazed Left-wing extremists'.

Some police officers, however, favoured explanations drawn from the basic social and political flaws category. Colin Couch, for example, who was Chief Superintendent in Tottenham, said that social disadvantage and unemployment were important factors, and a similar approach was taken by Commander Alex Marnoch, Head of Police in Lambeth. Occasionally Conservative politicians also espoused these views. Jonathan Sayeed, MP for Bristol East, said 'those who feel rejected by society will tend to reject the rules of that society', but he also stressed criminality and cultural factors.[45] The Labour and Alliance parties, and church and community leaders, adopted 'basic societal flaws' explanations, though after the Handsworth disorders two Labour MPs, Roy Hattersley and Jeff Rooker, articulated law and order theories.

By mid-October Mr. Rooker was ascribing the riots essentially to 'economic decline, deprivation and disintegration' and 'the obscenity of unemployment'. John Fraser, Labour MP for Norwood, the constituency in which much of Brixton falls, spoke of 'the violent harvest of bitter fruit' sown during the past 6 years by the Government:

> It is impossible to divorce the catastrophic cuts in housing, the catastrophic increase in unemployment and the catastrophic cuts in all sorts of services in the constituency and borough that I represent, from what has happened in that area, where deep hatred, disillusion, despair and alienation lie beneath the surface and are the cause of these riots.[46]

Black community leaders blamed police harassment and abuse, as well as racial discrimination and disadvantage. Asians seemed to be more divided in their views, but a number of Asians from Handsworth blamed poverty and police 'heavy-handed' treatment for the disorders.

The reactions from those with liberal and radical perspectives tended to emphasise unemployment, deprivation and particularly poor housing, racism, and police relations with the local communities as the principal problems. Some drew attention to perceptions of unjust treatment, relative deprivation and unrealised expectations. A few also highlighted political exclusion and alienation as causes of the disorders.

Five common characteristics

Gerald Kaufman, the Shadow Home Secretary, listed many of these factors as causes of the riots. He was particularly scathing of the Government's argument that they were simply crimes. Why, he asked, if the disorders were not related to social and economic disadvantage, did they occur in inner-city areas and not in the Home Secretary's constituency of Witney, Oxfordshire?

It does seem that in 1985 and 1986, as in 1981 and 1980, the areas in which disorder ocurred share certain common characteristics. In addition, it seems that the riots themselves began after similar events. The *immediate precipitants* or *trigger events* in each case involved police officers and black people. The trigger events are the sparks which ignite the tinder. There seem to be five characteristics which are common to the areas where rioting has occurred in the 1980s:

(1) *Racial disadvantage and discrimination are major afflictions.* A significant proportion of the population in each area in which rioting occurred is Afro-Carribbean or Asian. These are the people who tend to experience social and economic disadvantage particularly acutely, and who

also suffer from racial discrimination, racist abuse and sometimes physical attacks.[47] As quoted earlier, Lord Scarman reported:

> Racial disadvantage is a fact of current British life. It was, I am equally sure, a significant factor in the causation of the Brixton disorders. Urgent action is needed if it is not to become an endemic ineradicable disease threatening the very survival of our society.[48]

Since he wrote this in 1981, the problems of racial disadvantage and racism seem in many respects to have become even worse.

(2) *Unemployment is high*, and particularly affects youth, and especially young black people. For example, in autumn 1985 the unemployment rate in Britain was 13 per cent but in Birmingham it was 20.8 per cent; in Handsworth it was 34.8 per cent. Of those who left school in 1984, 18 per cent of whites and 15.8 per cent of Asians, but only 4.9 per cent of Afro-Caribbeans, had found a job a year later. Youth unemployment in general in Handsworth was 50 per cent, while on Broadwater Farm Estate it was 60 per cent.

(3) *Deprivation is widespread*: environmental decay, poor educational and social service provision, inadequate recreational facilities and crime are problems. In particular, housing is often substandard and a source of great distress. The 1981 census showed that whereas under 1 per cent of households in Britain was overcrowded, in Birmingham the figure was 6 per cent and in Handsworth it was over 15 per cent. In Brixton, in 1981, 1022 new houses were completed, but by 1984 this had fallen to 552. The reason was the squeeze on local government expenditure, so that while in 1981 Lambeth Council spent £51 million on housing, by 1985 this had fallen to £34 million. Housing subsidies to Liverpool in 1980/81 were £18 million, but by 1984/85 this had fallen to £5 million; over the same period the city's rate support grant (RSG) fell from £141 million to £118 million.

(4) *Political exclusion and powerlessness are evident*, in that there are few institutions, opportunities and resources for articulating grievances and bringing pressure to bear on those with political power. Decisions tend to be imposed upon these communities through a 'top-down' approach by the professionals in local or central government, or by agencies such as the Urban Development Corporations. The lack of political voice affects all the residents in these areas, but particularly black people. As George Greaves, Principal Community Relations Officer in Lambeth, put it:

> Black people are hardly ever in a position to influence decisions made about them — decisions which sometimes alter the course of their lives in fundamental ways . . . on the rare occasions when they are consulted they feel their advice goes unheeded.[49]

(5) *Mistrust of, and hostility to, the police is widespread* among certain sections, particularly the young. There is disquiet about police tactics, such as stop-and-search, and allegations are frequently made about harassment, abuse and assault.[50] Lord Scarman found a 'loss of confidence by significant sections' of the Lambeth public. The incidents of misconduct which he found, led to a spiral of decline in relations so that many young people had become 'indignant and resentful against the police, suspicious of everything they did'.[51]

The repudiation of political authority

After each outbreak of urban unrest in the 1980s, among those who accepted societal flaws explanations, opinions varied as to which of the above five factors were the most significant. Lord Scarman, in 1981, came to the view that 'the riots were essentially an outburst of anger and resentment by young black people against the police',[52] and many people in the communities affected by riots in 1985 and 1986 also felt that this was the fundamental factor.

Taken together, the five problems are of great concern for two reasons. *First*, they result in frustrated expectations, cumulative disappointment and increasing resentment at the injustices. These lead to disenchantment with the established political procedures; they undermine confidence in, and the legitimacy of, political institutions and rules; and they erode social controls and the value consensus. The result may be the repudiation of political authority, manifest as civic indifference, a refusal to comply with laws and directives, or as open conflict and violence. Perhaps the least threatening outcome of this sombre possibility will be a continuing 'smouldering apathy' in the cities, which will sometimes flare up in violent disorder. Continued injustice will lead to further civil resistance and a developing political contention.[53]

The *second* reason for concern about the five problems is that it does not seem likely, at least in the short term, that anything very much will be done about them, for the reasons discussed in Chapter 19. In the aftermath of the 1981 riots there was a flurry of activity, but the momentum soon slackened, and 6 years later it is difficult to see any real progress with the problems listed above. After the 1985 disorders the Government steadfastly refused to hold another Scarman-type inquiry. It was made known that Viscount Whitelaw had been appointed Chairman of a Cabinet committee to examine inner-city policy and the Urban Programme. As a result some alterations and innovations have occurred, but overall the initiatives are modest. There seems to be a profound lack of political commitment.

The primary response is one based on the law and order or 'riff-raff' interpretations of the disorders. Police equipment, training and tactics for suppressing disorder have been developed and strengthened, and more stringent powers and penalties were provided in the Public Order Act 1986. Accounts of police operations since the disorders show that a tough approach is generally being adopted in a determination to eradicate disorder and crime. The police force areas in which riots occurred have been given additional officers and resources, and there is a clear demand from the lower ranks, articulated by the Police Federation, for a more vigorous form of policing.

There is, however, a danger that this response will make matters worse by diminishing further the cooperation and consent of people living in the inner cities. If this occurs it makes the task of the police in solving crimes even more difficult, which means that as their clear-up rate falls they may adopt even more rigorous methods. There is a danger of a vicious circle, in which the community and police grow ever further apart. Indeed, evidence produced by Gurr and others has shown that an increase in coercion by a regime very frequently leads to an increase in violent disturbances.[54] Unfortunately, as events in 1986 showed, there appeared to be a measure of understatement in the Home Secretary's remarks in Parliament in October 1985: 'I find what has happened deeply tragic and worrying. . . . We must not forget what happened, because it could happen again.'[55]

Notes

1. 'Anger in the streets', *Time*, 20 July 1981, p. 8.
2. For detailed accounts of the media coverage of the 1981 disorders see Chapters 1, 3 and 7 in J. Benyon (ed.), *Scarman and After: Essays Reflecting on Lord Scarman's Report, the Riots and their Aftermath*, Oxford: Pergamon Press, 1984; see especially Chapter 7 by G. Murdock, 'Reporting the riots: images and impact'.
3. *The Brixton Disorders, 10–12 April 1981: Report of an Inquiry by the Rt. Hon. The Lord Scarman, OBE*, London: HMSO, 1981 (Cmnd. 8427), para. 1.7.
4. *Ibid.*, para. 9.1.
5. House of Commons Official Report, Parliamentary Debates (*Hansard*) Session 1984–85, Sixth Series, Vol. 84, 23 October 1985, cols 350–51.
6. Daniel Defoe, *An Effectual Scheme for the Immediate Prevention of Street Robberies and Suppressing of all other Disorders of the Night; with a Brief History of the Night-houses and an Appendix Relating to those Sons of Hell Call'd Incendiaries*, London, 1730, cited by A. Silver in D. J. Bordua (ed.), *The Police: Six Sociological Essays*, New York: John Wiley, 1967, p. 1.
7. Cited in E. Halevy, *A History of the English People*, New York, 1912, Vol. 1, p. 292.
8. House of Lords Official Report, Parliamentary Debates (*Hansard*), Session 1981–82, Fifth Series, Vol. 428, 24 March 1982, cols 1005–1006.
9. Select Committee on the Employment of Military in Cases of Disturbance, 1908; see also R. Geary, *Policing Industrial Disputes: 1893 to 1985*, London: Methuen, 1986, pp. 14–19.
10. MORI poll for London Television, *Weekend World*, 3 March 1985.
11. *Hansard*, 23 October 1985, *supra* note 5, cols 356–61.
12. *Ibid.*, col. 365.
13. *Ibid.*, col. 374.
14. House of Commons Official Report, Parliamentary Debates (*Hansard*), Session 1984–85, Sixth Series, Vol. 84, 21 October 1985, col. 39.
15. See for example J. Stevenson, *Popular Disturbances in England 1700–1870*, London: Longman, 1979; E. J. Hobsbawm, *Primitive Rebels*, Manchester: Manchester University Press, 1959; G. Rude, *The Crowd in History 1730–1848*, London: Lawrence and Wishart, 1981; C. Hampton (ed.), *A Radical Reader*, Harmondsworth: Penguin, 1984.

16. *Substance of the Speech of the Rt. Hon. Lord Grenville in the House of Lords, 19 November 1820*, London p. 23, cited by A. Silver, *supra* note 6, p. 16.
17. Geary, *Policing Industrial Disputes*, *supra* note 9, pp. 25–47.
18. J. Button, *Black Violence*, Princeton: Princeton University Press, 1978; S. Taylor, 'The Scarman Report and explanations of riots', in J. Benyon (ed.), *Scarman and After*, Oxford: Pergamon Press, 1984, pp. 20–34.
19. J. Skolnick, *The Politics of Protest*, New York: Ballantine Books, 1969, p. 15.
20. *Ibid.*, pp. 330–6.
21. *A Different Reality: Report of the Review Panel*, Birmingham: West Midlands County Council, February 1986; *The Broadwater Farm Inquiry Report*, London: Broadwater Farm Inquiry, 1986.
22. *The Brixton Disorders*, *supra* note 3; *Report of the National Advisory Commission on Civil Disorders* (The Kerner Commission), Washington: US Government Printing Office 1968; reprinted as *Report*, New York: Bantam Books, 1968.
23. *The Brixton Disorders*, *supra* note 3, para. 2.35.
24. Taylor, 'The Scarman Report and explanations of riots', *supra* note 18.
25. *The Brixton Disorders*, *supra* note 3, para. 2.38.
26. Rude, *The Crowd in History*, *supra* note 15.
27. J. Davies, 'The J-curve of rising and declining satisfactions as a cause of revolution and rebellion', in H. Graham and T. Gurr (eds), *Violence in America: Historical and Comparative Perspectives*, London: Sage, 1979.
28. J. Dollard *et al.*, *Frustration and Aggression*, New Haven: Yale University Press, 1974; T. Gurr, *Why Men Rebel*, Princeton: Princeton University Press, 1970; see also contributions in L. Masotti and D. Bowen (eds), *Riots and Rebellion*, California: Sage, 1968; L. Festinger, *The Theory of Cognitive Dissonance*, Stanford: Stanford University Press, 1968; D. Schwartz, 'A theory of revolutionary behaviour', in J. Davies (ed.), *When Men Revolt and Why*, Glencoe; Free Press, 1971; H. Eckstein (ed.), *Internal War*, Glencoe: Free Press, 1964.
29. P. Bachrach and M. Baratz, *Power and Poverty*, New York: Oxford University Press, 1970; A. O. Hirschman, *Exit, Voice and Loyalty: Responses to Decline in Firms, Organisations and States*, Cambridge, Mass.: Harvard University Press, 1970.
30. J. Lea and J. Young, *What is to be Done about Law and Order?*, Harmondsworth: Penguin, 1984, especially pp. 198–225.
31. *Ibid.*; see also J. Lea and J. Young, 'The riots in Britain 1981', in D. Cowell, T. Jones and J. Young (eds), *Policing the Riots*, London: Junction Books, 1982, pp. 5–20; 'Britain's Inner Cities', *The Economist*, 16 July 1981, pp. 34–6.
32. T. Carlyle, *Chartism*, London: Chapman and Hall, 1892, p. 23.
33. T. Gurr, 'A causal model of civil strife', *American Political Science Review*, Vol. 62, 1968, pp. 1104–24; D. Bwy, 'Dimensions of social conflict in Latin America', in Masotti and Bowen (eds), *Riots and Rebellion*, *supra* note 28; D. Russell, *Rebellion, Revolution and Armed Force*, New York: Academic Press, 1974.
34. *Hansard*, 23 October 1985, *supra* note 5, col. 358.
35. G. Tullock, 'The paradox of revolution', *Public Choice*, Vol. 11, 1971, pp. 89–100; E. Banfield 'Rioting mainly for fun and profit', in J. Q. Wilson (ed.), *The Metropolitan Enigma*, Cambridge, Mass.: Harvard University Press, 1968.
36. Banfield 'Rioting mainly for fun and profit', *supra* note 35.
37. G. Le Bon, *The Crowd*, New York: Viking Press, 1960, p. 32.
38. R. Clutterbuck, *Britain in Agony: The Growth of Political Violence*, Harmondsworth: Penguin, 1980; R. Clutterbuck, *The Media and Political Violence*, London: Macmillan, 1983.
39. *Hansard*, 23 October 1985, *supra* note 5, col. 385.
40. R. Clutterbuck, 'Terrorism and urban violence', *Proceedings of the Academy of Political Science*, Vol. 34, 1982, p. 170; S. Spilerman, 'Structural characteristics of cities and the severity of racial disorders', *American Sociological Review*, Vol. 41, October 1976, p. 790; E. Moonman, *Copycat Hooligans*, London: Centre for Contemporary Studies, 1981.
41. G. Murdock, 'Reporting the riots: images and impact', in J. Benyon (ed.), *Scarman and After*, Oxford: Pergamon Press', 1984, pp. 73–95.
42. *The Brixton Disorders*, *supra* note 3, para. 3.108.
43. *Hansard*, 23 October 1985, *supra* note 5, col. 385.

44. *Ibid.*, col. 375.
45. *Ibid.*, col. 378.
46. *Ibid.*, cols. 379–84.
47. See for example C. Brown, *Black and White Britain: The Third PSI Survey*, London: Heinemann, 1984; J. Benyon (ed.), *Scarman and After*, Oxford: Pergamon Press, 1984, pp. 163–229; Home Office, *Racial Attacks*, London: HMSO, 1981.
48. *The Brixton Disorders*, *supra* note 2, para. 9.1.
49. G. Greaves, 'The Brixton disorders' in J. Benyon (ed.), *Scarman and After*, Oxford: Pergamon Press, 1984, p. 71.
50. *Police and People in London*, Vol. 1: D. J. Smith, *A Survey of Londoners*, London: Policy Studies Institute, 1983 (PSI No. 618); Vol. 4: D. J. Smith and J. Gray, *The Police in Action*, London: Policy Studies Institute, 1983 (PSI No. 621); J. Benyon, *A Tale of Failure: Race and Policing*, Coventry: University of Warwick, 1983 (Policy Paper in Ethnic Relations No. 3); J. Benyon and C. Bourn (eds), *The Police: Powers, Procedures and Proprieties*, Oxford: Pergamon Press, 1986.
51. *The Brixton Disorders*, *supra* note 2, para. 4.1.
52. *Ibid.*, para 8.12.
53. For a discussion of four forms of collective violence (political contention, civil disorder, class struggle and civil resistance) see T. Davis, 'The forms of collective racial violence', *Political Studies*, Vol. 34, March 1986, pp. 40–60.
54. Gurr, 'A causal model of civil strife', *supra* note 33; Bwy, 'Dimensions of social conflict in Latin America', *supra* note 33; Russell, *Rebellion, Revolution and Armed Force*, *supra* note 33; C. Johnson, *Revolutionary Change*, London: University of London Press, 1968.
55. *Hansard*, 23 October 1985, *supra* note 5, cols 361–2.

Appendix: Disorder in the devil's decade

A strange myth seems to have developed that, despite high unemployment, the 1930s was a period of relative public tranquillity. Mrs. Thatcher, for example, has remarked on a number of occasions: 'we had much higher unemployment in the 1930s, but we didn't get violence then'. This view of the interwar years is a dramatic case of historical amnesia, for the period was far from peaceful. Indeed, as noted by two historians who have made a special study of the 1930s, 'the Government was seriously alarmed by the threat to public order' (Stevenson and Cook, 1979, p. 218).

It might reasonably be asked of those who claim this was a time when unemployment was high, yet civil order was assured, why two successive governments considered it was necessary for Parliament to pass public order legislation. The Incitement to Disaffection Act 1934, and the Public Order Act 1936, were passed to meet the perceived challenge from extra-parliamentary movements. Public disorder was seen as a threat not just by the governments in the 1930s but also by the media. For example, *The Times* (29 October 1932) said of the National Unemployed Workers' Movement (NUWM) Hunger March:

> The evil will grow if it is not checked. There are plenty of ways in which legitimate discontent may be rationally expressed. The government must seriously consider whether the spurious importance which these mass marches are bound to be given at home or abroad should not be countered by special restrictive measures.

Two years later, under the headline BIG PLANS TO CURB 'HUNGER MARCHES', 'Foiling a New Red Plot', the *Sunday Pictorial* (22 February 1934) carried the report:

> It is known that sinister influences are at work to provoke trouble of a grave character and the authorities have not overlooked the possibility of repercussions in London following the desperate street fighting which recently took place in Paris and Vienna.

In the autumn of 1932 Sir Oswald Mosley formed the British Union of Fascists (BUF). In 1934 Lord Rothermere's newspapers (the *Daily Mail*, the *Evening News*, the *Sunday Dispatch* and the *Sunday Pictorial*) started to support the fascists. On 15 January 1934, for example, the *Daily Mail* carried an article entitled 'Hurrah for the Black-Shirts'. But BUF meetings were often accompanied by violent clashes, and its anti-semitism led to many attacks by fascists on Jewish people. On 4 October 1936 a march led by Mosley was confronted by a huge crowd of opponents, and the 'Battle of Cable Street' ensued in London's East End. The BUF continued in existence until May 1940, when Mosley and some of his followers were detained under the Emergency Powers Defence Regulations.

As the following *selection* of incidents shows, with good reason the 1930s earned its tag of the 'devil's decade'.

1930

Jan: NUWM reports membership still rising; its slogan is 'on the streets with mass demonstrations'.
Mar: Third National Hunger March sets out.
Apr: Race riots in North Shields.
May: Struggle between hunger marchers and police at the House of Commons.
Jul: Riots between Roman Catholics and Orangemen in Everton, Liverpool.
Aug: Baton charge on strikers in Cardiff.
Nov: Affray at political meeting in Derby.

1931

Jan: At Highbury, crowds sweep police aside.
Mar: Crime wave reported.
Jun: Gang disorder in London.
Jul: Orange riots in Liverpool (50 hurt).
Aug: Street battle in Oxford; riot in Manchester: 1000 fight police.
Sep: Clashes between police and Welsh hunger marchers at Trades Union Congress in Bristol; police baton unemployed marchers in Whitehall; violence between unemployed and police in Dundee, Birmingham, Glasgow, and Manchester; Royal Navy mutiny at Invergordon; trouble in Liverpool.
Oct: Mounted police charge unemployed in Salford; more rioting in Glasgow; 80,000 unemployed march in Manchester: police turn fire hoses on them; many people clubbed by police; violent clashes between police and unemployed in London, Blackburn and Cardiff; riot at Moseley meeting in Birmingham; trouble at Leicester meeting; more disturbances in London and Cardiff; National Government under MacDonald elected.
Nov: Disorder in Shoreditch, elsewhere in London and in Coventry; marches and demonstrations against the means test.
Dec: Police and unemployed clash in Liverpool, Wallsend, London, Leeds, Glasgow, Wigan, Kirkcaldy, Stoke-on-Trent and elsewhere.

1932

Jan: Unemployed protest in Leicester; clashes between police and jobless in Keighley, Glasgow, Rochdale and Glasgow again.
Feb: Violence in London and Bristol.
Mar: More clashes in Glasgow.
Apr: Riots in London; crowd rescue arrested men in Leeds; strike protests in Hinckley; growing crime wave is a source of concern.
Jun: Police break up Communist march in Hendon; mounted police charge march in Bristol; batons drawn on Leicester crowd.
Aug: Disorder in Burnley.
Sep: Extraordinary events in Birkenhead: raids by police on working-class homes after clash between unemployed and officers; many reports of people badly beaten; over 100 taken to hospital with severe injuries; violence between police and jobless elsewhere on Merseyside and in London.

Oct: Police charge demonstration in Glasgow; violence in Croydon; riots in London; cameras forbidden to film NUWM Fourth Hunger March; marchers and police clash in Stratford-upon-Avon; in Belfast police baton-charge march; second march is banned, but goes ahead; widespread fighting; barricades erected; police stoned; great violence by police; two people shot dead by police, several more wounded; troops called in; Tom Mann, Hon. Treasurer of NUWM, arrested; disturbances at North Shields and West Ham; disorder in Lambeth; 'uproar' in Leicester; at Hyde Park it is claimed that special constables attack hunger marchers after abuse; violent scenes ensue; mounted police charge into crowd; 70 public and seven police injured; 3 days later, in Trafalgar Square, trouble between police and demonstrators.

Nov: When NUWM petition is taken to Westminster violence occurs; 3174 police clash with unemployed; fierce fighting; police seize petition; police raid NUWM headquarters, without a warrant, and confiscate documents [damages and costs are later awarded against the police]; Wal Hannington, leader of NUWM, is arrested for incitement [he is sentenced to 3 months in prison]; Home Secretary Gilmour warns Cabinet that during the recent disturbances 'the position had become extremely critical'.

Dec: Sid Elias, Chairman of NUWM, gets 2 years in prison for sedition; Tom Mann and Emrys Llewellyn (NUWM secretary) each sentenced to 2 months in prison.

1933

Jan: Unemployment reaches 3 million.
Feb: 20,000 in TUC demonstration at Hyde Park.
Mar: Disorder when Prince of Wales visits Glasgow.
Apr: Means test riot in Durham.
May: Violent clashes between fascists and opponents in London; violent anti-Hitler demonstration in London; more trouble at fascist rally in London; unemployed storm meeting in London; clash between police and jobless in Great Yarmouth.
Nov: Violence between Blackshirts and others in Coventry; trouble at fascist meeting in London.

1934

Feb: Fifth National Hunger March under way; National Council for Civil Liberties formed by, amongst others, Attlee, Brittain, Herbert, Laski and Wells.
Mar: Trouble with fascists in Bristol; serious street disorder in Glasgow (one dead, three injured).
Apr: Fight in Newcastle between fascists and communists.
Jun: Disturbances at BUF meeting at Olympia; anti-fascist disturbance at BUF meeting in Finsbury Park; police use batons in Plymouth at clash between BUF supporters and opponents; disorder after Blackshirt meeting in Leicester; trouble and arrests at BUF meeting in Sheffield.
Jul: Cabinet discusses proposals for strengthening public order law.
Sept: Trouble at BUF meeting in Leicester.
Oct: Disorder at fascist rally in Plymouth.
Nov: Incitement to Disaffection Act receives Royal Assent.

1935

Jan: Agitation against the new unemployment relief scales.
Feb: Protests all over the country; in South Wales 300,000 on the streets; disturbances at Merthyr, Arbertillery, Nantyglo and Blaina; large-scale protests in Yorkshire and Scotland; heavy fighting in Sheffield; trouble in Tyneside and Lancashire; MP attacked in Lincoln; new relief scales withdrawn.
Apr: Crowd stone police in South Wales; trouble at BUF meeting in Leicester.
Jun: Police baton charge in Belfast; woman dies at Blackshirt meeting in Bootle; Stanley Baldwin becomes Prime Minister.

Jul: Orange disorders in Glasgow; riots in Belfast.
Oct: Violence at fascist meeting in Leicester.
Nov: Stormy scenes at election meetings; in the General Election Labour win 154 seats (a gain of 102), Conservatives win 437.

1936

Mar: Trouble at fascist meeting at Albert Hall; police accused of attacking anti-fascists.
May: Disturbances at BUF meetings in Leicester and Oxford.
Jun: Further disorder at BUF meetings in Oxford and Manchester.
Jul. Disturbances at BUF rally in Hull; trouble on Orange march in Glasgow.
Aug: Disorder at BUF meetings in Bristol and Leicester.
Sept: Violence at fascist rally in Leeds.
Oct: British Union of Fascists' march in East End is confronted by crowd estimated at 100,000; fighting ensues; in the 'Battle of Cable Street' many are injured, over 80 arrested; Jarrow 'Crusade' arrives in London; unemployment in Jarrow is 73 per cent; march receives much favourable publicity; Sixth National Hunger March by NUWM arrives in London; although much bigger than Jarrow 'Crusade', it receives less attention.
Dec: Public Order Act receives Royal Assent.

1937

Apr: City Road Police Station reports continued disturbances in the East End.
May: Neville Chamberlain becomes Prime Minister.
Jul: Irishmen riot in Huddersfield; serious disturbances in Bermondsey and south London at BUF march; 113 arrests and 28 casualties.
Oct: Fascist riot in Liverpool.
Nov: Commotion at the Cenotaph.

1938

Mar: Uproar at Leicester meeting.
May: Mosley's Leicester headquarters stormed.
Jun: Reports of anti-semitic attacks and abuse in various areas.
Dec: 200 men sit down in Oxford Street, with banners saying 'work or bread'; Ritz is occupied by unemployed asking for tea for twopence.

1939

Jan: Unemployed threaten police in Brighton; invasions continue of expensive restaurants in Piccadilly and Regent Street; several 'chain-gangs' are arrested, after chaining themselves to public buildings.
May: Further reports of attacks on Jews.
Jul: Rent strikers fight with police in Middlesex; crowd tries to lynch Irishman in Liverpool disorder.
Aug: Trouble at peace demonstration in Downing Street.
Sep: War against Germany is declared.
Nov: Disorder at fascist meeting in London.

Sources: C. Mowat, *Britain between the Wars*, London: Methuen, 1968; P. Kingsford, *The Hunger Marchers in Britain 1920–1940*, London: Lawrence and Wishart: 1982; J. Stevenson and C. Cook, *The Slump*, London: Quartet, 1979; I. Waddington, Department of Sociology, University of Leicester.

PART 2

Urban Unrest in Britain and the United States

CHAPTER 3

Urban unrest in Britain

STUART HALL

I have to confess that when I was invited — not only to contribute but to do so first — I had two principal reservations which I should share with you. The first is a confession. Urban unrest is a topic about which I find it impossible to muster the scholarly detachment and academic calm which is often felt to be appropriate in discussions of this kind, and if I transgress in any way that frontier I hope that you will forgive me.

Secondly, I have a reluctance about entering once again into what seems to me a terribly familiar and recurring cycle. The cycle goes something like this. There is a problem that is followed by a conference; the conference is followed by research; the research reinforces what we already know, but in elegant and scholarly language. Then nothing happens. There is another problem which arises out of the conditions which the research investigated. Everyone expresses surprise that the problem has arisen and calls another conference. I regret to say that I feel we are still at some strategic point in that ever-recurring circle.

Deprivation in the cities

I am therefore very pleased indeed that this conference has been organised on such an important and timely topic, but I do hope that some time will be spent directing attention to an important aspect of unrest: the way in which a particular definition of the causes and background to these events is rapidly established. It is true that some time afterwards alternative explanations of a deeper and more searching kind may occasionally come to the fore and raise matters for the agenda, but never with the urgency or vigour or commitment or collective political will necessary to bring about fundamental change.

With what I suspect are controversial opening comments let me go on perhaps to be even more provocative. What seem to be the principal underlying causes of the urban unrest which Britain has experienced in recent years? These events are not *exclusively* related to the question of race, but race is a substantial factor. The central question concerns the

45

extensive alienation of the black population in this society, and urban unrest flows from that sense of deep injustice. That is undoubtedly one definition of the situation and I offer it as a place from which to start.

If we are seriously interested in understanding why during the 1980s there is this kind of unrest in British cities we need to consider three fundamental themes. *First* there is the question of social deprivation and disadvantage. I do not propose to try to catalogue in any deep sense what that social deprivation and disadvantage is like in our society, for it has been extensively documented and the evidence is easily accessible. It is an affront to research work, and to those who have directed scholarly and academic attention to this problem, even to question whether we know the extent of social deprivation and disadvantage, especially that amongst the black population. Its existence is well established.

However the data do not tell the full story. One of the dimensions which is constantly missing from the debates about social deprivation and disadvantage in the black population is *any real sense of what it constitutes as the lived reality of those who experience it.* Disadvantage and deprivation are general terms. They describe general social and economic processes, but it is quite difficult to try to imagine what it is like to experience the results of a set of social processes. What is it like to be an ordinary black person living an everyday life, trying to work and to keep a family together in an urban environment? Such a person may not understand many of these processes in an analytic way, and they do not know precisely where they come from, but they constitute their everyday, everynight, lived reality: simply the facts of what life is like.

Another aspect of social deprivation and disadvantage is, of course, that they are not race-specific in our society. However, we would be not facing up to the facts if we failed to recognise that where deprivation and disadvantage occur those who are black are doubly disadvantaged. Black people consistently find themselves at the bottom of the pile of every indicator of deprivation and disadvantage, and that position within the structure of social, political and economic life is then compounded and doubled by the additional factor of race. The question of deprivation cannot be isolated from the particular and specific ways in which disadvantage affects the experience of people who are black, and is compounded by the fact of their racial identity.[1]

The assault on collective social provision

The *second* theme concerns the political context of urban disadvantage and unrest. We have to recognise the degree to which those who are at the bottom of the social and economic pyramid in this society have, over the past 10 years, had their position exacerbated and compounded by the general economic recession. More specifically, one must recognise the way in which the processes of deindustrialisation in large sectors of society have undermined the following: the opportunities of the worst-off for material sustenance; their capacities to maintain an adequate standard of life; the hopes, especially of those who are young, for permanent and secure employment; and their chances of advancement, whether they are men or women, in the employment field. We must recognise the way in which this impacts on the whole of the rest of their living experience.

In addition to the actual way in which the economic position of the poorer sections of our society have been damaged by economic trends over the past 10 years there has been an additional factor, namely an assault on the very idea of collective social provision itself. That is a political choice. It is one thing for a society to say 'we are in an economic situation where, even if we wanted, it is not possible to offer to those at the bottom of the social ladder the forms of social and collective support which would enable them to survive in a decent way'. It is quite another thing for a society to enter such an economic condition committed to a public view that the collective social provision for the deprived and disorganised in the society is some kind of moral sin, and that what they should do is what we are told people used to do in the past, which is to lift themselves up out of poverty and disadvantage by their own moral bootstraps.

When a society commits itself to that as its public philosophy, and when public policies are reconstructed and redirected so as to enable the combination of possessive individualism, a strong and disciplinary state and the wild and untutored forces of the free market to prevail, it is slightly obscene to ask the question why those who are at the receiving end of those processes sometimes get so angry that they throw a brick. So the questions of social and economic disadvantage are in my view compounded by a quite specific political and ideological climate which has come into existence in the past decade, and which has seriously affected the way in which black and white people at the bottom of the society — but black especially — have to survive.

Racism and social exclusion

The *third* point to which I need to draw attention is simply the question of racism. It is now considered slightly *de trop*, slightly outdated, to refer to the question of racism at all. It was noticeable, when the 1985 riots were being discussed and debated publicly in the media and elsewhere, that the question of racism was regarded as an already established fact which we all know and are trying to do something about, but which we do not have to look at specifically. The experience of those who are at the receiving end of racism in this society is *not* that it is something they experience in this or that situation, when they go to this or that public authority, or turn up for this or that job, or when they encounter this or that authority figure in society. It is simply now the modality in which they live their lives, it is how they relate to almost every institutional and organised form of life in this society, because it is how the society relates to them.

Racism is seen and experienced by black people as having much more to do with the way in which institutions work towards them than it has to do with the particular attitude of this or that individual. It is quite true in our society that attitudes based on race and colour, and attitudes of discrimination towards black people, are very prevalent, and we have only to look at the long-standing history of this society to know both why those attitudes are present, and why they are not in any sense confined to one sector of the society. If the problem of racism was simply a problem of altering the personal and interpersonal attitudes of one group to another, or one set of individuals to another, that would be intractable enough, but it would not describe the real position that exists.

The actual problem is one in which groups of people in this society — perfectly well-minded, full of liberal sentiment, indeed wanting in their overt commitment to do something significant about the situation — nevertheless so operate in institutional settings that they work, towards the people who are powerless and who do not shape the decisions that affect their lives, in such a way as to discriminate particular sections of the population from others along the line of closure which is defined by race and colour. In this way one particular section of the society comes to understand itself as a targeted population. These people feel that the institutions work towards them not in terms of their specific needs and demands as individuals with the full range of good and bad differences which affect and characterise all individuals in society. They feel the institutions work towards them as a block. They are seen first in the stereotype of their racial and ethnic identity, and only then are they seen as people, individuals, and groups, with a specific social or economic problem.

When one group in society systematically works towards another group in the society over time — and it is now 30 years and more — in this consistently stereotyped way, it produces at the other end of the institutional processes a group in the population that identifies itself as the excluded. No social scientist is able to say on this day or that day, at this hour or that hour, X or Y will trigger off social unrest, but it will follow, as night follows day, that such an excluded population with a deep sense of social injustice will sooner or later explode.

The responses of the news agenda

This is the simple, lived, factual background. That is all that social science can tell anyone about why there is urban unrest of the kind we have experienced in Britain in the 1980s. There is not any mystery; there is no hidden factor; there is no new news to bring to you. The news is that this is the way in which society treats second and third and fourth generations of black people, born in Britain, whose entire hopes and aspirations and futures are tied up with whether this society succeeds or not in delivering the goods to its population. They have no other future anywhere else.

Black people have come to understand that British society works towards them in that way, which is not to suggest that every individual and particular moment of social interaction is one of racist discrimination. It is not to suggest that at all. It is also *not* to suggest that black people are not involved in illegal activities — that they are not like other sections of the population involved in crimes arising from the context of social poverty and unemployment. They are a population like any population, with the same mixture of good and bad, of legal and illegal, of criminal and respectable. At one time, it ought to be reported, the black population was specifically identified by public authorities in this society as being astonishingly law-abiding. It requires some social explanation as to how a particularly law-abiding population in the 1950s became a characteristically and stereotypically illegal and lawless population in the 1980s.

The points I have been making are not news to anybody who has given more than a few moments thought to the subject. Nevertheless when the startling events, which occurred in 1980, 1981 and 1985, come onto the news agenda, and when they break across the news pages, it is increasingly the case that these factors are not any longer taken into consideration.[2] It is not even considered appropriate to mobilise them as an initial response to the disorders. What we saw in 1985 was the notion that after all thousands and millions of pounds had been spent in the inner cities without any consequence, that after all was it not true that people had undertaken and involved themselves in illegal activities, that of course there is social deprivation, of course there is economic hardship, of course there are problems of the alienation and unemployment in the second, third and fourth generations, but nevertheless (we are told) there must be something else — something else which accounts for the way in which people acted in those events.

Now undoubtedly there was something else. There were other things because the actual triggers of such events, we know from history, we cannot predict, and are often of a small, sometimes slight, even indeed trivial, nature. It is not the importance of the event which moves a person to behave in a particular way on this day or that. It is the accumulating circumstances which predispose large numbers of people to see the world in that way — to define it and to experience it that way, and to feel such a sense of being outside the way in which the society incorporates its citizens into its political and social life that they feel the society appears to owe them nothing, and they owe the society nothing in return.

The real, underlying roots of urban unrest

I am not a liberal, but the notion that so-called social order about which we are so preoccupied depends on a kind of contract between the powerful and the powerless does seem to me to carry enormous weight and importance. Unless a society operates towards its citizens as if there is some minimal sense in which they are intrinsically a part of that society, central to it, with a right to belong to it, with certain established formal and informal economic, political and cultural rights; and unless the society recognises, even in a general sense, an overall responsibility towards the preservation of life and the guarantee of a decent standard and style of life for the people as a whole — as a fundamental fact of their entering into the social contract at all — the society cannot call on the population to feel loyalty and sense of belonging. When an identifiable group in the society is so alienated from the processes of political, social and cultural incorporation that it feels itself to be the outsiders — 'the alien wedge' — they are open to the expression of anger, to the expression of a lack of commitment to social norms and social goals which at one point or another will produce a violent form of unrest.

I have chosen to articulate my views as strongly as I can because this does not seem to me, in 1986, to be a time for polite words. No doubt the definitions that I have given will be challenged from many quarters. I have tried to highlight what are the real underlying roots of urban unrest. There are many more specific problems, but unless these deep-rooted factors are acknowledged and tackled we will simply continue in the cycle of perpetual forgetfulness.

Notes

1. S. Hall *et al.*, *Policing the Crisis*, London: Macmillan, 1978.
2. S. Hall, 'Cold Comfort Farm', *New Socialist*, November 1985, pp. 10–12.

Lord Scarman: That moving and eloquent address by Professor Stuart Hall has certainly got the conference off to an excellent start, and I now call on Professor Martin Kilson of Harvard University to address us.

CHAPTER 4

Politics of race and urban crisis: the American case

MARTIN KILSON

I have been given the task of examining the contrasting, but not dissimilar, position of race and urban crisis in the United States. This issue in the United States is characterised by shifting boundaries between ethnic and racial groups in the past 30–40 years. I find Professor Stuart Hall's formulations, in Chapter 3, fascinating, and I think he is right. His views provide a pretty good understanding of the general context and causes of urban unrest as it affects the racial side of group relations, both in the United States and Britain, and elsewhere for that matter.

A question with two dimensions

The politics of race and urban crisis in the United States is essentially a question with two dimensions. *First*, it is still a question of extending the social contract that governs modern citizenship status to marginal and 'pariah' groups. Black people in the United States form the biggest of these groups, but there are many others, and their incorporation and involvement has been a central aspect of racial and urban crisis in American society. The *second* dimension entails the facilitation of the politicisation of marginal groups towards parity with mainstream American society.

When conceived this way we have an operational context within which to locate and diagnose the often high-profile events and dynamics which are associated with the politics of race and urban crisis. By this I mean dynamics such as tension between police and marginal groups, tension between marginal and mainstream groups (especially mainstream proletarian groups) and urban riots sparked by these tensions. The operational context within which the politics of race and urban crisis is managed or resolved — and it should be stressed that *it is more often managed rather than resolved* — will vary from country to country, depending upon differences in political culture.

Management of conflict may be all that can be achieved, and if you look at different types of conflict, other than those associated with racial and

51

ethnic boundaries, you will often see, there too, management rather than resolution of the problem. The variation in the management, of these dynamics and tensions, between different countries is an important point and hence there is no reason, for example, to expect that the politics associated with managing racial and urban crisis in Britain will necessarily be like the crisis-management politics in the United States. It may be or it may not be, because political culture intervenes and it can intervene in very fundamental and systematic ways. Political cultures of different nations have unique and peculiar ways of arriving at conflict management or conflict resolution. Social analysts must for ever be attentive to these peculiarities.

If we turn more specifically to look at the politics of managing the race and urban crisis in the United States, it seems to have gone through three distinct stages in the 40 or so years since the end of the Second World War. The *first* stage can be seen as the period of civil rights mobilisation, the *second* can be called the period of federalisation, and *finally* there has been the phase of deracialising police practices.

Stage one: the social contract inclusion and civil rights movement

Civil rights mobilisation proceeded from 1945 to 1964, and it involved fundamental changes in the politicisation of Afro-Americans as a marginal group. One feature that was associated with this politicisation was the establishment of new pressure groups. These were added to the older and well-established organisations such as the National Association for the Advancement of Coloured People (NAACP) and the National Urban League. During this first stage of management and/or resolution of the race and urban crisis new groups, each with their own special dimensions and attributes, are likely to occur.

In the United States an important new group was the Congress of Racial Equality (CORE), which emerged out of racial tensions during the war. In the south, the efforts to desegregate public facilities in the 1950s led to the Montgomery Boycott Movement, which overlapped with the Southern Christian Leadership Conference, headed by the Reverend Martin Luther King. In 1986 we started honouring his birthday as a national holiday in the United States — the first black American ever to be so honoured. Martin Luther King initiated and forged several of the new groups in this first stage and these groups emerged in the late 1950s and 1960s to politicise, way beyond anything before, the movement to expand social contract inclusion and civil rights for black Americans. This was primarily effective, in the first instance, in terms of the middle sector, or the middle class, among black Americans.

Another potent force which emerged in the early 1960s was the Student

Non-Violent Coordinating Committee, popularly known as SNICK. Students were also involved to some extent in another new development during this first phase. This was the rise of groups, such as the Nation of Islam, popularly known as the Black Muslims, which articulated the frustrations of blacks, especially lower-strata blacks, at their long-standing exclusion from parity of status in American life. A tension thus emerged for the first time with black leadership — a tension of a systemic sort. The tension was essentially social class in nature, but it took the ostensible form of black ethnocentrism *vis-à-vis* white society. The chief personality, of course, was Malcolm X.

Despite this tension, between upper-strata and lower-strata blacks, it did not degenerate into fully fledged intra-black conflict. There were several reasons for this. *First*, the middle-class leaders and membership of the social contract pressure groups, like NAACP, CORE, Southern Christian Leadership Council, and the Montgomery Boycott Association, all adopted a modified form of ethnocentrism themselves. I would call this an 'instrumentalist ethnocentrism' to distinguish it from 'the true believer ethnocentrism' of the Black Muslims. This instrumentalist ethnocentrism enabled the social contract inclusion, or civil rights expanding leadership groups and their members actually to outflank the Muslims and Malcolm X on the emotionalist fringe, which was mainly the working-class and lower middle-class or petty bourgeois fringe in black American life.

The *second* reason for the avoidance of major intra-black conflict was that throughout the 1960s the social contract groups sustained a majority preference among black Americans. A number of polls showed this. For example, Harris polls in 1963 and in 1966 showed that Martin Luther King's Southern Christian Leadership Conference had an 88 per cent favourable rating in both periods, and this support was drawn from among black Americans of all classes and economic and educational backgrounds. No other group was ever rated as high. The other groups all fell within the 60 per cent range of the social contract groups but none had as high a rating as the most effective figure of Martin Luther King and his organisation. Only 15 per cent gave a favourable rating to Elijah Mohammad, Malcolm X and the Muslims in 1963, and the figure had fallen to 12 per cent by 1966, by which time Malcolm X had died — murdered from within his own fissiparous ranks. King's Southern Christian Leadership Conference also outranked other social contract inclusion, civil rights expanding, groups including SNICK, which was the most socialist-oriented of the black civil and social rights groups in the 1960s.

The *third* reason why there was no collision between the social contract groups and the ethnocentric groups was the ability of the former, by the late 1960s and into the early 1970s, to achieve a large-scale federalisation of the social contract needs of black Americans. To use more general language, they achieved large-scale political nationalisation of blacks' social contract demands. So by the end of this first phase of crisis management, in 1964, a fully fledged social and political collision between the two contesting strands of black leadership had been avoided — and such a collision could have been very nasty and counterproductive.

Stage two: the complex process of federalisation

Between 1964 and 1975 the second stage of the management of the race and urban crisis occurred. It represented the most complex pattern of politicisation experienced by Afro-Americans, certainly this century. By 'complex' I mean that the process of federalisation both solved problems and created yet more. It occurred through a number of major public policy initiatives from the Federal Government, and a series of massive bureaucratic readjustments and tuning, and retuning and fine tuning, of policies. It takes 400 pages in a book to even begin to characterise the extent of this massive series of steps. Federalisation took place most prominently through the Civil Rights Act of 1964, the Voting Rights Act of 1965, the Economic Opportunity Act 1964, popularly known as the Great Society or the War on Poverty Act, but it also entailed many other pieces of legislation.

Federalisation represented the most complex process of politicisation heretofore experienced by black Americans in the twentieth century; its scale and complexity need to be appreciated in a number of respects. *First*, it expanded the social contract status of blacks on the road to formal parity with white Americans. This led to a fully fledged black political class that is today perhaps about 70,000 strong, of which about 7000 are elected officials and the remainder appointed. *Second*, at the same time as creating this political class and putting blacks *en route* towards parity with white American society, federalisation also stimulated tension within the conservative and reactionary segment of the white American mainstream, in so far as black social contract parity was pushed in the direction of black social *mobility* parity. This tension became politicised in the late 1960s, and especially in the late 1970s, among mainstream white Americans, and ultimately produced the neoconservatism and Reaganism that we have known for the past 6 years. *Third*, federalisation created within black American society, strangely enough, a form of rebellious populist urban militancy. This militancy lasted for five consecutive summers and of course the black urban riots had an enormous impact within black society, as well as between blacks and whites.

Thus federalisation, which at one level is so crucial to politicisation parity for blacks since the end of the war, produces a strange balance sheet. On the one hand, federalisation generates the greatest political and social thrust in twentieth-century America towards social contract parity for black Americans, thereby laying the institutional and social basis for a movement which is still going on towards social mobility parity for black Americans. On the other hand, the same federalisation stimulated riotous populist militancy among the marginal segments of urban blacks. Why should this contradictory, paradoxical balance sheet be found?

Federalisation and the black riots

The whole story is very complex, but one answer to this question lies in a closer look at the riotous, populist militancy. First, there was a high degree of riot participation by marginal segments of the society. Put another way, many rioters were drawn from the politically weak lower proletariat, which was the ramrod sector, the cutting edge, of populist insurrectionary militancy in the late 1960s and into the early 1970s. This high level of participation by the marginalised and weak proletariat is clearly evident in reports and studies of the riots. The easiest way of trying to get an idea of the rioters' social background was to survey people who were arrested. Data on occupational background, for example, showed the following in Newark, New Jersey: 50 per cent of the arrested people surveyed were unskilled workers; 61 per cent of rioters surveyed had been unemployed for a month or more in the year prior to the riot. In Detroit, Michigan, 60 per cent of rioters surveyed had educational levels of 1–6 grades, which in the United States means virtually no education at all.

In answer to the question 'why did riotous populist militancy break out at the federalisation stage?' one possibility is that the weak and marginal sectors of black Americans feared being passed over by the social contract and status mobility concessions associated with the federalisation stage. These federalisation concessions affected the coping strata sectors of black American society disproportionately. By the 'coping strata' I mean the stable proletariat or working-class (in American sociological jargon we call it the blue-collar working-class) and the middle-class and upper-class blacks.

The marginal sectors of the proletariat feared being ignored and excluded. This was a reasonable anxiety, and it proved powerful enough to sustain massive populist rioting for four or five consecutive years. Furthermore, this anxiety of being passed over was sharpened somewhat by some allies of marginal blacks — allies among new middle-class blacks who were themselves influenced by the ethnocentric-oriented organisations such as the Black Muslims and the Black Panthers. These bourgeois ethnocentrists cultivated populist outbursts among poor and marginal blacks. For example, survey data from the 1967 Detroit riot showed that 16 per cent of arrested people who were surveyed had college education, and in Newark the figure was 6 per cent.

Of course, the populist militancy among poor and marginal blacks did not amount to a revolution, although curiously enough some of the bourgeois ethnocentrists — influenced by a romantic form of Marxism in some cases — convinced themselves to the contrary. In reality we find that populist militancy and urban rioting by marginal groups among blacks is contained for three main reasons. *First*, as social historians who have studied riots in industrial societies during the past three centuries have shown, popular agitation does not itself make revolution. Some of the most interesting work is that by George Rude. His studies on the riotous elements in the nineteenth-century European proletariat show clearly that populist agitation burns out, as it were, and the populist-prone lower classes retreat to two things: either to quiescence, or to a high crime rate. Many similarities can be seen with what happened to populist militancy among marginal urban blacks in the United States from 1969 onwards. With extensive social disorganisation characterising the politically passive black poor, rioting petered out. And there was virtually no sign of either rehabilitationist or rebellious activity by the bourgeois ethnocentrists, who seemingly deserted the black poor.

The role of the new black political class

The *second* reason for the containment of black urban rioting and populist militancy concerns the role of the new black political class. As I pointed out earlier, the size of the black political class generated by federalisation was really quite incredible. To give an idea of the scale of the increase, in 1963 when I was studying black political representation my research revealed 325 black elected politicians in the whole of the United States. Today there are almost 7000, which is about 2 per cent of all American elected politicians, and each of the elected members of the black political class has a spin-off of about nine technicians or administrators involved in policy-making, so now there are about 70,000 blacks at least in the political class.

As an example of the new black political class consider the case of the mayor in Newark, New Jersey, who in 1986 was trying to get elected for a fifth term. He is a member of the new black bourgeoisie that surfaced as a result of federalisation. He is also a member of the new black political class. He is the son of a steel-factory worker and he himself became an engineer and then was elected the first black mayor in New Jersey in 1968, since when he has been the mayor of what is New Jersey's second major industrial area. This vast industrial, capitalist enclave is dominated by Newark and is governed by a black mayor.

He was one of the skilful members of the political class in politicising the coping segments of the lower class and splitting them off from the pathological lower class, often called 'the underclass' in American sociological jargon. And this is how the new black political class has influenced the containment of urban rioting and populist militancy. By politicising coping strata among working-class urban blacks they divide them off from the marginal underclass. This is not, of course, a novel phenomenon for it is not unlike the impact of the Labour and socialist parties in Europe, in the late nineteenth and early twentieth centuries.

Just as these parties did, so the new black political class socialises as it politicises; it helps to transmit coping standards of the middle class and bourgeois mainstream to the coping segments of the lower class. They will become ultimately almost a white-collar proletariat: they will become norm-deferring, norm-keeping, and 'respectable'. By and large the politicised coping strata of the black working class will behave conventionally and obey the social and political norms.

A *third* factor may help to explain why the populist militancy and urban rioting died down. The black political class has had a major impact on the urban police system. The growth of elected and appointed black people in the political system means that racialist and violent police behaviour comes to be more and more criticised and highlighted. The black political class politicised urban police practices, and it thus created the framework for the third stage in the conflict management of the race and urban crisis — that is, the period of deracialising police practices.

Stage three: the difficult task of deracialising police practices

It should be stressed that achieving the goal of politicising and deracialising police practices and systems is not easy — but it is necessary. It is not easy for three main reasons. *First*, police are part of the *parochial* or *localistic* sectors in modern society. In Anglo-modern societies, especially in Britain and in America, the political cultures have always ensured that the police are part of the localistic and parochial pattern. As such, the police mirror the worst localistic anxieties relating, for example, to class tensions, ethnic tensions, racial tensions, gender tensions. Thus to politicise or to repoliticise police patterns in order to alter them is difficult, because it inevitably stirs up localistic tensions.

It is worth looking a little more closely at these difficulties because policing is so important. If we glance back at the American experience from today's vantage point we can see all sorts of police malpractices towards minority groups, and in favour of others. Consider the Irish-controlled cities *vis-à-vis* the Italians, and the Irish and Italian-controlled cities *vis-à-vis* the Jews; or consider police behaviour, when these groups are in control, *vis-à-vis* the Orientals, or the first-generation Hispanics who entered the country in the 1920s and 1930s.

When changes and metamorphosis occur, as they always do in modern pluralist systems, the localistic police mirror the worst aspects of the tensions associated with the metamorphosis. Look at police behaviour towards the suffragettes and early feminists — the police mirrored the tensions, took the predominant view and attacked the women. In the early phase they even beat up bourgeois women — women beyond their own status. More recently, adopting the homophobic stance, they beat up people in the gay liberation movement and they beat them up for no reason other than that the localistic and parochialistic pressures said homosexuals were illegitimate. Police pick on pariah groups, reflecting localistic tensions and the only way to change this is to politicise policing — but, as I have pointed out, this is not an easy task.

A *second* reason why it is not easy to politicise a police system is because, as one attempts to politicise them in order to deracialise them, one is of course countered with the argument that politicisation is an illegitimate interference in what is claimed to be a technocratic function. This argument is just plain silly. Policing, like anything else in a modern society, is political and no matter how difficult it is police systems must be politicised.

The *third* reason it is difficult is that those who try to politicise or repoliticise the police are often 'outsiders' — either ethnic outsiders, bureaucratic outsiders or technician outsiders. It has been very hard to cultivate *cosmopolitan insiders* within police systems: deviants who say 'OK, I'm now in the local police system of Chicago but I'm cosmopolitan rather than parochial and I'm going to change the system'. In America, over the past 15 years, a group of cosmopolitan policeman has emerged who try to politicise on behalf of the black political class. Outsider policisation needs to be deftly sensitive when seeking to rationalise the behavioural distortions in police patterns.

In general from the late 1960s and during the 1970s, the black political class was reasonably skilful and successful at repoliticising and deracialising police systems. One reason for this success was the process of federalisation. By seeking central government influence and inputs, the new black political class managed to politicise and deracialise many local police patterns. This was possible under the Democratic administrations of Johnson and Carter — that is during the late 1960s and middle 1970s — and they even managed to mobilise federalisation under the moderate conservative Republican administrations of Nixon and Ford. It has proved less possible during the past 6 years under the right-wing conservative Republican government of Reagan. Federalisation supplies resources for providing localistic police forces a trade-off for permitting intervention strategies to alter racialist behaviour. It provides resources that help the different urban political classes give the localistic police forces the trade-off for letting someone intervene with deracialising strategies.

The black political classes have also used the federal axis to publicise nationally the recalcitrant police forces. This is relatively easy to do in American society. Any congressman in his first year can get a sub-committee to go into a city, any city in the United States, and bring the whole police hierarchy before it through its powers of subpoena. The *Washington Post* will be there, all the TV media, national as well as cable ones, everyone will be there to see the local police head dressed down and forced to admit the shortcomings. It is very important to publicise.

Another important aspect of the police deracialisation strategy of the black political class, at its best, has been to be sensitive of localistic white anxieties. They have been highly sensitive to the anxieties which are associated in-evitably with managing conflict along racial lines. Localistic white anxieties have been handled in a number of ways. One example is that some black mayors and city councils have simply moved slowly with respect to affirmative action practices, which they have as part of the federalisation process *vis-à-vis* urban police systems. In other cases they have moved relatively moderately and slowly with regard to racialist seniority practices in police systems. In yet other cases the black political class has intervened in police structures, but they have done so on a coracial basis. For example, instead of dismissing the white head of police they have appointed a joint black chief.

The long process of nudging politicians out of indifference

This gives some idea of the American experiences that are analogous to the policies of managing conflict and race and urban crisis in British society, and the more closely one turns the analogies around the more likely one will ultimately come up with responses that are useful and effective in the conflicts of race in the British political culture. There is not, of course, anything like a direct correspondence between the American and British experiences in managing the politics of race and urban crisis. Yet there are lessons the British can learn from the American experience. For one thing, the cosmopolitan elements in the British leadership must tackle the issue of ensuring social-status parity for non-white Britons: blacks and Asians. Changes in laws and in administrative practices required to bring about such parity must be achieved, and it is desirable that some politicians in all political parties embrace these changes.

Popular pressure groups can be important in respect of nudging politicians out of indifference and into a posture of concern. Though the more pluralistic and voluntaristic political patterns in America make this somewhat easier, it is nonetheless necessary to undertake in Britain even though it may be slow-moving, difficult and frustrating. And once the issue of social-contract parity is settled, the reformation of racialist police practices must also be confronted. There are clearly many ways to skin this cat, so to speak, but skin it we must — in the United States as well as in Britain.

Lord Scarman: We have had two stimulating and extremely informative presentations. Martin Kilson has added greatly to our knowledge and has given us something which, speaking for myself, was way beyond my experience as a resident of this country. And I think that to have heard Martin Kilson on how the social contract can work out, following upon the call by Stuart Hall for the initiation of such a social contract, was absolutely fascinating. John Clare is going to contribute next and then we will go straight on to David Smith and Richard Wells. Because of illness, Paul Boateng cannot take part but very kindly George Greaves and Devon Thomas have agreed to join us, so that when Richard Wells finishes we can have a discussion covering all the topics raised so far. Discussion can continue until we break for lunch, and if the discussion is as lively as I expect it will be we may even have a late lunch!

CHAPTER 5

The ratchet advances another turn

JOHN CLARE

Being here today in this company is something of an embarrassment for me. My problem is that over the past 10 years my work as a journalist in the field of race has been heavily influenced by the research and analysis of four of today's contributors: Stuart Hall, Usha Prashar, John Rex and David Smith. Furthermore, much of my reporting during that period has actually revolved around the views and activities of many of the rest, for example: George Greaves, Devon Thomas, Herman Ouseley and Richard Wells; and of course a good year of my working life was entirely dominated by Lord Scarman's inquiry into the first Brixton riot. So in the company of so many organ grinders, what is this poor monkey to do? I could perhaps don my BBC hat and spend the rest of my time summarising the views of all of you — and at 2 minutes each that would be roughly double the time I normally get!

Riots against the police

But I guess that is not why I have been asked to contribute. The 10 years that I have been reporting on race, initially for the London *Evening Standard* but mostly for the BBC, have coincided with 10 years of what in this debate we are calling 'urban unrest'. It was at the Notting Hill Carnival in August 1976 that I covered my first riot in Britain, leaving aside, that is, Northern Ireland where, like Lord Scarman, I first became involved in these matters in the late 1960s. I moved on to Lewisham in 1977, to Southall in 1979, to Bristol in 1980, to Brixton and Toxteth in 1981 and to Handsworth, Brixton again, and Tottenham in 1985. With two exceptions, each of those riots was directed explicitly against the police. And each outbreak of disorder, if not actually provoked by the police, was triggered by a police action. The exceptions were Lewisham and Southall, where the provocation came from the National Front.

The other elements all these riots had in common were that they occurred in run-down inner-city, crime-ridden areas, and the majority of the participants were black: most were also under 25, and they were more

61

likely to be out of work than in it. This, you may recall, exactly echoes the conclusions of the Kerner Commission in its study of the riots in the United States in the late 1960s. Until the night of 6 October 1985 in Tottenham I would have said that only three things have really changed. First, whereas at Notting Hill in 1976 the police had only milk crates and dustbin lids with which to defend themselves, they turn out at riots now in steel helmets, visors, body armour and flame-proof overalls. They are equipped with special truncheons, two sizes of riot shields, video cameras and helicopters. CS gas and plastic bullets are not usually far away.

The second change, perhaps only of passing interest, is that representatives of the media who used to be cordially ignored by the rioters are now a prime target. This is the direct consequence of two decades of distorted and racist reporting. The third change is striking but largely cosmetic. The triangle at the centre of the St. Paul's District, Bristol, the area around Upper Parliament Street in Liverpool 8, and Railton Road, the front line in Brixton, have all been transformed by the combined attentions of the landowners and the local authority architects. Waste ground formerly encased in sheets of corrugated zinc have given way to carefully-tarred playgrounds. Crumbling terraces have been replaced by low-rise developments in red brick. And the space in between have developed surprising humps where tired grass grows and young saplings are clamped to stout poles.

So much for the visible changes. Whether the events of 6 October 1985 on the Broadwater Farm Estate in Tottenham — incidentally an architect's idea of paradise — represent a watershed in these affairs, or merely a deviant quirk, we do not yet know. What made Tottenham different from all that had gone before, in this country at any rate, was that a policeman was hacked to death with appalling ferocity, at least two different guns were fired by the rioters and there was an unusual degree of organisation. This was not, however, as great as the police pretended, and maybe no more than a function of the restricted nature of the battlefield. But what makes me suspect that Tottenham *does* represent a significant and sinister development is that the anger, hatred, and determination of the rioters there seemed to me no different from that which fuelled every other riot I have observed over the past 10 years: bullets, it would seem, go hand in hand with bullet-proofing. The ratchet has advanced another turn.

The police get more resources

Something else that all the most serious of these riots have in common is that they occurred under a hard-nosed right-wing government, which at least gives one the opportunity to study the whole gamut of Conservative responses to urban unrest. One of those responses has been constant. After every riot the police have got more: more money, more manpower, more equipment, more riot training. Indeed at the Conservative Party Conference in 1985 they even got a blank cheque, personally signed by the Prime Minister, and I see that the Metropolitan Police Commissioner, Sir Kenneth Newman, is even now trying to cash his. The economic response has apparently differed, but in fact remains the same. In 1980 after Bristol, Timothy Raison, then at the Home Office, said it was not the sort of problem at which you could throw money. In 1981 after Toxteth, Michael Heseltine, then at the Department of the Environment, decided it *was* the sort of problem you could throw money at, so long as the money you were throwing with one hand was less than the money you were taking away with the other. This is a phenomenon which was analysed recently by the Economic and Social Research Council which is sponsoring today's conference.

And so Liverpool got a garden festival (an American wheeze, we were told) along with coach-loads of rising young capitalists, drafted in for the day to see how the other half lives. Brixton in 1981, of course, got Lord Scarman, which was not the sort of mistake the Government were going to make again, so that by the time the 1985 riots came along they had rather run out of responses. Douglas Hurd, the Home Secretary, left Handsworth shaking his head over what he called 'sheer criminality' and acts of 'pure wickedness'. Phrases echoed, depressingly enough, both by the Deputy Leader of the Labour Party and the area's avowedly left-wing MP. Mr. Hattersley asserted that Handsworth in 1985 and the Brixton riots in 1981 were two very different events. Brixton he described as a spontaneous outburst, very largely generated by the conditions of the area, the absence of jobs, the behaviour of the police, the quality of the property. And yet, he went on, 'I don't believe the same situation applied in Handsworth'.

Mr. Hurd, though, went further than that, having apparently read the Scarman Report on his trip up to Handsworth. He declared when he arrived that its recommendations had been largely implemented. This is such patent breath-taking nonsense that one can only conclude that the Minister must have fallen asleep in the back of his Rover and, like Martin Luther King, had a dream: the difference being that Dr. King knew what he was doing.

Lord Scarman made two sets of recommendations, distinct but inextricably linked. Those affecting the police have in some measure been implemented. You will remember that Lord Scarman observed, in that mildly apocalyptic prose with which we have all become so familiar, that if the police did not change their methods, disorder would become a disease endemic in our society. As if to confound us before last year's riots, the policing of Handsworth and even of Brixton were widely regarded as Scarman made flesh.

Riots and injustice

But be not confounded, for of his second set of recommendations, concerning what he called 'the basic flaws in our society'. Lord Scarman said that unless they were tackled and eliminated, all the necessary improvements in policing would be of no avail. And what were those basic flaws: racial discrimination and disadvantage. They are, Lord Scarman said, and so long as they remain will continue to be, a potent factor of unrest. He recommended that they be dealt with by a central government policy of direct coordinated attack, which he added (mistakenly in my view) inevitably means that the ethnic minorities will enjoy for a time a positive discrimination in their favour. I say mistakenly, because the *simple absence of negative discrimination* would be a fine start, and because any call for positive discrimination is the only excuse needed for this Government and many of the institutions of our society to do nothing at all.

And nothing at all is precisely what has been done, as Lord Scarman himself noted in November 1985 in a carefully coded but damning address to the annual conference of NACRO. The full extent of that nothingness has been exposed recently by Colin Brown in the latest instalment of the Policy Studies Institute continuing study of racial discrimination and disadvantage: a study to which we have all been indebted for the past 20 years. In the field of discrimination and work, he concluded that a third of all private employers in Britain still routinely discriminate against appropriately qualified black and Asian applicants, who are three or four times more likely to be denied even an interview for a job than similarly qualified whites. And if we are going to talk about 'sheer criminality' and 'acts of pure wickedness' that might not be a bad place to begin.

Indeed I believe it is the only place to begin. People do not riot out of pure wickedness or because someone has told them to, but out of a common sense of injustice, both comprehensive and specific. This is why if you wanted to start a riot you could not do better than have the police go to Brixton and shoot an innocent black woman in her own home. An accident, no doubt, but immediately identified as entirely symbolic of the police's customary behaviour towards black people. And since people keep asking, that is also why no-one rioted when, in similar circumstances, the police in Birmingham shot and killed a 5 year-old child who was white.

On the Broadwater Farm Estate in January 1986 I listened to a young black man contemptuously dismissing the ludicrous rumour spread by the police that the estate's basement garages had been flooded with lakes of petrol. To the assembled white media he said two things we would all do well to remember. The first was 'You know people don't just get up in the morning and say "shit this is a nice day for a riot".' And the second was 'You won't understand what happened here until you know what it feels like to be black.' Well the fact is that no-one any more has any excuse for not knowing what it feels like to be black. The trouble is that our society is accumulating an unenviable history of not hearing what it is being told. Three months before the 1981 riots in Brixton a Working Party set up by Lambeth Council published a report on the state of police/black relations in the borough. It bore a prophetic slogan: the community may not survive this sort of policing. Dismissed at the time by both the Government and the media as the loony ravings of a tiny left-wing minority, that conclusion was to be fully and explicitly borne out by Lord Scarman's Report on the subsequent rioting.

Is anyone listening?

More soberly, and more recently, the Economic and Social Research Council, in the report I referred to earlier which is an introduction to a forthcoming study of five inner cities, came to the following conclusion. Society cannot for long corral a significant percentage of its population into a few areas of extreme disadvantage without courting social costs which will impinge on the plausibility of its economic strategies. Is anyone, I wonder, listening? The evidence would suggest not, for it is not only the Government, and now sections of the Labour Party, that react to urban unrest with impatient incomprehension. So too, as has always been the case, do the police and much of the media.

The day after Handsworth, the *Sun*'s leading article began scornfully: 'In no time the sociologists will be picking among the debris for evidence of social protest. They'll be eager to find signs of resentment over deprivation and unemployment.' The *Mail* commented: 'No need for another analysis of urban deprivation, ethnic values and the politics of protest. One Scarman is enough.' It was left to the police to come up with the explanation everyone, including presumably Mr. Hattersley, had been waiting for. And they were not to be found wanting. The Chief Constable, Mr. Geoffrey Dear, rejected any suggestion that tension might have arisen after a switch to high-profile policing. Instead he declared: 'The rioting was orchestrated by local drug dealers who had become fearful for the demise of their livelihoods'; and again: 'It was fuelled and organised by persons who require a supply of drugs to continue their normal lifestyle.'

As long as we go on offering and believing explanations like that we are never going to understand anything about urban unrest. In which case, Mr. Chairman, I fully expect to be back here in 10 years' time with another litany of the riots I have covered.

Lord Scarman: Thank you very much indeed, John Clare: powerful and very much to the point. Now, I do not think I need introduce David Smith. Everyone is aware of the distinguished services of the Policy Studies Institute, which is one of the better creations of our times. David Smith is a respected Senior Fellow at the Institute.

PART 3

Policing and Urban Unrest

CHAPTER 6

Policing and urban unrest

DAVID SMITH

I am going to make an effort to be genuinely brief — or at least a genuine effort to be brief! Let me first though take up just one point made by John Clare. The Policy Studies Institute's work on racial discrimination and disadvantage has been carried out now over a twenty-year period, first by Bill Daniel, then by myself and most recently by Colin Brown.[1] The research shows that the levels of racial discrimination continue to be much the same as they were when the 1968 Race Relations Act was passed, and the actual gap in economic living circumstances between white and black people has, in most respects, not significantly narrowed over the 20-year period.

The subject that I have been asked to address is policing and urban unrest. It seems to me that in the title policing *and* urban unrest, the most important word is the conjunction 'and': small words are often the most important. Breaking it down, there is one set of questions which focus on the relations between policing (styles of policing, policies of policing, methods of controlling the police and so on) and the outbreak of urban unrest, and there is another set of questions which arise in terms of the impact of urban unrest *on* policing. Relying to a large extent (but not exclusively) on the research that we carried out at the Policy Studies Institute, published as *Police and People in London*,[2] I will briefly examine the nature of these relationships.

I start with the question: to what extent is the past pattern of policing and policing policies an important cause of the urban unrest that we have seen? The first thing is that I agree entirely with John Clare's forceful statement that the riots in 1981 and in 1985 were fundamentally anti-police riots. There is a lot of evidence to support that view. The fact that they were fundamentally anti-police riots makes it all the more important to consider the first of my two sets of questions: what is the relationship between policing and the outbreak of civil disorder? There is a mistake which is quite often made, which is to jump from the fact that they were anti-police riots to the conclusion that the riots were caused by the style of policing. Life is not as simple as that.

It is necessary to distinguish between the individual level and the collective or the political level. At the individual level we can carry out anlayses of, for example, our survey data for Londoners in 1981 to see whether there is a relationship between people's own personal experience of contact with police officers and their general level of hostility towards, or liking of, the police. At the political and collective level one must consider whether hostility towards the police amongst certain sections of the population is partly, or entirely, based on the collective consciousness of the whole group, rather than on people's own individual experiences. A further factor is whether the hostility is directed at individual police officers in particular encounters, or at the whole police organisation and as a symbol of authority, and perhaps an oppressive kind of authority, in society at large.

Police behaviour and individuals' experiences

If one looks at the evidence of the link between policing and urban unrest at the individual level, one *first* finds that there is strong hostility to the police among certain specific population groups, but good perceptions of the police among other large sections of the population. Broadly speaking, the groups among which there is strong hostility are those within which one finds those people who participated in the rioting. Put another way round, the people who participated in rioting were drawn from groups which are known to be extremely hostile to the police.

Secondly, one finds that attitudes to the police, and views about what the police actually do and the way they do it, and also the different patterns of actual experience that people have at the individual level of contact with the police, are strongly related to the general lines of demarcation that exist within the society. There are extremely strong contrasts between different groups in their attitudes to the police, and in the nature of their experiences with the police, and these contrasts basically relate to fundamental lines of demarcation and divisions that exist in society. This relates very much to points made by Martin Kilson in Chapter 4: the experiences, impact and divisiveness of different styles of policing is an expression of, and relates to, a wider set of divisions that exist in society.

The *third* point from our own research is that there proved to be a strong relationship between people's hostility towards the police and their perceptions of their personal experience of contact with police officers. We showed in *Police and People in London* that the more adversarial contacts a person has with the police, the more hostile they are likely to be to them. Since we published the study I have carried out further analysis on this particular point, and I have found that if one classifies people according to the way they evaluate their adversarial contact one finds no relationship between adversarial contacts that are evaluated as OK by the people concerned and how hostile they are to the police, whereas there is a very strong relationship between adversarial contacts evaluated as bad and the degree of hostility which the person feels towards the police. I would say these are among the strongest relationships that I have ever observed in survey research.

A *fourth* point worthy of note is that there seem to be rising expectations among sections of the public about standards of police conduct, and there are changes all the time about what constitutes an acceptable level of rudeness and of violence by the police. In addition, there is the specific dimension of racial prejudice and the racism that is sometimes involved in policing. The introduction of substantial numbers of ethnic minority groups in cities has changed the pattern of expectations on both sides in the relationship between the police and the public. There have been changes in what is expected, and accepted, both among the police and the community, and this may be quite an important factor in the links between policing conduct and the way that people respond.

It is often reported that 40 years ago the police used to behave extremely badly in the East End, and yet in general that did not lead to anti-police riots in the same sense that we have seen them recently. Maybe this is connected with changes in expectations which are in turn connected with the introduction of racial minorities in the cities.

Fifthly, of course, it must be said that there is considerable evidence of bad police behaviour that actually takes place. Perhaps, as I suggested, there is no more of it than at earlier times, perhaps even less than at earlier times, but there is a substantial amount of bad police behaviour and there is a substantial amount of racial prejudice, certainly within the Metropolitan Police.

Collective consciousness and hostility towards the police

Let me turn now to evidence on the relationship between styles of policing and unrest, in terms of the collective level of analysis. One reason that one has to look seriously at the collective or political level as well is that although the relationships I have been describing are strong, they are by no means strong enough to account for the very big differences between individuals, and between different population groups, in their levels of hostility to the police. In particular, if you look at the views of people of West Indian origin they are much more hostile to the police than white people or people of Asian origin. Following from what I have reported, adversarial-type police contacts tend to be more common with people of West Indian origin, and that is a partial explanation of the hostility towards the police among black people of West Indian origin.

Nevertheless, people of West Indian origin who report *no* personal adversarial contact with the police are still far more hostile to the police than white people, who have not had contact with the police of this kind. Similarly, if one compares people of West Indian origin, who have had a stated amount of adversarial contact, with white people who have had the same amount of negative contact, and control for age and sex as well, one still finds huge differences in the opinions that they express. Thus, there is evidence of some extra element in the formation of the views of West Indian people.

There is a substantial evidence of collective consciousness: a sense of solidarity with all other people belonging to the same ethnic group and a collective perception of threats to themselves from various forces in society, symbolised most strongly by the threat that they feel is posed to them by the police. In social anthropological research it has been found that individual young West Indian boys or young men will respond in quite an emotional way to accounts of experiences quite remote from their personal lives of some kind of bad behaviour by the police, or any kind of oppression as they see it towards members of their group. A particular event which showed that sort of process in action was the Deptford fire in 1981 and the response to that by large groups of black people in the organisation of the Black People's Day of Action on 2 March 1981. It was quite clear through the whole development of that response that it was a collective political response to events which were remote from the personal lives of many of the people taking part. People came from as far afield as Manchester and Leeds to take part in the Black People's Day of Action about an event about which there was very little information as to what had really occurred.

There is also some evidence — and it is interesting to compare the position in Britain with that in the United States, described by Martin Kilson in Chapter 4 — of the development of a kind of political ideology. By this I mean a coherent view within the collective consciousness about what is to be done in response to what is perceived as being police oppression and also oppression by wider forces in society. One should stress, though, the point made by John Clare, that there is very little evidence of any degree of practical organisation of an effective kind underlying any of the riots that have taken place. They seem to have been largely spontaneous. Nevertheless, the beginnings of the development of some kind of political ideology do seem to be evident. So in summary, it does appear that racism and racial prejudice within the police, and the concentration of certain kinds of policing on young people generally and particularly young black people, has brought forth a response both at the individual level and also at a more collective level. Both of these responses are involved in the development of unrest.

Urban unrest and changes in policing

What of the second set of relationships between urban unrest and policing? How is urban unrest related back to changes in the pattern, the style and the methods of policing? I should start by stressing that some of the relationships seem to me to be quite paradoxical and contradictory. The *first* point is that there is a danger, and probably a reality, that urban unrest will lead to some more abrasive, more insensitive and more 'over-the-top' policing. This factor has been described by Bittner in the United States as 'the 20 foot jump over the 5 foot ditch'. Put another way, a police officer always tends to deal with any particular threat or difficulty with more force and more counter-threat than is really required.

If I was a police officer I would do this, and so would you, because there is always the exceptional case where the particular threat turns out to be much greater than you initially realised. The police officer's mind is on the exceptional case when the threat might turn out to be really serious, rather than on this usual case which is not a serious case at all, and therefore he is always liable to take, as Bittner eloquently puts it, 'the 20 foot leap over the 5 foot ditch'. This was visible to us as we were actually inside the Metropolitan Police at the time of the Brixton riots in 1981. What tends to happen inside the police force in response to these kinds of event is the perception, on quite a massive scale, of a threat to the organisation and to the individual. This leads, at least in the short term and maybe also in the longer term, to a tendency to take a bigger leap than is necessary. Policing thus becomes more tough and robust.

Second, as John Clare clearly put it, urban unrest leads to more policing resources generally and specifically to the introduction of strategies and hardware for containing incidents of public disorder. A feature of these strategies is that they are a *collective* style of policing, where police officers are doing things in a disciplined way in obedience to commands, rather than an *individual* style of policing. The collective style of policing conflicts and contrasts very markedly with the style of policing which the rest of the time everybody is expecting. It is perhaps worth emphasising that the disciplined, militaristic response of the police to public disorder is not only inevitable but is also desirable. This point is often misunderstood, particularly by people on the left, but it needs to be recognised that when things have gone wrong on these occasions it has been because individual officers have acted on their own — have taken the law into their own hands — and have *not* acted in a disciplined, paramilitary way under the command of supervising officers.

A *third* result of the impact of urban unrest on policing is that it tends to lead to the organisation of policing in larger units. The trend is thus towards more national kinds of organisation of the police forces, or the sharing of resources between police forces, and this conflicts with the objective of trying to make policing responsive to local needs.

The *fourth* feature is that there are hidden implications in the fact that urban unrest leads to more policing resources. The reason for providing these additional resources is of course the fear on the part of government, and indeed the fear on the part of respectable parts of the population generally, of what would happen if there is major public disorder on a large scale. There is a fear of an epidemic of disorder. The paradox is that most of the time those resources cannot be used for this kind of purpose, and so they have to be used for something else. The result of urban unrest, then, is that it creates a problem about how to make use, in a useful, constructive, creative way, of the substantial increase in police resources.

Curiously, I do believe that urban unrest can lead back to a serious attempt to bring about policing reforms. I was a bit depressed by Martin Kilson's point in his contribution, that one of the major significant things that has happened in changes in policing in the United States was the introduction of large numbers of black police officers. I agree that this is certainly a significant change. I have been told, however, by the Director of the Police Foundation in America, that they evaluate the standards of policing in terms of what they call the 'kill-rate', that is how many people are killed by a police officer in a year, and I was informed that the kill-rate among black police officers is higher than among white police officers.

I just do not think that the relationship between solving the problems of policing and introducing more black police officers is as direct and straightforward as has been suggested. I think there is genuine evidence of a serious attempt, certainly in the Metropolitan Police and in some other police forces too, at medium and high levels in the organisation, to rethink what policing is about and how you can get control of the actual services being delivered at the sharp end. I would like to draw attention to the fact that it is easy to talk about reforming police forces, and it is easy — or quite easy anyway — to change the law; it is easy to be rather sententious about standards of police conduct and about the failure of the police to achieve, with increasing resources, a reduction in the increasing level of crime. It is *much more difficult actually to change what really happens on the ground*.

The real problem is how one goes from having ideas about policing reform and a genuine commitment to it, as I believe there is in large parts of the medium and higher echelons of the police forces, to changing the actual pattern and style of policing that occurs. This is the really difficult question in the real world. I think urban unrest is leading to a serious reassessment of policing, and this comes back to the points made by Martin Kilson about the relationship between policing policy and politics more generally. There is evidence that there are real, if slow, developments in the way in which the political process approaches the vital discussion of what policing policy is, and what it ought to be.

Notes

1. W. W. Daniel, *Racial Discrimination in England*, Harmondsworth: Penguin, 1968; D. J. Smith, *Racial Disadvantage in Britain*, Harmondsworth: Penguin, 1977; C. Brown *Black and White Britain*, London: Heinemann, 1984.
2. Policy Studies Institute, *Police and People in London*, 4 volumes, London: Policy Studies Institute, 1983.

Lord Scarman: I thank you very much indeed. Now I ask Richard Wells to address us. Richard Wells is, as many of you know, a Deputy Assistant Commissioner of the Metropolitan Police, and Director of the Public Affairs Department at New Scotland Yard. This will be the first time at this conference that a police voice has been heard — and as a judge I think it is time it should be!

CHAPTER 7

The will and the way to move forward in policing

RICHARD WELLS[1]

Shortly after the Tottenham riots in 1985 I was asked by Granada's *World in Action* team to give my assessment of the causes of the disturbances. My immediate response is now a matter of public record: 'I see a three-fold pay-off for people involved against the police. I see a move from boredom to excitement, from what they see as poverty to obvious profit — and I mean in physical terms from looting — and from a sort of helplessness, that they seem feel, to a feeling of power'.[2]

I have not moved away from that belief, though others' complementary views have contributed to our joint understanding of violent unrest. There are those who speak of deep feelings of injustice felt by some minority groups, those who acknowledge violent behaviour as a cry for attention, or as realising either ideological, group or even individual ends, or on the other extreme there are those, apparently devotees of some latter-day concept of 'original sin', who see the behaviour as caused by inherent badness.

Search for causes is necessarily retrospective and is particularly susceptible to feelings of recrimination and revenge; likewise, it focuses on past failure. A search for a sane way forward clearly cannot be undertaken without some appreciation of past causes, and will still be rendered problematic by the likelihood of interested parties bringing to the forum the impedimenta of their cumulative experience and attitudes. But, at some stage, there has to be a conscious decision, by those who wish to progress, to move from the retrospective mode to the prospective mode of analysis.

In an attempt to make that transition, I have produced a simple model, shown in Table 1, which may help to rationalise and clarify at least the cluster of police/community tensions. It will be insufficient to address these alone, for other agencies, ranging from the government to voluntary groups, as well as significant individuals, must play a parallel role in illuminating and easing tensions in other parts of the constellation of urban unrest. Nor can the police/community tensions be resolved in isolation; responsible agencies must involve themselves in that work, as must the police involve themselves beyond strictly 'police matters'. For each it turns on both point of focus and depth of field.

Table 1   Some of the areas of police/public tension,
showing the required responses

	Police responses required	
Public search for	**In the organisation**	**In the individual**
Trust	Openness	Local and recognisable
Familiarity	Show care: share concern	'Traditional' image/role
Avoidance of arbitrariness	Consultation	Communication
Legitimacy of force/stealth	Accountability	'Fair play and a sense of proportion
Effectiveness	Some success in agreed areas some sense of rationality	

Two caveats should be entered about the model. The first is that the reference to a 'public' does not assume a homogeneity of public. Recognising that there are many 'publics', each with its own profile of expectations about the police, nonetheless I believe there to be common denominators, concentration on which will allow the nuances of differences in expectation to be acknowledged and respected by the police. Secondly, the boxes leak! Complex ideas do not lend themselves readily to compression into such limited space and overspills are to be anticipated.

As I see it, then, the public at large searches for a number of qualities in its police and the search demands those qualities, explicitly or implicitly, in both the police organisation and in the police individual. There is likely to be some differentiation between what is looked for in the Force as against what is expected from the individual. Most of us, it seems, can accommodate disparities between our broad view of, say, a large bureaucracy and our more closely focused view of its individual representatives. We may be intolerant of the postal service, but we still brighten to the smile of our postman!

The search for trust: the importance of openness

Wherever in society we ascribe to an organisation, or an individual, a delegated power, there is a strong element of trust involved in the process. If the trust is called into question by the way in which the power is exercised, then those who have ascribed power and those who are subject to its effects (and these may not be one and the same group) will seek reassurance that their trust was indeed well-placed.

So it is with the police. Not for the first time in their history there has been some falling away of uncritical trust placed in them. It is unlikely to have been either a precipitate change or a change in absolute terms. Much more likely the change from substantial trust to less trust will have been incremental and unequal in its points of origin. There may have been less change, for example, in the attitude of the lower socioeconomic groupings whose contacts with the police are likely to have been confrontational or adversarial through time than in higher groupings, with whom first the advent of the internal combustion engine, then legislation on aspects of sexuality or consumption or narcotics, have seen police more lately arrive on the scene as enforcers of the law rather than providers of a service.

Inevitably the growth of interest in, and promotion of, civil rights has combined with an assertively investigative press to offer easier access to views of the man in the street confronted by bureaucracy. This development has lent considerable weight to the questioning process of the purpose and style of policing. And the police service — for all its merits and comparatively high standing in public regard when seen alongside counterparts in other countries — has indubitably failed on some noteworthy occasions to come up with answers of sufficient assurance to still public unease.

Symptoms of unsatisfactory answers are public inquiries, Royal Commissions and changes in controlling legislation. The repeal of the 1824 Vagrancy Act and its 'suspected person' provisions reflected unease at officers' subjective judgement of people loitering; the Bail Act 1976 was enacted in the wake of regrettably cavalier attitudes towards custodial remand by some officers and some courts. The Police and Criminal Evidence Act 1984 has brought very clear constraints upon any arbitrary whims of police officers to detain suspects. In each case of newly enacted legislation Parliament seeks to balance not only concern *about* the police but concern *for* the police, permitting some room for manoeuvre in bringing offenders to justice but requiring that room to be more measurable and certain. Given the unprecedentedly long passage of the Police and Criminal Evidence Bill through Parliament, its public airing and now, on enactment, its criticism in some police circles as being too restrictive, and in libertarian circles as having endowed the police with too many new powers, it seems to have struck at least that balance.

The worst fear in the face of any power is that it will be exercised secretly and arbitrarily. The public search for trust in the police turns on both fears and I shall deal with arbitrariness later. The search for trust in openness reflects not just attitudes towards the police service. In the present climate, which urges greater freedom of information, a closed organisation is almost inevitably — and sometimes unwittingly — a suspect organisation. The police service — born into a climate of marked hostility and perhaps uncertain of its broader social role — put up some prickly defence mechanisms, not least of which was keeping itself to itself. Along with that inward-looking culture came policies, practices and attitudes which were largely determined *within* the police group rather than in free exchange with the community. That had to change and has, in my estimation, changed enormously.

Openness seems to me to be an absolute requirement in generating trust.

However, there will be some areas in which the police cannot be open. I would not expect police officers to discuss publicly, for example, surveillance techniques of robbery teams. Those people who are engaged in crimes against the community, or indeed against the nation as a whole, are able to choose their time and their ground, and we should not concede another significant advantage in telling them the methods that we are developing in preventing and detecting their anti-social activities. There will always be some areas of necessary secrecy, and the difficulty will constantly lie, of course, in defining precisely what those areas should be, and indeed in who should define them.

Ironically, there is a closeness of ideology between those who, being 'the professionals', would prefer no interference in their judgement of what is 'necessary' and on the other hand those who, at the extremes of libertarianism, countenance no arbiter save him who is strictly acceptable in their eyes. The balance between these twin arrogances must remain, *faute de mieux*, our sane though fallible parliamentary and judicial processes.

If secrecy is occasionally necessary to ensure effectiveness of operations, it should never be used to draw a veil over moments of inefficiency. The learning curve of the Metropolitan Police has shown a sharp rise in this regard under Sir Kenneth Newman (though there were auguries of that change before his arrival), and there are now many stories that can be told of policy decisions and operations around which we do not put such a protective arm as we may earlier have done. The openness has made the Force — and the pressures and stresses under which its officers work — much more understandable to the critical viewer.

For openness to thrive, the *tone* of criticism directed at any organisation is vital. A constant drip-feed of vitriolic attack — as opposed to constructive criticism — may have the effect of closing down, prematurely, a body which is in the early stages of coming to terms with its own greater accessibility. If criticism of the police continues to be strident, without measure or reason, it will reduce the range of options for some police officers to speak freely about their work. Doubtless this will admirably suit the ends of some critics, in whom an open police service causes acute feelings of personal and political dissonance.

The search for trust: police who are 'local and recognisable'

As Table 1 shows, I believe that the search for trust at the individual, constable level is for an officer who is, so far as possible, local and recognisable. This will be particularly difficult in a large organisation such as the Metropolitan Police, or even in county forces of some size, given human parochialism from which inhabitants of even neighbouring villages can be viewed as 'foreigners'. Nonetheless, Force policy and philosophy should be aimed at making ranks from commissioner to constable more obviously tied to community structures. At chief officer level no more may be possible than to ensure that the incumbent emerges as a humane, sympathetic character with a genuine interest in the householder's problems. Television and its ubiquitous living-room impact will ensure at least an illusion of 'local and recognisable'. At constable level, even in dense city environments it will be possible to achieve a real sense of 'belonging' through the provision of, ideally, home beat officers or at least continuity in the posting of constables with a 'geographic' rather than a 'shift' responsibility.

It is helpful for the police organiser to focus on what is best to be avoided: any move which makes the police appear as impersonal, external to the community and, accordingly, anonymous must be resisted. In city life, and given current trends in public disorder, some rationalisation of police man-power into rapidly mobile support units seems inevitable and there is clear evidence that, on occasions, a swift display of manpower has nipped disorder in the bud. In the short term, restoration of immediate peace is an important and necessary achievement. We must remain, however, unsure of the feelings for the future which such units reinforce in all of the participants — the police and the policed.

One way forward is to ensure that support units have some clear linkage with the locality to be policed. This can be achieved in part (and to be realistic usually only in part) by use of locally based officers as members of the unit itself, by deploying unit members in conjunction with locally known and recognised officers or, if nothing else, making sure that officers emerge from the transit carriers to patrol, individually or in pairs, *on foot*. The Metropolitan Police are only too aware of the dangers of the ominous image of what Sir Kenneth has called 'the gathering storm'[3] of support units lying in wait for emergent trouble and much can be done, through constructive and thoughtful leadership of the units, to reduce that sense of threat.

Besides giving mobile units a geographic responsibility, one can also give them creative as well as reactive responsibilities. For example, a force-wide organisation like the Special Patrol Group (SPG) has been allocated a role in combating burglary rather than in just the control of public disorder. The recent reorganisation of the Metropolitan Police shows clearly the competing needs — and policies — of, on the one hand, conserving the peace, and, on the other, keeping in touch with the people. The first has sired the recent creation of a new, enhanced SPG in the form of Territorial Support Groups (TSG), now based on the eight new Areas and demanding rigorous selection, training and leadership. But, in the opposite direction — from the centre outwards — has been the massively conceived and executed plan of de-volving decision-making from New Scotland Yard to local divisions, making the chief superintendents in charge of police stations more autonomous than ever before.

This is surely as it should be. Although there has been some difficulty in accommodating London borough boundaries as the Force has abolished a whole intermediate level of command (the former 'District' and its commander), nonetheless the chief superintendent, fingers familiar with the pile of the local community carpet, emerges as the officer who is known by, and knows, people of the locality. Both of these new directions will need constant attention if the 'local and recognisable' need is to be satisfied. Particularly in the case of the new Territorial Support Groups, efforts will need to be made to ensure that they do not emerge as what has been called 'an alien force of occupation'. The fact that they will be drawn from their own areas will contribute towards the objective, though, to be realistic, 100 men from such a massive 'wedge' of Greater London will stretch the concept of 'local' to vanishing point. A more practical method will be to follow the practice used by the SPG (who will be absorbed into the TSGs) of deployment with locally recognised officers in each new place which they visit in their preventive patrolling role.

For divisional superintendents to become 'local and recognisable' will be much easier, provided that we can ensure continuity of personnel at stations. Unforeseen consequences bedevil long-range planning, where threats to alter pension conditions precipitate a rash of premature retirements, or where there is a series of unexpected moves of Metropolitan officers out to other Forces in career progression. But we really do need senior officers who continue to identify with, and be identifiable within, the community. This is equally true of the best officer, who is recognisable day-in and day-out and, in that, provides an element of reassurance. That has to be weighed against other considerations: for example, continuity has to be weighed against staleness. Questions of continuity also need to be weighed against individual career considerations, and these are part of the internal dilemmas in police organisation.

It will remain difficult, then, for a large Force like the Metropolitan Police to achieve high levels of 'local and recognisable' officers, not least where initial recruitment draws necessarily from outside London (though, in an improved ratio now of some 60:40 outside to London-born), and where officers gravitate towards housing which is not local to their daily police duties.

Familiarity: showing care and sharing concern

Under such circumstances the general public may look at least, if not for a known face, then for faces which allow a familiar sense of approach. This leads us to the second line of Table 1, which concerns the importance of the 'familia' in the original sense of the word: that is recognised as belonging to the same broad group as the observer, rather than as an 'outsider'.

If the police organisation is, or appears to be, a centrally imposed anonymous body, as in many states of Europe and elsewhere, there will be little sense of the 'familia': rather than intimate and integrated, the police will seem remote and out of sympathy with local needs. At an organisational level the Force must be able, through its philosophies and policies, to show care for its work and share concern with the community. Constables must receive direct training which helps them to understand those policies, as well as clear encouragement and example from the top. The police task in inner cities is fraught with physical danger, moral dilemmas, and, in preventing and detecting crime, shortage of time and length of odds. This should be carefully weighed before critics rush to judge 'young officers' who seem to find no time to smile or to talk to their parishioners. Moreover, there are countless daily examples of sterling service being rendered by officers, not only in response to public demand, but in quite remarkable creative initiatives.[4]

The care–concern model will normally dominate, and the police 'service' theme will be uppermost. When violent crime intervenes the emphasis will — and must — change, demanding the emergence of the control/enforcement model of the police 'force'.

The general public appears to have a strong feeling for an individual police officer who is 'traditional' in style, image and role. Few would dare to define what is meant by 'traditional'; it is, I suspect, a largely intuitive drive for both police officers and members of the public to retain immediately recognisable dress and modes of working. But change constantly intervenes and today's 'short-term' measure is always potentially tomorrow's expectation. The immediate postwar period saw the revolutionary introduction of the blue-shirted collar and tie for constables and the 'traditional' button-up collar passed on; in 1976 the Metropolitan Police introduced the egalitarian white shirt for all ranks and the 'traditional' blue shirt disappeared; the helmet chinstrap has gone; the army-style belted tunic has been replaced (in some ranks: there are curious anomalies) with a broader-lapelled 'civilian' style. These moves away from the 'traditional' and 'military' style are cumulatively significant, but are largely unnoticed by the public. Occupying higher profile are the more compelling — and compelled — changes of protective shields following Notting Hill's 1976 dustbin-lid debacle; flame-proof overalls following petrol bombs; and NATO-style helmets following head injuries from flying missiles.

It is significant that each escalation of police equipment *follows* attack, whereas it is often described by adversaries as proactive change and, therefore, evidence of police oppression of the people. That a chief officer has a statutory responsibility for the health and safety of his officers is less often adduced. Also, it is important to note that such change is still cause for public concern and news headline material. By implication, the British police officer is *still* viewed substantially as unarmed and civilian, with riot equipment the exception rather than the rule. That status of exception is under-written by other developments towards greater sensitivity, especially in a training model which, though not free from criticism, has been described as among the best of its kind.[5]

There is, however, no room for complacency, since critical edge can be dulled by habit; new undesirable 'tradition', appearing at first as a barely evident but creeping accretion on the familiar body, can become metamorphic. Some fascinating and more encouraging breaking-away from popular stereotype is interesting to note; even as I review this text, in a BBC broadcast, a police superintendent is stoutly championing the status of an unarmed police in the face of an assertive interviewer protesting that, surely, the police must be effective against violence![6] The same will to retain our traditional unarmed image has recently been manifested in the Met's reduction in strength of its authorised firearms officers from 4600 to 3300: a cutback of 28 per cent. In effect this is a successful example of winding back against the 'rachet' effect of escalating force.

I am concerned about riot protective equipment in all its manifestations. I am concerned about police officers carrying Heckler and Koch MP5's at Heathrow Airport. But such steps are taken only with great deliberation and when the likely alternative consequences of *not* raising levels of protection are unthinkable. The 'traditional' image must be a benchmark against which to orientate ourselves and defer undesirable and unnecessary change. But it cannot afford to be a nostalgic groove in which we stick against the compelling weight of a society changing about us. Our action should be to resist impulsive change, winding back to the 'traditional' wherever we can, not out of sentimentality but in recognition of the real worth to democracy of the civilian and unarmed police officer. Parallel action is needed to ensure that the expectations of the general public are educated and realistic.

Avoiding arbitrariness: consultation and communication

Closely linked in the public eye with irrational and impulsive change must be any activity in the police service which is arbitrary, and this takes us to the third line of Table 1. There is a growing search for consultation in the way in which a police force performs duties within the localities for which it is responsible. The search is still patchy in application, as is the police response. It should be noted, however, that there are many people in our different communities who are quite content for the police to manage 'their own business' and there are police officers who believe that, too.

There are areas, as well, usually at the critical and significant fringes of civil rights, in which there is an uncomfortable conflict between the security of specific operational facts and a generalised freedom of information. There will always be covert intelligence about criminal activity —

terrorists or bank robbers — which cannot be publicly discussed or the subject of consultation. Police activity which arises under such circumstances appears arbitrary, and though styles of police authority may change in structure or political hue, I believe there will always be an irreducible minimum of material which will be judged, in the public interest, not to be capable of open discussion.

In most other areas, however, there is a need for genuine consultation. A real search for consultation entails shared interest in the prevention and detection of crime, and necessitates often quite determined and strenuous effort to match the priorities of the police with the priorities of those outside the police service. There are occasional mismatches of priority which need to be resolved, particularly at divisional police station level, where the wishes and anxieties of the community can best be felt.

However, we need to aim for more than just a type of consumer poll of what ought to be given priority. Although such dipstick sampling is valuable in its own right, we also need to try through *discussion* to share perceptions about the quality of policing. Consultation should aim to enable police officers to learn more about the perceptions of the community, who not only pay for those services but who are also in receipt of them. The community should learn more about the affective side of policing as well as the effective. There ought to be a real preparedness, in individual officers and individual community representatives, to change minds if points raised in the consultative process so require. This is very difficult for all of us; the convenience of inertia is a dominant force against the effort required to revise views. Thoughts need to be given to all aspects of consultation, ranging from appreciation of non-verbal communication, the dynamics of the group, hidden agendas, and even the structure of the room in which consultation takes place. Only in this way will we facilitate real dialogue, free of feelings of threat to earnestly held positions.

The frame of mind of *all* parties towards the consultative process will, then, be critical. Some police officers will, in the early stages, find it difficult to discuss policing issues which they saw formerly as entirely and solely within their own 'professional' remit; some community representatives will, on a number of widely differing grounds, be unwilling to accept limitations upon what decisions police officers are prepared to relinquish from their professional grasp.

This willingness to change must be omnilateral. The police service believes that as an organisation it has made attempt after attempt to change its stance; it has become more sensitive, particularly at middle and senior levels, but we have found more frequently than not that olive branches have been taken from our grasp and dashed at our feet. We can do that only so often before officers start wondering about the wisdom of offering olive branches of any sort. This position is a matter for grave concern.

Within individual contact between police officers and members of the public, a police officer has, perhaps, the greater responsibility for communication. This arises not only from the power of the constable's office which confers a temporary psychological advantage in even the most innocuous of police/public interactions, but also because the officer will often have been the only party in the exchange who has been trained to communicate. Whatever the spiral of mutual discontent that the officer is locked into, whatever biographical baggage he or she brings to the daily work, there is, then, an added responsibility on police officers to be the person to try, in the face of non-communication, to communicate. I would concede, sadly, that often it is the other way round; there is some evidence that, on occasions, others try to communicate with police officers, and it is the officers who put up the shutters against communication. This can arise from officers who adopt a defensive position — either generalised or particular to the occasion — and may be a response to the stridently critical atmosphere in which officers feel they are working. The best that we can do in the service in the selection and recruitment of mature personnel and in their training will help to overcome that. In this most imperfect of worlds, it is taking us some time to do it, but there ought to be more ready recognition that there has been genuine and substantial progress.

Officers ought to be able to account for the rationale of their actions, ought to be able to articulate the feelings that are leading to this or that particular course of action, and should be able to express the conflicts that they feel in some extremely demanding police problems. These may range from the tensions of a violent domestic intervention to the frustrations of short resources which mean they arrive minutes, if not sometimes hours, late at the scene of a distressed victim. They need to be able to put into words these conflicts, to share perceptions, and to talk through the ambiguities, which they often feel in the role of policing in the late 1980s. This will not always be possible, or appropriate, at the scene of an intervention into another's crisis, but it will be possible, appropriate and *necessary* in the process of formal consultation. Likewise, the police must listen and hear. I believe that for several groups, including the police, the 1981 disorders were a cry to the deaf.[7] We should have heard and we did not.

Another example is in the area of racial attacks, where for a long time we took the view that attacks on minority ethnic groups were simply and statistically reflective of a growing violence in society. It took some time for the real phenomenon of racial attacks to be accepted.

The police and community alike must be able to listen to, and hear, the messages rather than adopting mechanistic, and therefore sterile, forms of consultation and communication. At an individual level, 'mechanistic' communication reverts to the stereotypic police officer, who can recite only acts and sections or, more subtly, speaks only with the voice and the views of the police subculture; likewise there are those for whom, in the so-called debate with the police, the off-the-shelf prepacked slogan rules. Both are anathema to genuine dialogue.

The search for legitimacy: accountability and 'fair play'

At no point has there been more domination by slogan than in airing the vexed question of police accountability. For some time the stridency of the sloganisers deafened intended audiences. As a result, important messages were not heard. This was not helped by 'accountability' being advanced, from some quarters, as the more acceptable face of what was no more than an aspiration to party political control of the police. At least that argument is now advanced more openly, and can be judged on its merits.

Our position is clear, and again a matter of public record.[8] Police must work within the legal and constitutional framework of the moment. Seeking to make the police service more accountable is a perfectly legitimate political aspiration, provided that it, too, is pursued within the democratic process. At no point is our accountability more sought than in establishing the legitimacy of force, when it is used, and also the legitimacy of what might be called 'stealth', or covert operations, used to achieve police objectives. This is highlighted in the fourth line of Table 1. The extent to which we are seen to be acting with the support of the law in these spheres is vital.

At an organisational level we should seek to be accountable. There are, I believe, two sorts of accountability. There is a *de jure* accountability, a constitutional accountability; which may or may not suit individuals according to their political or their practical and pragmatic viewpoint. The legal framework can be changed through the democratic process, if that is what is desired, but the existing position of accountability is the one within which the police have to work.

There is also a style of a *de facto* accountability to which chief officers, and indeed individual officers, are subordinate day-by-day. To what extent do the general public feel that, in operating, the police officer has met the public need? If the feeling is that the police have *not* met with public expectations how will the responsible chief officer know and be persuaded to meet those expectations? The difficulty is to discover what the public need is; which public or which community? Frequently communities will have conflicting needs, conflicting priorities and conflicting views about what the police should, or should not, do. In both '*de jure*' and '*de facto*' accountability the role of communities' elected representatives is important in easing the dilemma of which to choose of many disparate views.

The problem is made more complex in London where 'elected representatives' appear at different levels. The Metropolitan Police is constitutionally responsible — and accountable — to the Home Secretary and through the Home Secretary to Parliament. But locally elected representatives in some boroughs have appointed 'police committees' which seek to create a reporting relationship between the police and themselves. Whilst this aspiration is understandable, it is in conflict with our constitutionally established accountability to the Home Secretary of the day, and is resisted as official policy.[9]

Until this uneasy relationship is formally resolved, in my view the Metropolitan Police should nonetheless attempt to hear and respond to views from such locally elected representatives, but only under such circumstances which make it quite clear that it is not a 'reporting' relationship. This would complement the exchange of information and decision-making on important matters of mutual interest in the other body of locally elected representatives, the consultative groups, set up under the auspices of Section 106 of the Police and Criminal Evidence Act 1984. Real impact can be made within these groups on the policy and operational thinking of the police, and likewise by the police representatives on the groups' awareness of some finely balanced conflicting interests with which officers are repeatedly called to deal. The groups' meetings are open to the press, and such media coverage — at times leading, and at others led by, public opinion — is a persuasive factor in exposing local policing to scrutiny and change. The press is in itself a very powerful forum for practical if not formal police accountability.

The public search for legitimacy — and reassurance — in police accountability, will be based upon a whole range of activities including the questioning of the Home Secretary in Parliament and the scope of answers given; the passage of significant cases through the courts and the judgements passed; the response of the Force to the Public Accounts Committee; the evidence given to formal public inquiries; answers in publicly broadcast debates; letters and replies in the press; our own unsolicited publication of Force plans and policies, either generally or at specific moments of shared police/public concern; and not least in our carefully observed and minuted reaction to discussion in all manner of local meetings from consultative groups, through neighbourhood watch, to residents' associations and social councils. Although acknowledging that it is tangential to the argument of *police* accountability, it is tempting nonetheless to ask what other public bodies have their policies and practices so thoroughly reviewed, including those of some of our more vociferous critics. At the individual constable level, the general public will formulate and express its own views on the legitimacy of force applied. It is necessarily a subjective and emotive series of judgements.

The degree of force used at any one stage by a police officer must in law be matched against the circumstances in which that force is used. To take the argument for a moment out of the police context, consider the example of a harassed parent trying to get a 5-year-old child out of the supermarket past the sweet counter when the child has a very fixed determination to leave with a chocolate bar. When the persuasion stage has passed and the child moves to the bucking and wriggling stage, some degree of coercion will become inevitable. The amount of what Bittner calls 'situationally justified force'[10] which can be used in such circumstances will be viewed with greater or less legitimacy by the onlookers, according to the way the child is managed. If you extend that concept to the throwing of bricks, lumps of cast iron fencing, petrol bombs and the firing of guns, the amount of force used against the police, almost regardless of what the police role has been in the time leading up to the unrest, will govern the level of legitimacy with which the force used by the police is viewed. To be acceptable, force must in the end be judged by those observing to be proportionate.

The concept of minimum force, which is based on an objective sense of proportion applied to any given set of circumstances, is closely linked to our national preoccupation with 'fair play'. Police use of 'fair play' in force will probably be assessed at two levels. In the face of violence directed against officers, it will be judged initially as whether it was, inherently, an expected and proportionate response. In the aftermath a greater span of evidence will be weighed: to what degree was there dialogue designed to defuse growing tension, what positive steps were taken to meet diverse public expectations, what persuasive measures were adopted before force was contemplated and what warnings were given before force was finally employed? The much overworked objectivity of that Clapham bus-rider will have a necessary role to play in reaching such judgements and, in a world of self-interest, this is sometimes an elusive voice.

The same point applies to use of covert activity. Whilst few object, it seems, to teams of anti-robbery officers dressing up in disguise to keep surveillance on, and to arrest, a team of thieves, yet there is something intuitively sneaky about the police officer who hides behind lamp-posts to pounce upon hapless motorists in bus lanes. It would be difficult in law to unpack the distinctions between the two examples. Extending the argument, the violence of terrorism or the violence of other extremes of political protest is planned secretly and needs equally covert counter-measures if society is not to be seriously disadvantaged. The difficulty with such areas of operation is that because they are covert they are not subject to the same degree of public scrutiny, and not susceptible to any popular review of their fairness or otherwise. For the overwhelming majority of people — including police officers — such work is consented to only as a generality, and then as an act of faith.

Most people place that faith in the fact that there are laws strictly governing telephone and postal interceptions which require the personal fiat of the Home Secretary of the day, regardless of political party. For others, the existing safeguards of the law and any general expression of trust is inadequate. The growing openness of society favours the demands of that minority, and there is little doubt that there will be gradual development towards freedom of information; it seems likely that, as in the United States, such freedom will remain hedged about by cautious amendment. Nonetheless areas where there *are* increased openness will, at one and the same time, convince the broad majority of people of the legitimacy of revealed practices, and yet will ensure in police officers a continued commitment to strict compliance with legal requirements. Once again, there will remain a minority, more inspired than realistic, who will not be satisfied with anything but total revelation. The Data Protection Act epitomises those processes of a growing openness precisely.

Effectiveness and police fallibility

In all of this, the general public nonetheless requires an effective police, and this introduces the final line of Table 1. But, for the British at least, whether at the organisational level of policing or at the individual officer level, total effectiveness seems accepted as neither practicable nor, curiously, desirable. Enter, once again, sense of fair play and proportion. Sir Robert Mark drew attention to the phenomenon of the police 'winning by appearing to lose', and this apt theory relies upon the human and fallible face of policing and is directly related to healthy British scepticism towards over-formal authority. The PSI Report[11] indicated that victims of crime are as influenced in their attitude towards the police by the helpfulness of officers, as by their strict capacity for solving crime.

There is also a public search for some rational, planned style of police approach to prevention and detection of crime, and to the maintenance of order. However, that style should not lose its sense of humour, its appreciation of the local nuance, and should not ride roughshod over local feelings in a mechanistic scramble for some notional 100 per cent effectiveness. Unprecedented levels of enforcement and necessary parallel expansions of the judicial and penal system would rapidly erode the concept of broad public consent, and coercion would be the order of the day. There is, in the end, a balance to be struck between the fear of crime and fear of the crime-fighting force.

The trust which is placed in the police is still high, with a sample of young people between 18 and 25 years of age rating the service second only to doctors in terms of respect.[12] Although that picture will mask pockets of very considerable mistrust, it is a finding in which police officers will find some encouragement to go forward. If the Metropolitan Police can continue to respond to the search for trust and reassurance in the directions shown in the model in Table 1, then I think that the police/community contribution to parliamentary democracy in London is safeguarded. If we do not, I think that the chances of urban unrest — given other existing factors — are significantly greater.

To return to the 1985 Tottenham riots, I shall restate my belief that answers are not to be found in the will of the police alone to move forward:

> You must go to society at large for its solution to find a way in which young people can healthily and legally channel their aggressions, in which they can find a slice of the profit and in which they can find legitimate ways to gain access to power.[13]

Notes

1. The views expressed in this paper are those of the author and do not necessarily reflect the views of the Metropolitan Police Commissioner, or the Force policy.
2. *World in Action*, broadcast on Independent Television on 14 October 1985.
3. *Report of the Commissioner of Police of the Metropolis for the Year 1984*, London: HMSO, June 1985 (Cmnd. 9541), p. 12.
4. *Report of the Commissioner of Police of the Metropolis for the Year 1985*, London: HMSO, 1986 (Cmnd. 9790), pp. 19–20.
5. Bull and Horncastle, *Metropolitan Police Recruitment; an Independent Evaluation*, 1985, p. 10 (Executive Summary).
6. BBC Radio Four, *Today*, 1 October 1986.
7. It is interesting and perhaps significant in terms of communication to have found, following this address, that a London-based television producer present at the Warwick Conference misheard this as a 'cry to the *death*'.
8. *Report of the Commissioner of Police of the Metropolis for the Year 1985*, London: HMSO, 1986 (Cmnd. 9790), p. 2.
9. *Ibid.*, p. 2.
10. E. Bittner, *The Functions of Police in Modern Society*, Public Health Service Publication No. 205Y: NIMH Monograph Series on Crime and Delinquency, Washington: Government Printing Office, 1970.
11. *Police and People in London*, Vol. 1: David J. Smith *A Survey of Londoners*, London: Policy Studies Institute, 1983 (PSI No. 618), p. 30.
12. MORI Poll, *The Times*, 3 September 1986.
13. *World in Action*, broadcast on Independent Television on 14 October 1985.

Lord Scarman: Thank you very much for a most interesting and stimulating presentation.

CHAPTER 8

Policing and urban unrest: Discussion

Lord Scarman: We have concluded some extremely interesting addresses and I now wish to encourage as free a discussion as possible. You may make a proposition or ask a question, whichever you choose, or you can do both. If anybody should wish to ask a question off the record, he or she can do so, but as you probably know asking questions off the record is never a very impressive operation and can lead to misunderstandings! However, we do not wish to impose any patterns upon the conduct of the conference.

We are being joined for the discussion session by two noble volunteers standing — or rather sitting — in for Paul Boateng. We are joined first of all by George Greaves, who will be well known to many of you, and is very well known to me, as the Principal Community Relations Officer of Lambeth Community Relations Council. His contribution both as a man of action and a man of ideas in the area that we are considering is a notable one. We are also joined by Devon Thomas who also comes from Brixton and is Chairperson of the Brixton Legal Defence Group, and of course his knowledge is considerable and will be extremely useful. Now who would like to begin?

Dissatisfaction with the police

Chris Adamson, Community Relations Officer, Camden: Richard Wells is an easy target, and he has an unenviable task. I do have to say, though, that I feel his address was rather bland. The theme of this conference is the crisis of policing in cities and in the part of Inner London that I know the crisis is considerable. David Smith said that he had found a lot of dedication and real desire for change at the top of the Metropolitan Police Force, and I am sure that is true. I do not believe that the police are governed by wicked men any more than any other organisation, but there are strong reasons for believing that with their present structure, and by training, and perhaps for other reasons, the police are quite incapable of confronting the task on their own. The whole question of political accountability, which Martin Kilson brought out in the United States setting, seems to me to be central. Without it the police are incapable of dealing with the alienation, partly produced by the police themselves and partly arising from other social factors in the inner cities. The police, and politicians, need to wake up to the ways in which black people, and many white people, in the inner cities and elsewhere have just come to feel that the police force is totally unaccountable to anybody but themselves. It is only through proper accountability that politicians can actually govern what the police do, because at the moment they are out of control.

Joe Darden, Michigan State University, United States: My question is addressed to David Smith, concerning his assessment that the attitudes of West Indians towards the police differed from the attitudes of those who are white. I would like to indicate that there is some research that deals with the dissatisfaction of the police in the black community in the United States, and the differences that exist between blacks and whites. It is worth considering the research of David Grundberg and Howard Schuming, carried out in the United States, and published in an article entitled 'Dissatisfaction with Social Services'. [Editors' note: the article is reprinted in J. T. Darden (ed.), *The Ghetto: Readings with Interpretations*, New York: National University Publications, 1981.] The result of this analysis was that there is a high correlation between the racial composition of a neighbourhood and the dissatisfaction with the police. When you have racially integrated neighbourhoods, the differences between the dissatisfaction of blacks in that neighbourhood and the dissatisfaction of whites in that neighbourhood seem to diminish. Where you have residential segregation, there is a large difference in the dissatisfaction with the police on the part of blacks and dissatisfaction on the part of whites. Their conclusion was that it is not race *per se* that explains dissatisfaction with the police on the part of blacks and dissatisfaction on the part of whites. Their conclusion was that it is not race *per se* that explains dissatisfaction with the police, but the racial composition of the neighbourhood. The implication of that is that the racial composition of the neighbourhood must be an important variable when you are assessing whether or not there is a difference in dissatisfaction with the police on the part of blacks and whites.

David Smith: The short answer is that from our data it is quite different in London, and the racial composition of the neighbourhood does not explain the differences that I was talking about. However, you have to bear in mind that we have overall a much smaller proportion of people of West Indian origin in London than you would probably have black people in American cities. There are no totally segregated districts in London so the whole social geography is different. It is the case that black people living in areas of low West Indian concentration tend to be *more* hostile to the police than those living in areas of high West Indian concentration. In other words, black people in Wimbledon are more hostile to the police than black people in Brixton. This is a surprising finding, but it is true.

The rapidly changing and deteriorating policing context

Anon: I wonder how David Smith would view the question of the accountability of policemen. Does he foresee any constructive developments of better or closer understanding for the future? From my own knowledge police committees are the most extreme, right-wing of all groups. I have served on one for the past 5 years, and you cannot even discuss the issue of black people. Recruitment and training is partly my responsibility, and even to look at that with the police seems a difficulty, indeed it is difficult even to mention the word 'black'. How do you view the future in light of the abolition of the police authorities in a number of sensitive areas? Furthermore, I take exception to your criticisms of Professor Kilson from America, in light of our present increased use of guns. It is a development which comes very close to us, and on which we have to make a decision on our committee next month. And I feel supportive of what he said: everything he said, in my estimation, is perfectly true. I hope that you can give us some constructive answers for future developments, because unless something positive is done to help the decaying inner-city areas things can only get worse, and there will be more people being attacked, like me in public and in private, for speaking out.

Lord Scarman: I do not know whether anyone feels he is able to give, off the cuff, a constructive answer that you want. I think we have got to consider very carefully indeed the extremely interesting information that for some of us is being received for the first time from our American friends. Stuart Hall, would you like to say anything about this?

Stuart Hall: I do not want to respond to that because in a sense I can only ask the question in another form. It does seem to me that there is an increasing urgency needed. We ought to recognise the rapid changes in terms of policing, and police responses to disorder, because we are not dealing with a static position. If I felt that Richard Wells omitted a dimension it was the recognition of how rapidly the policing situation has changed and deteriorated even over the past 5 years. We are not simply dealing with relationships on the ground between groups in trouble and police who have a difficult problem.

We all know that that is the underlying situation. But over and above that, we are dealing with the hardening of collective attitudes on both sides. This does not arise because people, as somebody said, get up one morning out of the wrong side of the bed and think it is a good day to attack the police. As a result of long collective experience collective views come into existence, and they shape and structure every single set of interactions. 'Who was to blame?' is a secondary question, because before that one already has the institutional relationship between the two groups. They shape the field in which individual policemen and individual black people actually meet in the areas of conflict in our cities.

Then we must add to that not only what was called earlier the political blank cheque, but also the clear expansion of those kinds of powers which allow the police to spread and display their effective authority on the ground locally, without taking on board either accountability or sensitivity to local conditions. In addition, there is the increasingly high profile of the police as a group in articulating policies with respect not only to crime but towards the disciplining of social and economic problems.

When one adds all these factors together one is dealing with a totally changed and transformed policing environment, which has very little bearing or relationship to the traditional history of the police as we knew it from the middle of the nineteenth century until the 1970s. We are dealing with rapid transformation of the police, of authority and of the law and of the policing of communities in the inner cities. That is a dramatic shift. It has been changing gradually over the past 20 years but in the past few years it has raced away. We are talking about a different quality and character of policing altogether from what we have known in the past.

The notion that here are the traditional policing functions which can be slowly evolved and gradually adapted with a population which has a basic trust in the institution, but feels there is this or that which can be wrong and enters into a genuine and gentle dialogue about how it can be improved — that is just simply not what the situation is like on the ground. We seem to be expecting a gentle conversation to be happening whereas no conversation is going on at all. In this sort of situation, which is one potentially explosive like dynamite, it is only a question as to who takes a match out of his pocket and the whole thing blows up.

That I think is what the policing question is really like, and I am not trying to raise the emotional temperature, but I am saying that unless we begin with that recognition of the reality of policing in these areas, including the problems for the police themselves in carrying out their traditional task in these changed technical and social conditions, we are not actually addressing the problem.

Racial attacks and police consultation

Leon Donnellan, North East London Probation Service: I would like to endorse the remarks of the visitor from America who gave us his view of what I think is a very real fact in the East End of London where I work.

This concerns the importance of the mix of ethnic minority groups in a particular area, possibly leading to unrest in the inner city. I have been helped by Martin Kilson's picture of the process of politicisation and social contract. However, I have observed with regret during the past 2 years the actual policing in the East End which has caused considerable concern to the Asian community and to other minority communities. In particular, the police have been very slow to recognise the importance of racial attacks on Asians and their homes. I feel that consultation at all levels has broken down because of the lack of awareness of the complexity of the community.

There was earlier reference by David Smith to the relationships between the criminals in the East End, who have been very famous over the years, and the police. There seems to have been a certain respect among the police for the masculinity of the East End criminal, which I am afraid is not extended towards the mixed minority ethnic groups. In the probation service we try to a certain degree to have a helpful role with offenders who appear in the courts, but I question whether we do an effective job and whether the courts necessarily do an effective job, when one looks at the recent cases of the Newham Seven and the Newham Five. I would like to ask David Smith and Richard Wells whether the East End is just one example of a difficult community of mixed ethnic groups that the police have not dealt with appropriately, and whether in the light of Handsworth, Tottenham and Brixton we may have had too simplified an approach.

Richard Wells: Of course, all communities are different in their different ways. It is difficult to highlight the East End as a particular problem. What the police find is that constantly we are caught between conflicting interests and, as hackneyed as it may sound, with resource deficiencies, and there is only a certain amount of work that can be done. As I said earlier, awareness grows slowly. When awareness does grow the police tend to be doers and the police are now far more aware of, and far more responsive to, the problem of racial attacks. Senior officers go to each scene to make sure that there is a supervised commitment. I am sorry to hear you say that consultation has broken down, because our feedback from the community has never been better. That is not to say that it is perfect, but just that it is better than ever before: I am referring to your particular locality. We find mixed messages and I very much doubt if the absence of consultative groups is because police officers have been slow in coming forward to offer them. Usually the obstruction comes from other quarters.

Policing and the political process

David Smith: A good part of what I said in my talk was in support of the points just made by Stuart Hall very eloquently. There is a collective and political dimension to race and policing which is extremely important. I do not disagree with the questioner who was very dissatisfied with the developments in getting a political dialogue about policing policy and real consultation on policing issues and policy. Obviously, despite what Richard Wells has just said, although there might have been some progress, there is an enormous way to go before there is any really serious discussion within the political process of policing, or policing policy. All that I meant to indicate was that the urban unrest has begun to make developments in that direction a bit more likely.

Can I just come back very briefly on the point about black police officers and the use of guns? I was perhaps speaking too quickly and I did not intend to criticise the views of Martin Kilson. What I do not believe is that getting more black police officers into the police force is *in itself* either a credible, or anywhere near a complete, answer to producing better standards of policing: the whole thing is much bigger than that. Finally, in response to the questioner from the East End of London, it does seem to me just from personal experience, and without being able to quantify it, that the East End of London is a very special and unique place, where the ethnic mix is quite unlike anywhere else. There may be special conditions which make it particularly difficult to get the consultative process going.

Lord Scarman: Well, the East End is one of the prides of London and I speak as a Londoner. Indeed, perhaps it is the best part of London. I now want to call on our two speakers who stepped into the breach to have the last word; first, Devon Thomas, and he will be followed by George Greaves.

CHAPTER 9

A question of power

DEVON THOMAS

Perhaps I should just make it very clear from which perspective I speak, as people may not know me or the organisation in which I am involved. I have something of a feeling of *déjà vu*. I was at the *Scarman and After* conference in 1982, and in my talk there I attempted to torpedo the one-dimensional view of life in the so-called inner cities.[1] My view is that the problem is not that people are living in totally bad conditions — which indeed many people are in these areas — but the central question is one of power. If we look at the analyses that were made in the United States, many people there found that the riots were the cry of the unheard. In the British context, I feel that this is very much what the urban uprisings were about. However, I want also to paint a picture of the inner-city areas as places where the communities are very active. The community in Brixton is organising itself on many levels, and the kinds of picture, which so many have portrayed, of helpless people only being able to respond by throwing bricks and petrol bombs is not an accurate one.

Are the cries from the active inner cities being heard? This is where the frustration comes in. I was interested in the approach of Mr. Wells, and the terms he used to look at the causes of unrest, suggesting that perhaps one of them may be original sin. This provides a good insight for me into the working minds of senior police officers. Perhaps I could take a moment to look back at my experiences. When I was a teenager I was involved in the establishment of one of the first institutions that tried to respond to the needs of black youths in the Brixton area. We tried to develop a 'help on arrest' scheme, which was a kind of first-stage consultative approach. This was in the mid-sixties. Basically, the scheme was established because there was great concern about the amount of harassment of local young people by the police, and we decided to set up a means by which each young person, with whom we had contact through the youth club work and so on, had a card which set out their rights and the procedures to be followed. One of the aims of the scheme — and perhaps this shows how naive we were, or maybe indicates how far matters have deteriorated — was to try gently to ensure that police officers handled young black people with the same respect and approach that they would any other sections of the public. Unfortunately our hopes were dashed, and as others have said this kind of experience has built up with the end result of the gulf which now exists.

Another point concerns the different findings in British and American experiences. It has been suggested that in the United States in areas of high black settlement there may be more hostility to the police, whereas the opposite situation may occur in the United Kingdom. This is another issue I attempted to address in the aftermath of 1981, because obviously there are similarities and lessons we can learn from across the Atlantic. I spent much of my time trying to see what I could learn from the American experience. We do, though, have to recognise the many differences in the nature and the history of the black community in the United States. The way racism has operated has been different. So the responses of black people in the United States compared with Britain are likely to be different.

Dealing with the wrong agendas

You will find what might at first seem to be a surprising response if you talk to people about housing in Brixton, or Southall, or the East End of London. Asian people who are offered housing outside these areas often turn it down in spite of the fact that they are being offered better properties. The reason, of course, is that if they move out of their areas of prime settlement they feel unsafe, they experience additional hostility and pressure and they lack protection. They feel much safer in areas where they are with people of their own communities. Perhaps this helps to explain why black people who have moved out of those areas with a large black population to places such as Wimbledon, which was mentioned earlier, feel isolated. In such areas, black people feel particularly conscious if they are being stopped and asked questions to a much greater degree than their white peers in the community, and this is no doubt one of the reasons why you have greater hostility towards the police by black people living in Wimbledon.

Again, I would agree with David Smith about the dubiousness of believing that an increase in the number of black police officers will solve the problems. This view appears to suggest that the problem resides within black people. The view we take is that the position we find ourselves in is not conducive to black people joining institutions such as the police. If only black people saw the police and other institutions behaving with fairness — if there was justice for blacks, as one of our slogans goes — then one might find the situation changing, and the development of an environment in which black people feel they can make a contribution by joining the police force. Until these kinds of issues are resolved we will continue to deal with agendas which are not really the right ones at all.

Note

1. D. Thomas, 'Black initiatives in Brixton', in J. Benyon (ed.), *Scarman and After*, Oxford: Pergamon Press, 1984, pp. 184–90.

CHAPTER 10

Can the police solve the problems?

GEORGE GREAVES

I must of necessity be very brief. I must also confess that I find the whole position most confusing: I suppose that is my weakness. Perhaps I can just say a few things and probably raise some more questions. Stuart Hall reminded us that in the 1950s and early 1960s the police were saying of the West Indian community that we were particularly law-abiding. As late as 1967, when I went to work in Lambeth, the Brixton police said that there were only two problems they had with the West Indians. First, the police said that black people wanted them to solve their domestic affairs, which as the police they could not do, and second, black people had noisy parties at weekends! As far as crime was concerned the police reported no problem. I wonder if anybody would say such a thing about Brixton today. If that is true it is a powerful comment on what society has done to British black people between 1967 and 1986. If we believe what we are told, we seem to have changed from a very law-abiding set of people into people who commit crimes and are bursting to riot.

The confusion in my mind is this question of accountability, and maybe I am seeing it differently as a black person. For example looking at the way the coal dispute in 1984–85 was policed, I feel that accountability is more apparent than real. It frightened me tremendously, I must confess, to think that police operations were being coordinated at the National Reporting Centre in New Scotland Yard by the chief constables' own organisation, and all that ministers seemed to be saying was 'we've got no responsibility for this. If that's what the police want to do: fair enough.' I found that a very frightening position, and I think that accountability is something that I would want to be looked at very closely, to see whether it has real meaning.

I agree with David Smith and Richard Wells that in the higher echelons of the Metropolitan Police people do want change. But I also feel very strongly — and listening to DAC Wells this morning has not moved me from that position — that the police are trying to solve difficulties and implement changes when they do not understand what the problem really is. Consequently, as we know, a great deal is happening in the police force in terms of training and reorganisation, but are these reforms tackling the real questions? Reorganisation is an interesting question because Sir Kenneth Newman seems to go to management consultants to find out how to police the community, whereas the community itself might be a better place to go! The only area in which the police appear to be succeeding is in the public relations field. For example, the Metropolitan Police can put out a story one day about petrol being flooded across basements, and the next day the small print will tell you it was not physically possible to do it that way. To say that the Broadwater Farm unrest was planned in such depth, to me with my experience, is utterly ludicrous.

There is much more that I would like to highlight about policing in areas such as Brixton,[1] but the central point is that the police do not appear to be able to reform themselves on their own. Outside pressure and influence are needed to bring about significant changes. The police cannot solve the problems without community involvement and public participation.

Note

1. For further discussion see G. Greaves, 'The Brixton disorders', in J. Benyon (ed.), *Scarman and After*, Oxford: Pergamon Press, 1984, pp. 63–72; G. Greaves, 'The police and their public', in J. Benyon and C. Bourn (eds), *The Police: Powers, Procedures and Proprieties*, Oxford: Pergamon Press, 1986, pp. 75–84.

PART 4

Unemployment, Racial Disadvantage and the Inner City

CHAPTER 11

Life in the ghetto

JOHN REX

In 1979 my colleague, Sally Tomlinson, and I published a book based upon 4 years' research in Handsworth.[1] We ended with a warning that unless real political progress of a peaceful kind occurred the future of Handsworth would be one of 'mindless violence and despair'. In 1981, however, when rioting broke out in other areas, there was no significant disturbance in Handsworth. Lord Scarman visited Birmingham and it was generally concluded that Handsworth was in some way different and better than other areas. The police claimed considerable credit and Handsworth was even said to provide a model of community policing.

The events of 1985 put Handsworth back on the agenda and I should like to take the opportunity of going back to our diagnosis of 1979. I do not in fact believe that the situation has altered much. It is still the case that no real political dialogue has been started, and it is still the case — even after September 1985 — that we are likely to see more mindless violence and despair.

Urban unrest and Birmingham's internal colonies

The first point to make about Handsworth, and one on which I am inclined to place an even stronger emphasis, is that Handsworth is a purpose-built ghetto. Let me explain what I mean. Around the year 1960 it was becoming clear that the population of Birmingham's inner-city wards was becoming increasingly black, that is, Afro-Caribbean and Asian. The Labour-led Birmingham City Council decided therefore to appoint a Liaison Officer for Coloured People — not, it should be noted, a Race Relations Officer to ensure that no citizen had his rights diminished on grounds of race, but a Liaison Officer to maintain liaison with an 'alien element' in the population. To this post it appointed a former colonial policeman, thereby making it clear that the task envisaged was a colonial one, and a policing one. This being the case, it was not surprising that decisions about the allocation of council housing were taken in a similar spirit. Newcomers were not allowed to go on the council housing list for

5 years, and even when they did get on the list they were not given points for length of residence. What was assumed, it seems, was that these workers were not entitled to share in the rights and benefits available to the rest of the population.

At first those who were excluded in this way from council housing were left to solve their housing problems themselves. The most enterprising among them bought large, old terrace houses and financed the operation by letting rooms. Under this system all those who had difficulty in getting council houses turned to the immigrant lodging-house proprietors, and the result was a concentration of all the problems of social pathology and of racial conflict in one area. This was the situation in Sparkbrook which Robert Moore and I studied between 1967 and 1969.[2]

After this time the council itself set about providing an alternative housing system for immigrants. This included a policy of giving council mortgages to immigrants in areas where the building societies would not lend, and also encouraging the housing associations to convert properties for letting to categories of tenant excluded from the council housing system. Together these two policies provided housing for immigrants, and especially West Indian immigrants, in segregated areas. While Sparkbrook became a largely Pakistani area, the Handsworth area became the Caribbean centre of Birmingham, alongside the Soho area which was overwhelmingly Indian.

Once it became clear to the whites of Handsworth and Sparkbrook that it was the intention of the council to use these areas, and also Aston, Small Heath and five other areas, as immigrant ghettos they fled. Each successive census in the years 1961, 1971 and 1981 showed an increase in the pro-portions of New Commonwealth immigrants and their children living in these areas. By 1981 Soho had 71 per cent of its population in this category, Handsworth had 57 per cent and Sparkbrook about 53 per cent. Some whites, of course, did remain — the old age pensioners for whom these were their birthplaces, and a few white immigrants settled, *but it was now clear that Birmingham's policy for black and Asian immigrants was to ghettoise them. When in due course it came to have race relations and equal opportunity policies there were also inner-city policies for the inner-city internal colonies where the colonial immigrants lived. Birmingham in fact was an apartheid city.*

It is still the case that race relations issues in Birmingham are dealt with as ghetto issues, and I want to emphasise that, so long as they are, no amount of attention to the social causes of unrest will solve the problems of such areas. It is all too common today to suggest that the radical view is that we should attend to these social causes rather than immediate triggering incidents which lead to unrest. What I am saying is that, however good the scientific information, however skilled the administration, so long as what is happening is that *we*, of the city, administrate *them*, in the inner-city ghetto or colony, there will be lacking that level of mutual respect which is the precondition of social peace. We will solve the problems of the inner city only when we see them, as we do the problems of the suburbs, as *our* problems.

Any solution of the Handsworth problem, or the inner-city problem in general, must involve the disappearance of the inner-city ghetto and the introduction of its population into the mainstream of our social life. What we need are not special inner-city authorities, which too often remind one of the Ministry of Bantu Affairs in South Africa, but an active policy of combating social discrimination so that our black and Asian citizens can claim their rights as citizens.

Having stressed this, and having made my main conclusion and policy recommendation clear at the outset, let me now look at the actual consequences of ghettoisation for our black and Asian populations, and for our society. I want to deal with three issues: education, unemployment and policing.

Segregated schools and the denial of opportunities

One of the ways in which the United States has attempted to deal with the problem of disadvantage in black inner-city schools is to bus a proportion of their children to the suburbs, while seeking to retain or increase the number of white children in these schools. Similar policies were once discussed in Britain, but usually in a very negative way, proposing a thinning out of the black children so that their presence would not prevent the educational progress of whites. Moreover, in the British case, such policies were actually prevented from operation by a refusal of the white suburban schools to receive those bussed. In the event we simply finished up by accepting segregated schooling.

In the Soho and Handsworth areas state secondary comprehensive schools now have not simply 71 per cent and 57 per cent of their population black and Asian. Because the whites who live there are either old people with no school-age children, or Irish who send their children to Catholic schools, proportions of pupils of New Commonwealth origins in the schools are much higher than the proportions of New Commonwealth origins in the general population. In fact the proportion is now above 90 per cent in nearly all the schools and above 95 per cent in several. The 30 per cent tipping point beyond which schools were alleged to get worse is now meaningless. For a black or Asian child there are two alternatives. If he or she is lucky, entrance may be obtained to a suburban school with a small minority of black and Asian children. But the majority will simply be assigned to black and Asian schools.

Of course a case can be made that in segregated schools there is more chance of the special needs of black and Asian children being dealt with effectively. It certainly is true that, where such children are only a small minority, they are likely to be classified as remedial or disciplinary cases simply because the school has no specialised ways of dealing with them. It is also true that the inner-city schools have actually benefited from positive discrimination.

For all this, however, such evidence as there is suggests that these segregated inner-city schools are not giving their pupils an equal chance, on completing their schooling, of surviving in an intensely competitive world. 'Ours', one teacher tells me, 'is a remedial school', while another tells me 'What we concentrate on is CSE Mode 3, which enables us to offer special syllabuses suited to their needs.' Unfortunately this is a world in which proper passes at 'A' and 'O' level and in CSE are the passports to jobs in an increasingly restricted employment market. Quite clearly, going to school in Handsworth does not give children as equal a chance as children from the suburban schools. It would seem that our experience reproduces that which was emphasised in the *Brown vs the Board of Education* decision in the United States: 'education which is segregated is inherently unequal'.

The minimal chances of employment

Not surprisingly, Handsworth children do not do well in the employment market. Handsworth as such does badly; young working-class children do badly; but a young Handsworth black does worst of all. Here are the latest figures for the area:[3]

> The overall rate of unemployment in the Lozells area is 38 per cent.
> The male rate of unemployment in the Lozells area is 46 per cent.
> The percentage of all school-leavers getting a job by November was 6 per cent.
> The number of Asian school-leavers getting a job by November was 7 per cent.
> The percentage of Afro-Caribbean school-leavers getting a job by November was 3 per cent.

The West Midlands Research project on the Youth Training Scheme revealed that while black youngsters make up 20 per cent of Birmingham's fifth-form population, only 8 per cent of those got jobs. The actual numbers finding jobs were 1410 for whites, 102 for Asians and 33 for Afro-Caribbeans. Only four Afro-Caribbean boys and four Afro-Caribbean girls from the whole of Handsworth got jobs.[4]

Quite clearly what happens to the young men and women of Handsworth is that when they have finished their segregated schooling their chances of obtaining any employment at all, let alone a good job, are minimal. They face lives of total emptiness except in so far as they can fill them with non-work activities. Asian children live under tight family control, and may be in part shielded from the consequences of unemployment by the sharing of the extended family, but for a great many young people, especially young blacks, there is little to do with one's time but to stand on street corners. There the question of policing becomes all-important.

Policing Handsworth

There has been little honest discussion of policing in Handsworth. What has changed most has been the ideology of policing, which have gone through four stages. The first was that discussed in Gus John's early book on Handsworth, *Race in the Inner City*.[5] The second was that of the attitudes expressed in John Brown's pamphlet *Shades of Grey*.[6] The third stage was that of the period when Superintendent David Webb was responsible for local policy under the benign and distant Chief Constabulary of Sir Phillip Knights. The fourth was the period, after the replacement of the Chief Constable, in which riots occurred. Consideration of these four periods should dispose of the myth that Handsworth has always been, compared with, say, Brixton, a model of community policing.

The usual account given of policing in Handsworth goes something like this. After an initial period in which there were complaints of police harassment of young blacks, community policing was introduced under Superintendent Webb. So successful was this form of policing that just prior to the riots the Police Authority was contemplating moving police to other areas. The riots came as a bolt from the blue and had little to do either with police harassment or with social causes. They were incited by a small criminal group of drug dealers, whose activities had recently been attacked by the police.

It certainly is the case that in the sixties and early seventies there were complaints of police harassment in Handsworth. These were chronicled both by Gus John and by Derek Humphry in his book *Police Power and Black People*.[7] It was also in Handsworth, as Stuart Hall and his collaborators showed, that what they called the 'moral panic' about 'mugging' began. It was in the light of the confrontation then that John Brown was called in to study policing.

Unfortunately, despite its undoubted importance and subsequent influence on policing, Brown's study *Shades of Grey* cannot be taken seriously as a social science document. After showing that Handsworth had the highest rates for one particular type of crime — street thefts and robbery with violence, although it was *not* the leading area for crimes of other kinds — Brown then boldy attributed these crimes to 200 so-called Dreadlocks, and devoted his report to describing the way in which the police dealt with this group.

The description of the Dreadlocks is far from objective. Brown described them as:

> 200 youths of West Indian origin or descent who have taken on the appearance of followers of the Rastafarian faith by plaiting their hair in locks and wearing green, gold and red woollen hats . . . whilst these youths claim identity as Rasta men, the nature of their criminality in fact represents a betrayal of the non-violent ideology of the Rastafarian faith. . . . Deprived and disadvantaged, they see themselves as victims of white racial society and attracted by the values and life-style of alienated Dreadlock groups drift into lives of idleness and crime, justifying themselves with half-digested gobbets of Rastafarian philosophy.

It is hard to read *Shades of Grey* without reaching the conclusion that what Brown thought needed to be done was simply to deal with the Dreadlock minority, though as he admitted:

> Superintendent Webb points out that he cannot use the police in a repressive role, nor can police take action unless the youths commit a criminal act or a breach of the peace, or unless specific complaints are brought against them by members of the public.

The situation was therefore one in which the police were subject to a double attack. On the one hand they were accused of harassing black youth. On the other they were criticised — by whites, Asians and older blacks — for not taking stronger action against them. Brown commended Webb for his activities in the area of community liaison, fostering youth work and assisting in the organisation of an African Liberation Day festival, and he called for the police units in the area to be brought up to strength.

Under Sir Phillip Knights, Superintendent Webb had in fact been given considerable independence to develop his own policies and he had encouraged youth work of all kinds, as well as developing liaison both with the social services and the community. More importantly, he had evolved a policy for dealing with the ganja question, which involved avoiding unnecessary arrests and recognising that ganja was a part of the culture of West Indian youth.

Whether Webb's policies added up to community policing is another question. Those who have been influenced by Chief Constable John Alderson's views on this question would be disappointed to find how little attention had been given to the basic question of the constable on the beat, knowing the people who lived on that beat and acting on their behalf. Nor could they have been entirely happy with the degree to which the police were involved in organising, as distinct from supporting, community activity. For all its apparent benevolence, and perhaps even because of it, Handsworth had tended to become a local police state in which the all-important question was not how Handsworth was represented, and its interests fought for on the City Council, but rather who was in charge of the police.

The resignation, first of Superintendent Webb, and then of Sir Phillip Knights, changed the policing situation and therefore changed Handsworth. Community policing was now an official policy and was spelled out in considerable detail by the new Chief Constable and his Deputy, but the adoption of this policy officially did not necessarily involve the maintenance of the tacit understandings which Superintendent Webb and his colleagues had worked out with the community. This was particularly true in relation to the ganja question, where the emphasis of the new policy was that all people were equally subject to the law. Pressure was mounting at national, as well as local, level for action to deal with the menace of heroin and in Handsworth this meant that all drug dealers and users, whether of heroin or ganja, were under attack.

Ganja, the police and social peace

According to the police report on the riots which occurred in September 1985, they were organised precisely by drug dealers whose operations had been curbed. What is not clear is why a triggering incident arising from a motoring offence should have brought the drug dealers into action and, secondly, how it was that a tiny minority of dealers could have mobilised the large-scale support which was evident in the rioting.

The answers to these last two questions must turn on existing police–community relations with persons other than drug dealers. For all the talk of police–community liaison over the past 10 years there still seems to be a minority whose response to police actions is one of distrust and violence, and that must be a matter for concern. If, however, it is true, as the police report suggests, that the 1985 riot was inspired by drug dealers, then problems of a different order arise. We should need to know whether police policy on ganja has changed, and if there were tacit understandings which were being broken. The problem is what level of law-enforcement there should be in relation to ganja and to what extent this had the support of the community.

It is not my intention here to advocate tolerance of ganja, except to say that it seems to me to be unwise to enforce the law against it severely because of the threat of heroin. Heroin and ganja are different types of problems. What I do want to suggest is that we have arrived at a very unhappy state of affairs if the maintenance of social peace depends on ganja.

The tolerance of a level of drug-use is a poor substitute for active policies of social reform. What we have to look at is the whole outlook on life of young people in the ghetto. If they are cast aside by the members of society to live in separate colonies, to be offered poor and segregated schooling, to have the minimum chance of employment, then this is the sort of situation which calls for a retreat from the world of some kind. Ganja provides just that. The answer to the ganja question is not therefore a better or more sensitive type of policing. The answer lies in the kind of society in which black minorities live and work with mainstream people, and in which the ghetto as we know it ceases to exist.

Notes

1. J. Rex and S. Tomlinson, *Colonial Immigrants in a British City*, London: Routledge and Kegan Paul, 1979.
2. See J. Rex and R. Moore, *Race, Community and Conflict*, London: Oxford University Press, 1967.
3. City of Birmingham Planning Department, *Handsworth/Soho/Lozells Inner Area Study*, Birmingham: City Council, 1985.
4. West Midlands County Council, *Unequal Opportunities — Racial Discrimination and Government Training Schemes*, Birmingham: West Midlands County Council, 1985.
5. A. John *et al.*, *Race in the Inner City*, London: Runnymede Trust, 1972.
6. J. Brown, *Shades of Grey: Police–West Indian Relations in Handsworth*, Cranfield: Cranfield Police Studies, 1977.
7. D. Humphry, *Police Power and Black People*, Harmondsworth: Penguin Books, 1970.

CHAPTER 12

Racial disadvantage, unemployment and urban unrest

IVAN HENRY

The fact that the urban unrest in Britain in the autumn of 1985 came as a surprise to the nation, and the fact that there is still an agonising search for the causes of the disorders, imply hypocrisy or a gross misunderstanding of race relations as they manifest themselves in the deprived areas of our great cities. I hesitate to refer to these districts as 'ghettos', for they are the only areas in Britain that can truly be defined as multiracial. In the case of Handsworth/Lozells, where the series of disorders broke out on the night of 9 September 1985, people of different races live in approximately equal numbers — but with unequal access to scarce resources. And since they coexist by force of circumstances and not from choice, every encounter is fraught with conflict.

The popular but erroneous analyses of race relations

Most of the popular analyses of race relations are based on false premises. One such definition is that of the 'assimilationists', who argue that in time white Britons will no longer consider blacks as strange, will recover from their xenophobia and this will hasten the process of assimilation into the mainstream of society. This thesis can be found in the works of Michael Banton, Ruth Glass and Sheila Patterson. It is defective because it overlooks the long history of the intimate relationship between black and white British subjects, both in the colonies and in the mother country.[1]

Another false understanding of race relations informs the massive literature dealing with personal prejudice and discrimination. It assumes that racial disadvantage is caused by personal dislike of blacks, and that if only whites would learn to like or tolerate them, then the problem would be solved.[2] Empirical evidence has led to legislation outlawing discrimination, and even though this has improved interpersonal relationships in public places it has not prevented the marginalisation and increasing deprivation of black Britons.

A third analysis, championed by neomarxists like Castles and Kosack,

RUU-I

concentrates on the function immigrant workers serve in Western European societies, and it belittles the salience of race. Though this thesis offers another plausible explanation of the crisis in the working-class movement, it fails to account for the failure of blacks to experience the same upward social mobility that white immigrant workers have historically experienced in Britain and elsewhere.[3]

The fourth, and most interesting, theoretical appraisal is that of John Rex and his associates.[4] This analysis emphasises the historical, political dimension of race relations, and argues that the conditions under which black immigrants entered Britain made marginalisation, conflict and truce inevitable. The scenario it outlines is that of the formation of a black 'underclass', acutely dependent on British institutions and somewhat de-moralised. Implicit in the concept of the underclass is overall subscription to the prevailing norms. My own research on the growth of corporate black identity threw up considerable evidence to refute this thesis of acculturation, identification and submission.[5]

The reality of the black Odyssey

What is significant about Rex and his associates' work is the insistence that the colonial, political antecedents would ensure the black immigrants would settle in internal colonies in the less attractive housing districts and occupations in metropolitan Britain. Their seminal work on Sparkbrook and Handsworth shows how the competition for housing accommodation, and the nature of the available employment and education, determined this pattern of settlement.

To all intents and purposes this mode of accommodation was considered temporary by all concerned. A careful study of newspaper cuttings of race relations in Birmingham in the 1950s and 1960s indicates that the 'host' society viewed black immigrants as target workers to be tolerated for a period before they returned to their homelands. The black settlers themselves expected to return home as soon as possible, or to achieve upward social mobility through their efforts or the achievements of their British-educated children.

The outcomes have been completely different. The 5-year Odyssey has become a life-time journey. Very few migrants have made it 'back home'. A large number of the black population has legally become black Britons, increasingly by birth, but their conditions have worsened. The comprehensive and periodic studies, carried out by Political and Economic Planning and its successor the Policy Studies Institute, have charted the plight of black immigrants from the 1950s. The most recent survey by the Policy Studies Institute found that in terms of location, housing, education and employment the position of blacks has not improved. In writing up this report, Colin Brown concluded:

For the most part, therefore, Britain's well-established black population is still occupying the precarious and unattractive position of the early immigrants. We have moved, over a period of 18 years, from studying the circumstances of immigrants to studying the black population of Britain only to find that we are still looking at the same thing. There is just the need now as in 1976 for action to give black people access to widening economic opportunities and life chances; and there is just the same need to pursue equality between racial groups in Britain.[6]

Lord Scarman in 1981 recognised the link between such deprivation and urban disorders.

The sustained recession, and in particular its manifestation in the form of high levels of unemployment, has heightened the insecurity of black people. A people preoccupied with finding employment — a people whose attraction to this cold, inegalitarian and unjust society was the lure of employment — had their social moorings cut during the spectacular labour-shedding era of the 1980s. Traditional industries collapsed in the West Midlands, and the rates of unemployment trebled between 1979 and 1985, and of course the area ceased to be a magnet for labour.

Within the black communities the high levels of unemployment came early and the impact has been severe and prolonged. No longer do average levels of unemployment have any meaning in parts of the inner city. For example, in Handsworth only eight school-leavers of Afro-Caribbean origin found employment in 1984. The employment career for many of our clients at Handsworth Employment Scheme follows the pattern of: 1 year on YOP/YTS, unemployment, voluntary work or pregnancy, 1 year on a Community Programme project, further unemployment, a repeat of Community Programme work experience and so on.

Competition, conflict and protest

The black response in purely economic terms has been two-fold. *First*, there has been renewed effort to find employment. People have been queuing up for jobs which in better times were dismissed as 'shit work'. The demand for places on our Community Programme, which offers work that is dirty, poorly paid and short-term, has increased. *Second*, there has been a phenomenal growth in interest in starting a business. Over 26 per cent of our clients express a wish to start a business. Indeed giving advice to potential entrepreneurs is now a growth industry in the inner city. However, frustrations build up when access to capital is blocked for what amounts to a lack of track record. The system obviously militates against newcomers.

Exacerbating the situation in Handsworth prior to the disturbances was the injection of money into the area, estimated at £20 million. In-stitutionalised racism embedded in the tendering system ensured that this money did not percolate down to the unemployed black, and other working-class, people in the area. One was faced with the scene of intense activity of houses being repaired by contractors who lived and recruited outside the area, while inside those houses sat unemployed people eminently qualified to do the work.

Enforced leisure increased the competition for space. Throughout the summer of 1985 one heard of cases of conflict over the use of cafés, bingo halls and public houses. On occasion local politicians would intervene on behalf of white residents' associations and debar black groups from using certain buildings. In this tense situation any spark could have caused conflagration.

On a wider canvas the stratification mould was hardening with blacks trapped at the bottom. Catalytic elements in the black community, drawing on African-derived identity resources, seized the time and protested. They transcended interpersonal conflict and attacked property and collective defenders of the status quo. Looters of all races capitalised on the breakdown of law and order. In the heat of the night lives were unfortunately lost. However, the protesters remain convinced that to do otherwise than protest would be to collude in their own oppression.

Notes

1. A more detailed critique of this approach can be found in I. Henry, H. Joshua and R. Sargeant, 'Power, culture and identity: the case of the Afro-Caribbean people', in Open University, *Minority Experience*, Vol. 3 of a course on Ethnic Minorities and Community Relations, Milton Keynes: Open University Press, 1983.
2. For a critique of such notions see C. Husband, 'Racial prejudice and the concept of social identity', in Open University, *Race and British Society*, Vol. 3 of a course on Ethnic Minorities and Community Relations, Milton Keynes: Open University Press, 1983.
3. S. Castles and G. Kosack, *Immigrant Workers and the Class Structure in Western Europe*, London: Oxford University Press, 1973.
4. J. Rex and S. Tomlinson, *Colonial Immigrants in a British City*, London: Routledge and Kegan Paul, 1979.
5. I. Henry, *The Growth of Corporate Black Identity Among Afro-Caribbean People in Birmingham, England*, unpublished Ph.D. thesis, University of Warwick, 1982.
6. C. Brown, *Black and White Britain*, London: Heinemann, 1984.

CHAPTER 13

Too much talk and not enough positive action

USHA PRASHAR

I should preface my views with a brief comment. When I sat down to put my thoughts together I felt a sense of anger and frustration at having to repeat the same things that many of us have been saying for at least 20 years. I also feel rather tired and jaded, because I am repeating the same things, and trying to find new words with which to express them. Yet despite all these years of discussion there is little sign that serious action is being taken. Perhaps it is frustration and anger which spurs us on; perhaps this is why we think 'we must not give up: we must fight on'.

I was involved in the conference *Scarman and After*, and there I said that Lord Scarman had made a well-founded case for positive action to deal with unemployment, racial discrimination and all the other problems facing the communities in the inner cities.[1] He argued strongly for positive action within the context of a realistic strategy directed at specific areas of racial disadvantage. Since his report was published in November 1981 a few initiatives have been taken, but on a very piecemeal and *ad hoc* basis. This has been nothing like what was recommended, which was a direct and coordinated attack on racial disadvantage. Lord Scarman argued that the task of tackling social problems was even more urgent than that of establishing good relations between black communities and the police.

The sorry story of inaction since 1981

So what has happened since 1981? I am afraid it does not really add up to very much. The first thing was that Sir George Young was appointed as a junior minister in the Department of Environment, with special responsibility for race. However, no interdepartmental committee, or Cabinet committee of relevant ministers, was set up. Some attempts were made to develop a new role, with an emphasis on facilitating action to ensure the more efficient functioning of the existing machinery of government, and some more money was given to black and ethnic minority groups. Even this small impetus seems to have waned in recent years. The

115

Department of the Environment, and to some extent the Home Office, encouraged local authorities to adopt equal opportunity policies. However, in the 1986 government reshuffle the unit in the Department of the Environment, which had responsibility under Sir George Young for positive action and for promoting initiatives for black people, was abolished.

The response of the Department of Education and Science to Lord Scarman's recommendations was that they were awaiting the outcome of the Swann Committee Report. When this report was published the Department of Education and Science responded with two consultative documents, one on the recruitment of more black teachers and one on monitoring and record-keeping. So far that is all. If we look at housing, what was suggested? Lord Scarman called for a major programme of rehabilitation based on community participation, and a review of council housing allocation. Five years later the Housing Renewal Unit has been established, and its job is to pull together private funding and local authority money to rehabilitate all housing stock. This unit has an annual budget of £300,000! And the money which has been allocated to the Housing Investment Programme has also been declining. The story on the provision of jobs is the same. There has been a grave increase in unemployment, but the Government tinkers with the problem. For example, in 1985 the Home Office put all of £20,000 into a scheme for small businesses in Handsworth, and Deptford in south-east London.

We have had nothing like the 'concerted effort' recommended by Lord Scarman. Instead, we have been given bits and pieces, which have come too late and have been minuscule compared to the scale of the problem. What has been happening as far as discrimination is concerned? A number of the contributors in this book refer to the two PSI studies: *Racial Disadvantage in Britain* and *Black and White Britain*.[2] Both these reports showed that racial disadvantage is certainly getting no better: they document a devastating record of continuing discrimination, and lack of progress as far as the material conditions of minorities are concerned.

Let us look at the sort of structural changes which have been taking place in cities such as Birmingham. Between 1978 and 1984 Birmingham lost one-third of all its manufacturing jobs, and a similar decline in employment opportunities has occurred in many other inner-city areas. There has also been a significant decline in the real amount of money which has been directed to these areas. Although ministers talk about how the Urban Programme has increased, it must not be forgotten that larger amounts of central government funding for rate support have been siphoned off. In fact there has been a net *loss* of finance.

In summary, we find that there has been minimal action since 1981, there is evidence of grave and continuing discrimination and there is continuing economic decline which is damaging the inner cities. The response to these problems has been inadequate. Few initiatives which have been taken have been handled properly. For example, £20 million was spent in Handsworth in the years before the 1985 riots, and the result, we were told, was a better environment. However, it was admitted that few if any jobs were created for local people. Following the 1981 disturbances, a number of local authorities embarked upon 'enveloping schemes' for the improvement of houses; outside contractors were brought in and there was no involvement of the local communities. The work was undertaken by contractors who, while doing the work on the houses, were racially abusive to the black residents who lived in them. It is not just how much is done — important though that is — but it also the *way* that it is done. The involvement of local communities is crucial.

Dissipating energy and promoting confusion

Another thing that we should be aware of is the danger of small amounts of money creating 'project mentality'. Little pots of money come in, and massive administrative arrangements are made for the allocation of that money; all the energy of the communities concerned is channelled into devising projects and making applications, and the local authorities spend vast amounts of time and resources on deciding how to allocate the money. All this activity does not add to very much in terms of jobs and real opportunities. Handsworth has a number of projects, but if you put them together what do they add up to? It is this piecemeal, *ad hoc* approach which also needs to be examined.

I would also like to draw attention to the way these issues have been discussed publicly. The quality of the debate has deteriorated enormously, and there has been a wilful attempt to create an illusion that a great deal is being done. Every time urban unrest occurs we hear ministers saying 'we are spending money in these areas; a great deal of money has been allocated'. There is an illusion that much is being done when in reality the position is very different. Indeed, what *is* happening is that black people are being pushed into a cul-de-sac where their energies are being dissipated on matters which do not really, in the long run, make much difference to their material conditions. The debate on these issues is like a pantomime where one side says 'Urban unrest is a problem caused by crime, drugs and law and order' and the other side says 'Oh no it is not' and the first group says 'Oh yes it is'. No progress is made and no meaningful discussion takes place.

We seem to be very long on analysis of what the issues are and why there has been social unrest, but very short on actually doing anything constructive. Following the race riots in America at least there were real discussions and positive responses. In the United States the people and the government recognised the nature of the problem, but here in Britain we spend time disagreeing about the causes of urban unrest. Unless we recognise the nature of the problem we are not going to get the right solutions. If anything there is now a tendency to confuse the issues and to deny that racism and social deprivation are the roots of the problem. This does not augur well for the future.

Notes

1. U. Prashar, 'The need for positive action', in J. Benyon (ed.), *Scarman and After*, Oxford: Pergamon Press, 1984.
2. D. J. Smith, *Racial Disadvantage in Britain*, Harmondsworth: Penguin, 1977: C. Brown, *Black and White Britain: The Third PSI Survey*, London: Heinemann, 1984.

CHAPTER 14

Unemployment, racial disadvantage and the inner city: Discussion

The different responses by the white majority to the 1981 and 1985 disorders

Marian Fitzgerald, Ealing Community Relations Council: May I take up one to two of the points that Usha has just made so well. It is clear from our discussions today, and from so much of the coverage of the urban disorders, that people are focusing on black people, focusing on the police, and talking a little bit about the policies of the current central government, but I think what is being left out of the equation is white majority attitudes and their political implications.

I would like briefly to point out some of the ways in which the ratchet was turned several notches by the 1985 riots. In 1981 there was a public response which was 'this cannot be allowed to happen again'. That gave rise to a vague political consensus between the parties that things *can* be done to improve the conditions which give rise to riots. OK, one cannot disagree with the view that the measures were palliatives and essentially *'ad hocery'*. They increased the Urban Programme, they set up Scarman, one might say, there was George Young and a lot of fingers crossed, and the opposition parties duly made some political capital out of it on the basis that it was an indictment of central government policies generally towards the inner cities, the economy, and towards law and order and police accountability. In all this response the race dimension was somewhat fudged, but there was a sort of consensus that something could be done about it: you could pander to public concern, and you could make sure that it did not happen again.

But in 1985 it did happen again, and the ratchet has turned several notches because those palliatives have not worked. Now the gloves are off. First of all there is public opinion: 'you said you could stop it and you didn't'. The cry for justice is not the issue any more. The Government and the media have redefined it as 'the enemy within and what are you going to do about it?', and we ignore this at our peril. The political reaction now has led to a consensus that the issue is one of law and order; this time there is to be no Scarman. The predominant response now is not that you can do something about the conditions which give rise to these riots; it is all a case

119

of 'human wickedness'. That is what Douglas Hurd said when he left Handsworth, and it is highly significant. The opposition parties are not overtly playing that game, but they are part of a consensus because they too are playing the law and order card. They are playing it under the guise of scoring points off the Government's record on law and order: 'the Conservatives said that they could solve the problems of law and order, but look what has happened: you have had riots; we can solve law and order better than they can'.

The political response this time is not just fudging the race dimension again, but it is also directly pandering to the baying for blood, the racist reaction, amongst the white majority. We really must realise how intractable this problem is, and we must address ourselves to the problem of white majority reaction and the political implications of it.

Social balance in schools

W. S. Walton, Chief Education Officer, Sheffield: I would like to comment on one or two of the things that Professor Rex said about curriculum in comprehensive schools in Handsworth, Birmingham. I agree, from the point of view of entering into higher education and of getting a job, it is important that we have courses that do have external accreditation. However, Mode 3 CSE also has external accreditation. It is exactly the same value as Mode 1 or Mode 2 CSE but the advantage of Mode 3 is that it enables the construction of a curriculum which is interesting and which provides an experience which is real and intelligible for young people. It seems to me that this is entirely commendable and I would applaud the people in Birmingham who are seeking to move in that sort of direction.

I am not so sure about the feeling that all-in integration is good in education. We have a lot of experience in this country at the present time of seeking to create and fulfil the principles of comprehensive schools by providing opportunities for the social mix. In all the cities in which I have worked there have been fleets of buses transporting children around the cities to seek to achieve social balance in the schools. I have no evidence at all about the success of those sort of policies in seeking to change social attitudes.

I also wonder about the curriculum effect if you seek to create integrated situations and if you accept the values that Professor Rex seemed to be putting forward about the traditional 'A' and 'O' level courses. It seems to me that, regardless of race, if you expose people of the lower social classes in this country to the traditional 'O' level curriculum you are doing them no favour at all. We already have in the order of a 70 per cent failure, or opting out, rate at 'O' or 'A' level in this country at the present time. We are offering a curriculum which is based on arbitrarily gathered-together single-subject chunks of knowledge, which have no intrinsic value whatsoever, and which often bore young people to tears.

It is worth thinking very carefully before one moves on the integrated path. I agree that given the present minority values that determine the direction of education in this country at the present time, that segregated schools are unequal, but I do not believe that it is inherently the case.

Hyacinth Parsons, Southwark Community Race Relations Council: I know this is an unusual question, but I just want to ask the last speaker how many CSEs did he require for the job he now occupies.

W. S. Walton: Fortunately I was in a situation, in the part of the country where I come from, where there was about 97 per cent employment at the time when I was looking for jobs. Certainly the situation in Sheffield at the present time is that regardless of the number of 'O' levels or CSEs it is extremely difficult to get a job. If you are black it is even more difficult to get a job. I do not deny that. What I was pointing out was that I think it is quite wrong to give the impression that the Mode 3 approach to CSE is of less value than the Mode 1 approach.

The perceptions of the majority of white people

Keith Harris, West Midlands Probation Service: We must be wary of not going back into the cycle that Stuart Hall spoke of earlier: of conference after conference. I do not suppose I am going to be able to produce a universal panacea, but I would like to offer two comments. One is that I think all human beings in Britain — all white and black people — need to be looking at ways in which they can get into the decision-making processes for change. If that means leaning on the government of the day, then we need to try and do so. What is vitally important is that black people should have access to the political processes.

The other point I want to make is about perceptions. I think it is a point directed at the mentality of the majority of white people in Western Europe. We tend to talk about race and people in terms of minorities, and today we are talking about race and black people, and discrimination and disadvantage, in terms of minority people. The white view is: 'it is a minority issue; it does not need much thought; it does not have to be handled seriously'.

However, if you look at the research done by *Faith in the City* (London: Church House Publishing, 1985) it suggests, for example, that Mexico City in the year 2000 will have 30 million people, and São Paulo in Brazil will have 26 million people. The point is that the majority of them are black, and racial discrimination and disadvantage are *majority* problems. If people in Europe begin to perceive that race is not a minority matter, but a very serious universal matter, we may begin to grasp the idea of what we have to tackle: not a minority issue but a serious fundamental world issue.

Anon: I would like to say one thing! As a member of this society I say to each and every one of you: until the colour of a person's skin is of no more significance than the colour of his or her eyes there is going to be war, in both a verbal and physical sense. We need equal rights, whether we are black or white.

PART 5

The Quest for Social Justice

CHAPTER 15

The quest for social justice

LORD SCARMAN

It is my pleasure to bring this part of the conference to a close. We have so far been looking either at the present or backwards in order to get the perspective and the analysis with which to tackle the final session. I think it is very fortunate, and we are all very glad, that Ann Dummett with her notable record can be in the chair for the final session. Hopefully the whole day's deliberations, and particularly the next session, can advance our thinking so that we help enable our society to make a step or so forward, no doubt leading to topics for another conference of this sort in the future.

I will just try to sum up, and to offer some reflections on, what we have heard so far. First, I would like to thank most sincerely, and with great appreciation, all our speakers who have taken immense trouble to prepare very careful submissions, beautifully presented to this conference, and that includes every one of those who has spoken to us. If Stuart Hall and Martin Kilson will allow me to say so, they got the conference off to magnificent start. They set a tone of debate the like of which I have seldom heard, and we are immensely indebted to both of them.

The search for the social contract

What was interesting, I found, was how complementary to each other the two contributions were. Stuart Hall, speaking with British experience, indicated that the basic cause of urban unrest is the sense of injustice — I shall return to that, because it is very important to bear in mind that it is from the perception or sense of injustice that most human disturbances in a gregarious society arise. But he went further. He said that there would be no way of eradicating this sense of injustice, unless — and he chose his words advisedly — we in this multiracial society can achieve a social contract.

These are very much jargon words, you may say, but of course they go straight back to the thinking of Jean Jacques Rousseau. This is where the modern idea of human rights and fundamental liberties of mankind originated, and of course as we know, Rousseau's thinking inspired the

125

French Revolution. He indicated that we need a social contract. The idea of the 'social contract' is a metaphor, but the sense behind it is tremendous. It is a lesson for everyone in our society, including the white majority whose attitudes have got to change.

It happens today that black people are largely concerned in urban unrest, because they live in the inner cities and they suffer the deprivations and racial disadvantage of which we know. In the past we have had urban unrest frequently in this country, other sections of the community having had in their generation a sense of injustice. Today, although it is not wholly the truth, it is the ethnic minorities, and the black minority in particular, which suffer social injustice and which protest about it. What Rousseau's ideas mean today is that society at large must open up to allow black people to participate like other citizens. Society must be prepared to receive the ethnic minorities into the establishment, to be councillors, magistrates, teachers, lawyers, accountants, entrepreneurs or whatever. Black people must be admitted to the power structure of our society. That is my interpretation of what Stuart Hall was saying with immense eloquence and tremendous power.

He was speaking of a society in which by and large that is not yet true. The social contract has not been achieved. How marvellous it was therefore that he should be followed by Martin Kilson, explaining the American experience in which the black social contract movement inspired by Martin Luther King has achieved if not complete success at least substantial progress. In Britain we must follow along this path. We need not blame ourselves for being less advanced than America, because we have had much less experience of racial discrimination and conflict than they have had. As we know, the United States has only managed to tackle it in a civilised way in the past 20 years or so.

We now have the value of their experience, and we must apply it. Of course, the society in the United States is different from our own, and of greater complexity, and we do not have to follow them into all the flexible and imaginative processes necessary to keep united a continent of almost infinite variety of population. In our little island, with our smaller numbers and our smaller differences, we still can learn, and what we have to learn is that all of us — the white majority, the ethnic minorities, the establishment, government, Parliament, the judges, the whole society, our families, our children — have got to say 'black people are part of our society and must be treated equally'.

The core of the problem: injustice

I did so much agree with Ivan Henry's comment upon the interesting analysis of the ghetto by Professor Rex. I do not think of any part of our society as a ghetto — that is negative and is in fact death-dealing — I think of our society as multiracial and multicultural, because that is what we are. And in our multiracial society both the white majority and the black minorities have to work together, and live together, without allowing the build-up of intolerable levels of injustice. And therefore in the first two contributions, in Chapters 3 and 4, we have not only been given various dimensions of the problem, and an interesting and informative lesson from Martin Kilson as to the considerable success that the Americans had in tackling them, but we have also reached the core of the problem: injustice.

In a conference dealing with the roots of urban unrest we really need to understand that if we cut away the specific problems, of racial disadvantage, racism, unemployment, policing, black people at the bottom of the social pile, we reach a more general answer, but one that has a specific application to the position of black people. The general lesson is that in any society where there is a substantial minority of fellow citizens labouring under a sense of injustice you will get urban unrest — and you may get much more. The French got revolution, but in Britain we have not quite reached revolution since the seventeeth century, because in a belated way our leaders always reacted just in time.

In his short, succinct but devastating analysis of what has happened since 1981, in Chapter 5, John Clare quotes a statement by Stafford Scott that we really must clasp to our hearts: 'you will not understand unless you know what it is like to be black'. This is what needs to be kept in mind by the white majority. But black people have similarly got to understand that however receptive the white majority become — and one must work to see that they do become receptive — black people have got to fight for their own success. They must make use of their opportunities. I will not say that black people have got to reach the commanding heights of power and the economy — to borrow Aneurin Bevan's phrase — but there is no reason why they should not be there. Let them move into the levels of power from the top to the bottom of society.

There was a most interesting leading article in *The Times* to celebrate the occasion of the first Martin Luther King public holiday in America, and the leader took note that there was no black leader in America now comparable to Martin Luther King. Does that mean that Martin Luther King had lived in vain? Of course it does not, for what is happening is exactly what Martin Luther King would want: ordinary, intelligent good-willed black people are moving into positions of power, as local politicians and state politicians, in the professions and so forth. They are not all of them men of genius or men of outstanding leadership, but they are good citizens making use of their opportunities to get into the system. And I believe that is really one of the lessons that is emerging from this conference.

I would like to say that I listened with interest to various comments on the Brixton Report. I happen to agree with the charmingly expressed criticism of John Clare that I could have been more explicit than I was when dealing with the problems summed up in the words 'positive discrimination'. I think in other parts of the Report it is perfectly plain the importance that I attach to improvement in social, economic, and political conditions of the ethnic minorities. I should have been more outspoken than I was about the necessity of affirmative action in order to overcome racial disadvantage.

I myself find the educational system's deficiencies one of the most disturbing, because unless a person is educated to a level necessary to make an impact in our society it is difficult to get anywhere. It does seem to me that affirmative action is needed to compensate black people, so that they can move into the professions, into higher education, into business and into a position of equality in the competitive labour market. Perhaps I did not see far enough, or maybe for once in my life I was mealy-mouthed, and for that I do indeed apologise.

The momentum must be sustained

But in Britain we have no reason to be in any way despairing. Admittedly there is one hell of a job to be done. Fortunately, I think we have realised this in time, but we must keep moving, and there is a danger of the momentum slackening. In Chapter 13, Usha Prashar mentions the lack of implementation of the social and economic recommendations to be found in the Brixton Report. This is sadly so, and I agree with the implication of her remarks that there has been a misdirection of effort, as well as in some respects a lack of effort. Without a carefully coordinated programme, which involves everyone from the local inhabitants themselves right up to and including the central government, we will not make the necessary progress.

Finally, one interesting thing is how little of our time has been spent at this conference discussing the police. We had interesting and valuable contributions from David Smith and Richard Wells, but the policing problem has somehow or other been submerged beneath the social problems. The truth of the matter is we will not get policing right unless we get the social context right. The problem in recruiting black policemen is a good illustration, and I end on this note. I support the programme for getting more black people into the police. It is invaluable, but I certainly do not regard it as a panacea.

If we can get black people into the whole of British public life, then no doubt they will come into the police and they will improve the police. Of course we must encourage black policemen, but I do not believe that that is a solution to the policing problem. There *is* a policing problem, and it is a continuing one, but let it be studied, as you are studying it in this conference, in its general social context. I really believe that your deliberations are leading the way forward towards a better understanding of the problem of urban unrest, and of the disadvantage of the ethnic minorities in our society.

PART 6

Looking Forward: Proposals and Prospects

CHAPTER 16

The way forward:
proposals and prospects

HERMAN OUSELEY

Ann Dummett (in the chair): It is my pleasure to introduce the two speakers for the last part of the conference, and it is a good thing that we have again one American speaker, as well as one British speaker. There have been divergent views expressed about what can be learnt from the American experience. I would only say that if one could only learn from experience that was *identical* at every point with one's own one would never learn anything whatever in this world. It is surely extremely useful that we have the opportunity for the sort of comparisons that this conference is enabling us to make. First of all I want to ask Herman Ouseley to give us his thoughts. Herman is Assistant Chief Executive in the London Borough of Lambeth and formerly was the Head of the Greater London Council's Ethnic Minorities Unit.[1]

Herman Ouseley: Thank you very much, Ann. I am delighted that we are starting to redress the gender imbalance: we have had Usha Prashar on the platform and we have you in the chair. In saying that, I am also sad that Lord Scarman has had to leave. I should point out that Ann Dummett has asked me to limit my talk to about 15 minutes, and the notes I had prepared run to about 16 pages, which will take at least an hour to deliver, so I will try to be disciplined, and I will scrap the notes!

Perhaps I could begin with a few words about Lord Scarman's 1981 Report. I do not wish to be offensive or disrespectful to a man who is undoubtedly a considerate and caring person. However we ought to recognise that although Lord Scarman is a prominent judge from the liberal wing of the judiciary, he achieved great kudos as a result of his Report into the Brixton uprisings in 1981. And what has that Report done? I am only going to mention two issues, because I could take an hour and a half just talking about the Scarman Report.

First of all, consider the case of police consultative committees. I have a lot of sympathy for the people who are involved in these bodies. I know some members and I have a great deal of admiration for them. In my own area of work, the person who chairs it is someone who has impeccable grass roots connections, and he has been prepared to get out there on the streets, but I believe he has been sold down the river by the structure with which he has been saddled. Immediately after the 1985 disturbances in Brixton he and his colleagues went along to the Home Secretary and pleaded for a public inquiry — all they got was a very polite message to go away. The reality of police consultative groups is that the people involved have no control at all over policing policies, behaviour and operations. This particular route is not taking us anywhere by way of improvement.

The experience of black people

The second issue area arising from Lord Scarman's Report is the question of positive action to overcome racial disadvantage and discrimination. Let me draw attention to what he says in Chapter 15. On this issue, Lord Scarman now accepts that he may have been mealy-mouthed and he apologises for not being more forthright. I do not want to be ungenerous, but he has had over 4 years since the Report to have done something about it. He is an important public person, a powerful judge and a very eminent person. What has he done in terms of affirmative action within the judiciary, to start bringing them closer to the real-life, everyday experience of black people? My fear is, as Ivan Henry and others have said, that in 10 years' time we will still be having this debate, and we will still be caught in a circle of protest, recommendations, debate, no action and more protests. Where is this getting us?

Another point which has been raised, by Usha Prashar and others, is the misdirection of effort. Presumably we are talking about local authorities who have allegedly been given a mass of money to spend in their areas just like the famous £20 million in Handsworth. But as John Clare points out in his eloquent presentation, in Chapter 5, what the Government gives with one hand they take away two or three times more with the other hand, in the form of rate-capping, cuts in housing investment and cuts in central government grants. This is surely the real nature of the misdirected effort. When one looks at all the things that black people have been doing in their communities to overcome their oppression, in their fight against racism on a day-to-day basis, what has happened is that their efforts and energies have been channelled not only into fighting racism, but also in fighting for crumbs.

The problem has been eloquently put today by John Clare, by Stuart Hall, by Devon Thomas and by other speakers. John Clare quoted the views of Stafford Scott, who is another black person who has actually come to the forefront off the streets, from the estate, to put forward very eloquently the experience of black people who have been involved in urban uprisings. Stafford Scott is from the Broadwater Farm Youth

Association Defence Campaign, and to quote him exactly: 'Unless you understand what being black in Britain really means, you will never understand why people are prepared to stand up and fight officers of the law.'

This is my real starting point because that is telling you why there are urban uprisings. It is because the way racism impacts through all the institutions of this society — every one including voluntary organisations run by white people — the outcome ensures that black people get nothing or very little. They are always second best, and that is the reality. So when we examine how to start dismantling racism we see it is a matter of power in society — and this is a point which has been raised several times during this conference, and indeed Lord Scarman said it. Racism is about power, and it is found in the way in which institutions and organisations operate, even when they have enlightened people in charge. In this I would even include the final administration at the Greater London Council (GLC), which was supposed to be one of the most radical, socialist administrations to run local government, at least in London. There were still whites predominantly in control, with only one black elected member on the GLC, and to a large extent the same situation exists at Lambeth, although we have eight elected members who are black.

Seven key factors in the way ahead

How are we going to tackle this problem of black people being more in control of these institutions that are making decisions all the time on their behalf? This is the shift in power which has to be achieved, and already various alliances between different groups have begun to be forged. There are several different factors of which we need to be aware, and in a necessarily abbreviated form I will summarise them. *First*, we must recognise that institutional racism exists. It applies to every institution in this country, and is found in the way they operate at the central government level, in the private sector and the voluntary sector, and at the local authority level. *Second*, we must realise that we have inadequate, ineffectively enforced race relations legislation which is supposed to try to deal with and correct inequalities which occur in society on a day-to-day basis.

Third, woefully inadequate resources have been made available to tackle the urban problems: urban deprivation, urban renewal, deteriorating living conditions. This has been pointed out by many contributors and, as Stuart Hall stresses in Chapter 3, there is a vast mass of research which documents the extent of urban disadvantage and which shows the lack of action taken to tackle it. *Fourth*, we must note that some of the alternative viable strategies for dealing with structural problems in inner cities have been tried. However, they have been tried by just a few local authorities, some with notable successes, *but not one* has been supported by the Thatcher

Government. In fact, the central government has moved quite dramatically against alternative strategies the moment they start to be successful. A classic example was the GLC working to mobilise people on a broad front in London. However, because ordinary poor people, including black people, were given a voice and were using a small part of the apparatus of power to express the view that is an alternative, the Thatcher Government decided to eradicate it completely: the GLC was abolished in April 1986.

The *fifth* point is that the police force is racist, and in this it takes its lead from a racist Government, which is backed by a racist news media. The police force continuously abuses the excess of power which it has, particularly when it is policing the inner-city areas and black people. The warnings were there in the 1960s, throughout the 1970s and by 1979 and 1980 things had deteriorated greatly. In January 1981 the final *Report of the Working Party on Community/Police Relations in Lambeth*[2] was published by the London Borough of Lambeth following the rejection by the Home Secretary of calls for a public inquiry, and it warned of the dangers of the police provoking serious urban unrest. Three months later it actually happened as predicted. The Report talked about the police being seen as an occupying alien force in the Brixton area. So the police are a technocratic, alien force with suburban mentality, trying to police people of whose conditions they have no awareness at all. In areas like Brixton, and Handsworth, and Broadwater Farm, we do not have local police, in their own local community where they have a local vested interest and can be accountable to their neighbours. Instead, we have mainly outsiders, with little or no knowledge, no feelings, no respect and no sensitivity for those they are policing.

The *sixth* factor is that anti-racist and racial equality programmes so far have been largely marginal and symbolic, and this is true even of the most radical programmes in the most committed local authorities. These campaigns have been marginal to the real needs of black people. Often they have been tokenistically insulting: at best all they have attempted to do is to equalise black people with the level of poverty shared by poor white people. There really is a lot of nonsense talked about moving black people into the middle classes — too many people have been reading papers emerging out of Thatcher's office, about the creation of a black bourgeoisie. All that *some* local authorities have tried is to bring black people in inner-city areas up to the levels of deprivation suffered by the poorest whites in these areas.

The *seventh*, and final, point is that in some areas we have seen the emergence of an alliance of 'usually excluded' groups of people. Perhaps this is similar to processes which have occurred in the United States, and which Martin Kilson mentions in Chapter 4. This alliance is a very important development. Race politics have developed, and black people have started to project themselves to the forefront of politics saying: 'We are going to deal with racism; we want a fair deal; we want equality; we want justice; we want to start dealing with your racism.'

Alongside the emergence of black politics we have seen the development of other movements: the Women's Movement, campaigns for disabled people, for old people, for poor whites in the cities, and of course for lesbians and gay men. The developing action on the part of these groups is very important, and there are interlocking features which are resulting in an alliance of the 'usually excluded'. This is of great significance for black people, because when one considers the limited successes in those areas of London, like Lambeth, Hackney, Brent and the GLC, where black people have made some partial progress, we still find that black women, or black elderly, or black disabled people, are the worst off. Thus, it is important to recognise that black people in all of those groupings — black women, black elderly, black disabled people, black gay people and black lesbians — are at the sharp end of disadvantage and discrimination.

A question of power

The fundamental question for the emerging alliance is how poor disenchanted, disenfranchised people can organise themselves to take control of those institutions, at local government but also central government levels, which make such an impact on their lives and in which other people make decisions for them all the time. At present, and in the past, it is these other people — 'them' — who determine what the environment will look like. 'They' built Broadwater Farm Estate in Tottenham and Stockwell Park Estate in Brixton; 'they' designed it, 'they' planned it, 'they' constructed it and then 'they' put the people to live in it. 'They' make the decisions about allocations of resources, jobs, housing, and so forth; and in short, 'they' determine who is going to get what. 'They' determine where to invest, and what to invest in. As Ivan Henry and other people said earlier about the money moving into Handsworth: it moves in and it moves straight through into the pockets of external white contractors who come in. This is happening in Brixton and in every black area: these areas are being plundered.

So the fundamental question is how ordinary people can actually take hold of the institutions and say: 'These resources are ours and we are going to determine the way they are to be deployed for our benefit.' It can be done; it has been done; it was beginning to be done, which is why the Government decided to attack, through rate-capping and other measures, those local authorities which have been attempting to align themselves with the disadvantaged communities and the 'usually excluded' groups of people. The policies of authorities like the GLC were seen as a threat, because they were encouraging ordinary, powerless, oppressed people to organise and to stand up for themselves.

Instead of this approach of enabling the powerless and the excluded to have control and to have a voice in their own lives, the predominant response by the Government has been piecemeal. Since 1981 — and before — we have had a process of 'buying off' local people in the inner cities. This boils down to the grant mentality; the dependency syndrome; the 'throw the crumbs and let them fight each other' approach. This is designed to ensure that blacks fight other blacks, that they squabble with whites, and that they compete with the disabled, the old people, and so on. And what are they fighting for? It is called the Urban Programme, but in reality it is the 'marginal programme'; it is tokenism. What it boils down to is a minute fraction of planned public expenditure. And when in 1985 the urban eruption took place we were told: 'what is the problem, you've had all this money: it must have been squandered?'. The money did not go into any black person's pocket: we would like to know where it went, as well. As someone said at the inquiry into the Handsworth disturbances: 'just think what you could do with that £20 million'.[3]

Nothing left to lose

That £20 million that was alleged to have been spent in Handsworth became a topic of great interest in the media at the time of the 1985 unrest. What role does the mass media play in this country? Unfortunately, the great majority of it plays an extremely negative role. Sadly, most black people, like so many white working-class people, read the *Sun*, the *Mail*, the *Express* and that sort of nonsense. And this section of the British daily media has launched savage and systematic attacks on black people. Since 1981 they have attacked the movements which have started to develop and they have attacked black politicians. Why?

The answer is because some black politicians are getting too near power, and might even begin to exert influence in local and central government. The mass media has attacked any gains made by black people, and when they vilify black people in power they go for them by the jugular. They create an image of 'when you give these nutcases a bit of power look what they do with it'. And so the moment black people start to express a view that represents the black experience they are mercilessly attacked. Look what happened to Bernie Grant in Haringey when he aligned himself to the black experience. Local black politicians, striving for recognition and trying to upgrade the legitimate demands of black people, are being lambasted.

And so the response to the uprisings in the mass media was entirely predictable. Consider, for example, what the *Daily Mail* wrote on 8 October 1985: 'Either they forego their anarchic luxury of orgies of arson, looting and murderous assaults against the men and women whose task it is to uphold the law of this land, or they will provoke a paramilitary reaction unknown to mainland Britain.' This is how the agenda is now being set. The media are also responsible in large measure for the so-called backlash. As I pointed out, where successes occur and where gains are made, the media attack them as positive discrimination — as black people getting more and being treated better than white people.

Throughout the period since 1981 we have seen this build-up by the media. The approach is that blacks want more than they should have: 'how dare they ask for these things?' Now we learn that it is not a question of white racism and racial discrimination; look at what the *Sun* wrote on 24 October 1985: 'The British people are not and never have been racist.' So now we know, of course — it is black people who are racist! The problems and issues have been redefined. In 1986, black politicians, black spokespeople, black groups, campaigning for better conditions and a fairer deal, have become, in the eyes of the mass media, black racists. This is the way the backlash is being orchestrated.

In the light of these developments it seems that black people have a choice of two courses of action. First, black people, especially the young, living in the inner cities can carry on down the road we are on. As Stafford Scott and so many others have said, young black people are prepared to fight against the police *because they have got nothing left to lose*. Plastic bullets and CS gas are part of the process of Ulsterisation of our cities, but they are not going to deter young people whose life experiences, and especially their encounters with the police, give them a deep sense of injustice and convince them that they have nothing left to lose.

The continuing long hard struggle

The second course of action is to continue to develop alliances, to mobilise support and to fight against racism. The limited successes so far achieved have shown that institutions can be successfully challenged, but it is a long, hard struggle. To coin a Reagan phrase, black people can take part in 'constructive engagement', that is, actually engaging the community in making constructive decisions for themselves. There is reason for a little glimmer of optimism in the limited experimentation which has taken place within those few authorities which have attempted to define the problem as the way in which they have operated, and which have sought to identify and mobilise the vulnerable communities — the usually excluded people — in the inner cities. Black people need to get rid of the Urban Programme, with its tokenism and marginality. The people of the inner cities need to get control of the millions of pounds that go into housing, education, social services, transport and the other areas of local government. We want to control the main programme. Energies must not be wasted on fighting between this cultural group and that, or on who is the community leader or the real youth spokesperson. We are talking about real people with real needs who have real problems.

In fact, in the inner cities, and particularly in the black communities, there is a welter of positive ideas and energy, of affirmation of their cultures expressing themselves in the most imaginative way with a lot of talent. And British society has been oppressing it. The local state apparatus has to be controlled by local people, and it can be. Power and resources have to be in the hands of local people. It is not just a matter of the election to local authorities of black members, because there is ample evidence of the capacity of black councillors to be ruled and manipulated by their controlling political Labour group. Councillors' accountability should lie, as should the police's, with the real people out on the streets and in their homes. In future, blacks and whites in the inner cities do not want other people creating their environment for them; they do not want people policing their areas who are not part of those areas; they do not want outsiders designing and planning their housing, their social services, their leisure and recreation provision. The outsiders ('the professionals') do not live there, and they do not understand. It is the people who have design awards, for these monstrosities that they put other people to live in, who are the ones who should be in the dock of the Old Bailey answering charges for creating urban unrest.

The indictment of British society

Dismantling racism in cities is not a new priority for black people: it has been an issue for the decades that they have been there. Dismantling racism is now a priority for white people, because it is whites who have the control, who have the power, who can do something about it. If every white person with some power started to do something, however limited, about racism, it might turn out to be tokenism, but just think of all that tokenism! If every employer in this country took on a black person we would have ended discrimination against black people in employment even though most would probably all be at the bottom of the pile making the tea.

I will end where I started, and that is with black experience. Black experience is a real-life alternative and vivid experience. It is here now, and it is not going away. Black experience is vibrant, it is creative, it is talented and it is positive. But in this society at present, the only way for black people to get their voice heard seems to be by being negative rather than positive, and destructive rather than creative. This is an indictment on British society. It is a waste — and it is really not very sensible, is it?

Notes

1. In 1986 Herman Ouseley was appointed Equal Opportunities Policy Coordinator for the Inner London Education Authority.
2. London Borough of Lambeth, *Report of the Working Party on Community/Police Relations in Lambeth*, Lambeth, 1981.
3. H. Ouseley, *et al.*, *A Different Reality*, Birmingham: West Midlands County Council, 1986.

Ann Dummett: Thank you very much, Herman, for a thorough and stimulating talk. We will now hear from Professor Thomas, and then we will take questions and comments on both speakers. May I welcome Professor Richard Thomas, who is Associate Professor of History and Urban Affairs at Michigan State University in the United States. We are delighted to have a second American guest with us.

CHAPTER 17

Looking forward: the Detroit experience after the riots of 1943 and 1967

RICHARD THOMAS

This chapter is based on the assumption that multiracial cities around the world can, and should, learn from each other's experiences in addressing racial problems and promoting racial unity and harmony. As the cities of the world become more racially, culturally and economically diverse, public officials and concerned citizens will have to become more aware of public and private practices that contribute to racial discrimination, conflict and polarisation. Although cities around the world differ in their historical and social development, cities presently being transformed into multiracial and multicultural centres might save themselves some of the traumas of change by learning from other cities' mistakes and achievements.

In the area of racial change in an industrial city, Detroit in the United States has the historical distinction of having experienced two devastating race riots in little over a quarter of a century. After each riot it was forced to 'look forward' in an attempt to seek remedies. Although the nature of racial problems in Detroit has changed since 1967, due to white flight to the suburbs and the emergence of black political power, 'race' is still thick in the air.[1] Detroit, therefore, can teach the world some useful lessons in the area of race relations. Notwithstanding its two race riots, and the present 'cold war' between this predominantly black city and its white suburbs, Detroit has one of the longest and most impressive histories of interracial cooperation of any city in the western industrialised world. Without this history, looking forward would have been far more difficult.

The 1943 Detroit race riot

In 1943 in Detroit, in the wake of the worst race riot up to that time in the nation's history, seeking solutions required tremendous hope. Thirty-four people, the majority of them black, lost their lives and over 200 people were injured. During the riot the police killed 17 blacks and no whites. White mobs beat blacks while white police looked on. After the riot, the Police Commissioner, ignoring the role of whites, placed all the blame on blacks. A fact-finding committee appointed by the Governor blamed the black press and the National Association for the Advancement of Coloured People (NAACP) for creating the racial tension which led to the riot. According to the committee's report, the black press and the NAACP caused the riot by their militant protests for racial equality. Although the report pleased the Mayor, one white newspaper, *The Free Press*, pointed out that the report had been 'largely drawn up by the Police Commissioner, who supplied most of the evidence'. The 'tragedy for Detroit', one writer stated, was 'that most whites were more than willing to believe the report'.[2]

The black community was outraged. The editor of the *Michigan Chronicle*, the most militant black newspaper in Detroit at the time, expressed the sentiments of the majority of blacks in the city when he wrote:

> The race riot and all that has gone before have made my people more nationalistic and more chauvinistic than ever before. Even some of us [he continued] who were half-liberal and were willing to believe in the possibilities of improving race relations have begun to have doubts . . . and worst, have given up hope.[3]

Fortunately, most black leaders continued to believe in and work for interracial unity and cooperation. Concerned blacks and whites decided to light some candles rather than to 'curse the darkness'. A citizens' committee met daily at the YMCA to discuss racial problems. And when the Mayor appointed an interracial committee of twelve members, several black leaders accepted appointments on it.[4]

The Detroit Interracial Committee

The Detroit Interracial Committee was formally organised in January 1944, six months after the riot. Among its major objectives was the development of a method to 'sift out and study rumours and reports of overt aggression in the city'. The Committee was seeking to determine the immediate causes of racial unrest, believing that once such causes were determined they could be addressed by the proper authorities. More importantly, the findings of the Committee 'could serve as a foundation for a well-rounded and realistic community programme in race relations'.[5]

Considering the fact that the Mayor had accepted the police version of the riot, his recommendation for such a committee reflected a particular view of the causes of the riots. For the Mayor, 'looking forward' in terms of proposals and recommendations did not mean addressing the root causes, such as police brutality and racial discrimination in housing and employment. His original instructions to the Committee charged it with making recommendations 'designed to improve those services which affect racial relations that flow from the several departments of government to the community and to work toward an improvement in the attitudes of white and Negro citizens toward one another'.[6] These rather broad recommendations ignored specific root causes of the riot and directed the Interracial Committee to concentrate on monitoring potential racial trouble spots, rather than addressing specific sensitive racial practices such as housing segregation and police brutality against blacks.

The Detroit Common Council reflected two views on future race relations. According to one view, since racial conflict had been a part of American history dating from the arrival of the first blacks, racial problems would always be with us. The other view held that racial problems could be solved by a 'programme of curative measures' which 'should be acted upon immediately'.[7] These measures included a Grand Jury investigation of the Police Department, the provision of additional housing and recreational facilities for black citizens, the hiring of black policemen in black areas, and the hiring of black teachers.[8] The local branch of the NAACP had recommended many of these 'curative measures' to a Mayor's committee in 1943. This action probably influenced the Mayor to recommend and support the establishment of the Interracial Committee, which became a new unit of city government with its own yearly budget. The Detroit race riot of 1943 not only led to the establishment of this committee, it also prompted 31 other cities with populations of 500,000 and over to establish similar committees.[9] Notwithstanding its shortcomings in the years ahead, the establishment of the Detroit Interracial Committee marked a significant stage in the manner in which large industrial cities with increasingly large black populations would seek solutions in the area of race relations.

The 1943 race riot also stimulated an increase in interracial cooperation among civic, religious, and labour organisations. In 1945 the Michigan Council of Churches issued a report entitled *Building Better Race Relations in Michigan*, which discussed 'interracial clinics' being held in several Michigan cities. The purpose of the clinics was to 'bring about the improvement of race relations within the community through the application of the principles of religion to the practical problems of interracial relations and practices'.

The United Auto Workers' Union (UAW) was a long-time supporter of black goals, and was in the vanguard of interracial cooperation in the struggle for social justice. Many whites in Detroit, however, still resisted the notion of social and economic equality for blacks. In 1950 Detroit veered dangerously close to another race riot when the Common Council held a public hearing to discuss a proposal for a cooperative housing

RUU–K

project to be built in northwest Detroit, a stronghold of white racism. Whites in the area wanted no part of the project in their community because three of the 54 families were black. White leaders supporting the project made no headway at the hearing. Blacks became angry. Mayor Cobo fired a black member of the Detroit Housing Commission who was also one of the black leaders criticising the Commission's vacillating policy. The crisis eventually led to the resignation of the Director of the city's Interracial Committee.[10]

This crisis revealed a basic flaw in the way city officials had approached the solution of post-Second World War racial problems. Inadequate, segregated housing had always been a major cause of racial problems in Detroit, and indeed elsewhere in the nation. But city officials had repeatedly delayed addressing the issue. Even after the 1948 Supreme Court ruling against the enforcement of restrictive covenants in private housing, Detroit housing officials continued their segregation policy in public housing. This blatant official intransigence encouraged white home-owners to use every measure at their disposal to keep blacks out of their neighbourhoods. As a result, racial skirmishes occurred throughout the 1950s as white home-owners challenged the legitimate rights of blacks to purchase houses in white neighbourhoods, and blacks continued to push for their right to live where they pleased.[11]

Ten years after

Ten years after the 1943 race riot, white racism still held sway in industrial Detroit. Interracial cooperation in the struggle for racial justice had increased but so had institutional racism. In 1953, according to one black newspaper, there were 'almost as many policies for handling Negro patients as there were [white] hospitals'. The Police Department's treatment of blacks had gone from bad to worse. Police brutality symbolised everything that was wrong with Detroit. Relations between the black community and the predominantly white Police Department had deteriorated to the point that the local NAACP and other civil rights groups spent most of their time processing various complaints against the Department. The black community found itself using the courts to clarify the use of firearms by white policemen in apprehending persons suspected of crimes.[12]

In 1953, black and white policemen did not walk beats together nor ride together in squad cars. Black policemen did not belong to the motorcycle, arson, or homicide squads. Although white policemen were assigned to black and white districts, black policemen were assigned to predominantly black districts to 'do a job with Negroes'. Out of the Department's 4200 policemen, only 101 were black. Only four held the rank of sergeant and only one was a detective lieutenant. No black policemen worked in administration at Central Headquarters or were assigned, except on special duty, to any precinct west of Woodward, the border of the black ghetto.[13]

Just after the 1943 riots the city had made an attempt to improve race relations between blacks and the police by appointing a progressive Police Commissioner named John Ballenger. Ballenger introduced intercultural courses in the Police Academy, promoted the first uniformed black sergeant, and initiated a general campaign against police brutality. He also created a policy study commission which included black citizens. During the decade after the riot, Ballenger became the last Police Commissioner to attend a meeting of the Detroit Interracial Committee, in which all Police Commissioners held membership as a function of their office.[14] The message was clear: other Commissioners placed little value on harmonious race relations; and their views were communicated to the rank and file. In fact the Police Department, the enforcement arm of a sometimes subtle, sometimes blatant, policy of racial containment and control, was really an extension of the racial policies of City Hall. The tragedy is that these policies persisted for years through the thick and thin of black protest.

Many community institutions failed to address the issue of racism while others did make an effort. Throughout this 10-year period, 1943–53, the YMCA, the Boy Scouts, and the schools led the resistance to racial integration. As the black population expanded, many white churches engaged in panic selling to escape racial integration. Yet a few, no less fearful of the unknown, decided to stay put and work towards a racially integrated city. Both the YWCA and the Girl Scouts, in contrast to their male counterparts, developed a policy of non-discrimination and practised it on all levels.[15]

Between 1943 and 1954 most blacks still remained locked into traditionally 'black jobs'. Blacks were rarely seen in business offices unless they were janitors or messengers. Hudsons, a large department store, had just begun hiring black salespeople, and the *Detroit Free Press*, a major white newspaper, had only recently hired its first black reporter. The CIO unions fought a constant battle to protect the rights of black workers, while the AFL unions worked just as hard barring blacks from membership.[16]

Detroit in the early 1960s

The persistence of racism in Detroit 10 years after the riot can be attributed partly to the fact that in 1943 public officials had refused to recognise the seriousness of racism. Few members of the white power establishment cared enough about racial discrimination to risk challenging the status quo. It would take another race riot to get their attention. White public officials largely ignored the protests of blacks against police brutality. Throughout the 1950s and 1960s, white public officials and private developers looked forward only to highway developments, medical centres, and other forms of urban renewal, completely oblivious of the net adverse effects of these developments upon poor blacks. Little did they realise that the ghettos they passed on their way to and from work bred a demoralising poverty and social pathology, along with a seething black hatred of everything white that had contributed to this condition. As if the racial fuse were not short enough in Detroit, racial violence associated with the civil rights movement in the South added to the tense racial atmosphere.

Metropolitan Detroit in the early 1960s was characterised by two opposing trends: sporadic interracial cooperation in the struggle for racial justice on the one hand, and institutionalised white racism on the other. On Labour Day in 1963, a white mob in Dearborn, a Detroit suburb with a history of blatant racism, nearly wrecked a house they thought had been purchased by blacks. This, along with other incidents, alarmed some white suburbans who did not want their communities to experience such traumas.[17]

Communities that cared enough to do something positive formed human relations groups, modelling them on similar organisations in Detroit, particularly the Detroit Commission on Community Relations, which had replaced the Detroit Interracial Committee. Human relations groups were organised in a dozen or more Detroit suburbs, partly as a response to the racism manifested in Dearborn. One of the main objectives of these groups was to foster an atmosphere of racial tolerance in the event that blacks moved in. It should be noted, however, that this move of certain white suburbs to establish human relations organisations was also triggered by several impressive demonstrations of interracial cooperation for interracial housing. The first event was the Metropolitan Conference on Open Occupancy held in Detroit in January 1963, and the second was the Martin Luther King Freedom March the following summer. Dr. King joined the march flanked by local black and white leaders. Several NAACP-sponsored interracial marches into the suburbs followed the main march.[18]

These events contributed to interracial cooperation in the struggle for fair housing; unfortunately, they were too few and too infrequent. The forces of poverty and institutional racism had already alienated large segments of the black ghetto population. In 1965, 2 years before the riot that would once again give Detroit the historical record for the worst riot in the nation's history, Judge George Edwards, a former Detroit Police Commissioner, wrote: 'hostility between the Negro communities in our large cities and the police departments is the major problem in law enforcement in this decade. It has been a major cause of all recent race riots.'[19]

During the 1943 riots Judge Edwards had issued a similar warning of 'open warfare between the Detroit Negroes and the Detroit Police Department'. In 1961, long before most observers noticed the undercurrent of tension in the ghetto, he ranked Detroit as 'the leading candidate in the United States for a race riot'.[20] Judge Edwards, therefore, was probably not too surprised when a police raid on a 'blind pig' in one of Detroit's worst black ghettos set off a bloody riot which left 43 people dead, destroyed close to 20 million dollars worth of property, and left in its wake a deeper chasm of racial fear and hatred.[21]

Hope grows from the ashes

To many blacks and whites, sifting the ashes of the Detroit 1967 riot for signs of hope seemed futile. As reports trickled in of black deaths caused by white policemen and the National Guard, black hatred, particularly of the predominantly white police force, intensified. Now, more than ever before, advocates of interracial cooperation had their work cut out. Planning for the future assumed as many forms as there were interpretations of the causes of the riots. Blacks and whites in Detroit began buying guns in anticipation of the next riot in what the Mayor called 'the arms race in Detroit'. Warren, a white suburb on the northeastern border of Detroit, led the way in organising for 'trouble' by forming a 'militia'. Black militants raised the clarion call for 'black power'. As deep as racial fears and hatred had cut into the collective psyches of black and white Detroit citizens, however, a deeper impulse held steady and true to its course. People of goodwill simply refused to let their dream of an integrated society die, so they rallied and began to build bridges and to heal wounds.[22]

Before the riot was 24 hours old an Interfaith Emergency Centre was organised by concerned representatives of the local Council of Churches, Archdiocese, Jewish Community Council, and the all-black Interdenominational Ministerial Alliance. This interfaith, interracial organisation set up shop in the general riot area within sight of the fires, sniping, and police–army patrols. The churches and the synagogue were used as distribution centres to meet the medical and food needs of the affected population.[23]

Less than a year after the riot in Detroit, *The Report of the National Advisory Commission on Civil Disorders* (the Kerner Commission Report) made the bold statement: 'What white Americans have never fully understood — but what the Negro can never forget — is that white society is deeply implicated in the ghetto. White institutions created it, white institutions maintain it, and white society condones it.'[24] Dr. Martin Luther King and Senator Robert F. Kennedy were assassinated. The murder of King was sufficient to have triggered another riot in Detroit as it had in other cities; instead, an uneasy calm prevailed. According to the then Mayor of Detroit, Jerome Cavanaugh, black and white Detroiters felt not only 'shock and shame' but a realisation that 'extremism in either direction was not a solution'.[25]

Throughout the Detroit metropolitan area, individuals and neighbour-hood organisations struggled to heal wounds and to work for racial harmony. Their first task centred on repudiating the insane arms race. One group distributed signs which said: 'This home is not armed.' Soon the signs appeared in windows and doors of over 2000 homes throughout the Detroit area. In Warren, a suburb noted for its white working-class racism, about 2500 whites rose to the occasion by signing a newspaper advertisement, entitled 'A Voice of Support', to encourage a racially mixed family to remain in the city after they were harassed by whites. One white resident of Warren organised a fund-raising drive that produced $11,000 for the purpose of improving interracial understanding. The organiser gave $2500 to help a black adult educational programme in Detroit develop a black history library.[26]

Focusing upon long-neglected root causes of urban racial unrest

After the 1943 riot the Detroit white power elite had placed most of the blame on black agitators and largely ignored institutional racism in planning ahead. In contrast, after the 1967 riot a few key white leaders in the public and private sectors began focusing upon long-neglected root causes of urban racial unrest. Recognising the historical conflict between Detroit's black community and the Police Department, Mayor Cavanaugh ordered increased recruitment of blacks. The state National Guard also began a recruitment policy among Detroit blacks. Fifteen Michigan cities including Detroit passed open housing ordinances following the 1967 riot. A statewide law banning discrimination in most real estate transactions was passed by the legislature and signed by the Governor.[27]

A few white religious leaders in Detroit had always been in the forefront of the struggle for racial equality. It did not take a riot to get their attention. But the riot of 1967, and the publication of the Kerner Commission Report in March of 1968 emphasising white racism as a major cause of the riot, encouraged such leaders to take bolder actions. Archbishop John F. Dearden, representing the Roman Catholic Archdiocese of Detroit and 1.5 million Catholics in an eight-county area, including the city, pledged 1 million dollars for a 'campaign designed to root out white racism, to win housing acceptance for Negroes, and to bring direct help to those trapped by ghetto life'.[28] About a month before the first anniversary of the 1967 riot the Michigan Catholic School Superintendents' Committee decided that black history would be integrated into all subjects taught in Michigan's 675 Catholic schools. The Committee also made plans to begin in-service training programmes for Catholic school principals and teachers to provide them with a 'better understanding of the problems facing inner-city children'.[29]

As important as these efforts were in addressing the causes of the riot, it was clear that the private sector would have to get involved if meaningful economic and social changes were expected to occur. To this end, during the week of the riot Mayor Cavanaugh and Governor George Romney formed the New Detroit Committee. Never before in the history of any American city had such a committee been formed. Its members included 'some of the world's most powerful men of industry', such as James M. Roches, Chairman of the Board of General Motors, the largest corporation in the world; Henry Ford II, Chairman of the Board of the Ford Motor Company, the third largest corporation in the world; Lynn A Townsend, Chairman of the Board of Chrysler; Max M. Fisher, major investor in the Marathon Oil Company; and Joseph L. Hudson, Jr., President of Detroit's J. L. Hudson Company, the largest privately owned department store in the world.[30]

Yet this was not the most impressive aspect of the Committee. Other members came from far different backgrounds; in fact, several members were *bona fide* local black militants. Hudson, the first chairman of the Committee, actively sought out aggressive grass-roots blacks to be voting members of the committee in an effort to reach out to 'the people on the level of the looter and the burned out'. Involving black militants caused some conflict, but their involvement in the Committee gave it the kind of credibility it otherwise would not have had. Before long, however, the militants became disillusioned with the Committee's approach to the problems.[31]

In its first report in the spring of 1968 the Committee declared its first responsibility to be to 'look forward; not backward': not to 'sift and study' what had happened during the riot. Although it did sponsor studies related to the causes of the riot, the Committee in its first 2 years spent 10 million dollars on various projects related to the needs in the inner city: 'from black arts and black theatre to black business'. The Committee also put the Police Department on notice that its racist practices would be under scrutiny and came up with $300,000 for a study of the Department. Unfortunately, the Police Department bureaucracy sabotaged the effort.[32]

By 1970, after a series of efforts resulting in both successes and failures, some corporate heads drifted back to their board rooms and chose to devote their time and energies to another project more in line with their vision of Detroit — namely, the physical and economic revitalisation of the city. To accomplish this end they formed an organisation called the Detroit Renaissance. This organisation would focus on the 'rebuilding of the central core of the metropolitan area, while New Detroit would be in charge of racial and social problems'.[33] What had started as a grand experiment had suffered its first serious compromise. Notwithstanding this division of labour, the New Detroit Committee provided at least some model of corporate involvement in urban problems. Furthermore, it contributed to the long history of interracial cooperation in industrial Detroit.

Building an interracial society — Focus: Hope

While corporate heads were meeting with militants and other elements of the black community to rebuild Detroit, another group emerged. Less powerful but no less determined to build something out of the ashes of the riot of 1967, this group was called Focus: Hope. This organisation was responsible for enlisting the volunteers who collected and published the 2500 signatures in the 'Voice of Support' campaign in major local newspapers encouraging the mixed family to remain in the city after they had been harassed. As a result of this support the family stayed. Several concerned people set up Focus: Hope in the spring of 1968 because they 'felt an urgent need to develop a metropolitan conscience regarding racial injustice and to enlist others in the task of forming a just and integrated society'. They produced a symbol of a black and a white hand reaching for each other, and reproduced it on buttons and bumper stickers. During the tension-filled months after the riot they distributed this symbol of hope throughout the area. By the early 1980s they had distributed over 1 million.[34]

Working through area churches, Focus: Hope trained a group of 50 ministers to discuss racial issues. Members of congregations were also involved by opening up their homes to discussions. For 3 weeks the ministers travelled through the area discussing sensitive racial topics. About 6000 heard their message in the follow-up home meetings, and 6000 people attended a concluding rally. The groundwork was laid. Slowly, bridges were being built. Focus: Hope had shown a way out of the darkness; they had lit the candle.[35]

Focus: Hope continued its work of uniting black and white in the common struggle, to 'resolve the effects of discrimination and injustice and to build integration'. A few months after its founding, Focus: Hope trained people to start up 70 human relations councils in a three-county area and conducted a public opinion campaign that contributed to the passage of a statewide open housing law. Focus: Hope workers also researched prices in poor neighbourhoods, disproving the Kerner Commission report that the poor did not pay more for food in ghetto stores. Two years later they sponsored a Brotherhood Festival in the middle of downtown Detroit. Many people were fearful that such an event might cause a riot, but it came off beautifully and became an annual tradition, sometimes drawing up to 250,000 black and white people from all over the metropolitan area. In 1975 this event was replaced by an annual Brotherhood March concluding with people signing the Brotherhood Pledge.[36]

In addition to these programmes, Focus: Hope developed one of the most effective food programmes in America. It also launched a training programme which has trained and placed hundreds of workers. During the bussing stage of race relations in Detroit in the 1970s, Focus: Hope staff helped relieve the racial tensions in the schools by setting up training conferences to teach communication skills to black and white students. Always in the forefront of the struggle against racism, Focus: Hope joined in a class action suit against the Automobile Club of Michigan, charging it with discriminatory practices. In 1986 Focus: Hope is still committed to racial justice.[37]

A city of racial and cultural diversity

These efforts to bridge the racial gap and heal the wounds of the 1967 riot occurred within a steadily declining urban economy. Whites continued to flee the city and many businesses followed. In the 1970s the white suburbs resembled a white noose round a black neck. Many blacks in Detroit became less interested in interracial cooperation and the vision of an integrated society and more interested in black political power. With the election of Coleman Young to the office of the Mayor of Detroit the trend towards black political and economic power accelerated.

Yet today, interracial cooperation continues to play a vital role in the political, economic and cultural life of both the city and some of the suburbs. Ethnic festivals on the riverfront in downtown Detroit attract people from all over the metropolitan area; Focus: Hope's annual Brotherhood Marches keep the vision of racial unity alive; periodic newspaper reports on the state of race relations in the city and the suburbs elevate the level of discussions of sensitive racial issues; suburbs such as Oak Park and Southfield lead the way in integrating their communities, and demonstrating that people of all racial and cultural backgrounds can live together peacefully. While much still remains to be done in the field of race relations, Detroit and a few of its suburbs are demonstrating how modern cities can handle complex racial and cultural diversity.

Notes

1. *The Detroit News*, 8 January 1985.
2. For information on the 1943 Detroit race riot, see A. McClung Lee and N. Humphrey, *Race Riot*, New York: Dryden Press, 1943; R. Shogan and T. Craig, *The Detroit Race Riot: A Study in Violence*, Philadelphia: Chilton Books, 1965; B. J. Widick, *Detroit: City of Race and Class Violence*, Chicago: Quadrangle Books, 1972, pp. 110–11.
3. *The Michigan Chronicle*, 13 August 1943.
4. *The National Urban League Report of the Detroit Race Riot and Recommendations for a Program of Community Action*, 28 June 1943, Executive Secretary general file, folder June–July, 1943, Box 5, Michigan Historical Collection, Detroit Urban League Papers, Ann Arbor, Michigan.
5. H. A. Kulka, *The Barometer of the City of Detroit Interracial Committee: An Attempt to Measure Racial Tensions*, unpublished MA thesis, Wayne State University, 1946, p. 1.
6. *Ibid.*, p. 10.
7. *Ibid.*, p. 9.
8. Statement and Recommendations to the Mayor's Committee from the NAACP, 27 June 1943.

152   *Richard Thomas*

9. Kulka, *The Barometer of the City of Detroit Interracial Committee*, *supra* note 5, p. 10.
10. A Report: *Building Better Race Relations in Michigan*, 1 October 1945; Michigan Interracial Clinics, 22 February–7 March 1945; Widick, *Detroit: City of Race and Class Violence*, *supra* note 2, p. 124.
11. Widick, *Detroit: City of Race and Class Violence*, *supra* note 2, p. 124; 'A northern city "sitting on a lid" of racial trouble', *U.S. News and World Report*, 11 May 1956, p. 38; *Annual Report, 1957*, City of Detroit Commission on Community Relations; *The Michigan Chronicle*, 16 February 1957 and 23 February 1957.
12. *The Michigan Chronicle*, 21 March 1953.
13. *Ibid.*, 21 March 1953.
14. *Ibid.*
15. *Ibid.*, 14 March 1953.
16. *Ibid.*, 7 March 1957.
17. *Annual Report 1963*, Detroit Commission on Community Relations p. 5.
18. *Ibid.*, p. 5; *The Detroit Free Press*, 3 and 4 January 1963; and 16, 22, 24, 29 June 1963; *The Michigan Chronicle*, 13 July, 27 July, 3 August 1963.
19. *Report of the National Advisory Commission on Civil Disorders*, New York: Bantam Books, March 1968, p. 85.
20. *Ibid.*
21. *Ibid.*, pp. 84 and 107.
22. *The State Journal*, 7 July 1968.
23. L. Gordon, 'Attempts to bridge the racial gap: the religious establishment'; L. Gordon, *A City in Racial Crisis: The Case of Detroit Pre- and Post-The 1967 Riot*, New York: Brown and Company, 1971, pp. 18–19.
24. *Report of the National Advisory Commission on Civil Disorders*, *supra* note 19, p. 85.
25. *The State Journal*, 7 July 1968.
26. *Ibid.*
27. Newsletter, *Action Time*, 15 June 1968: Archdiocese Archives of Detroit.
28. *The State Journal*, 7 July 1968.
29. R. Conot, *American Odyssey*, New York: William Morrow, 1974, pp. 602–3.
30. *Progress Report of the New Detroit Committee*, Detroit, Michigan: Metropolitan Fund, Inc., April 1968, p. 22.
31. 'Community dissension: black militants and the New Detroit Committee', in Gordon, *A City in Racial Crisis*, *supra* note 23, pp. 107–10.
32. *Progress Report*, *supra* note 30, p. 25.
33. *Ibid.*
34. *Focus: Hope*, pp. 4–16.
35. *Ibid.*
36. *Ibid.*
37. *Ibid.*, pp. 16–18

CHAPTER 18

Looking forward: proposals and prospects — Discussion

Ann Dummett: I would like to thank both Herman Ouseley and Richard Thomas. Following those two interesting and contrasting contributions, let me ask for points from the floor.

Alliances dictated by practical politics

Simon Hind, *The Voice*: Richard Thomas pointed out that alliances between black groups and white groups are important and indeed necessary, but should that be the result of an evolutionary process? Before making these alliances, do black people have to go through separatism and nationalism and on to the alliance?

Richard Thomas: I would not presume to come up with universal models of development applicable to all circumstances, and unfortunately we do not have time to consider in detail the history of how alliances developed in the United States. One thing, though, that is worth stressing is that when a group seeks alliances with others it is a process of negotiation, and this involves bargaining, making concessions but also stipulating conditions. For example, the alliances that Mayor Young was able to forge were effective because he was prepared to make concessions and also hold out for certain conditions.

Young had to move away from some of the romantic nationalism of the 1960s, and Detroit would not have had a black mayor had it not been for the fact that he realised that he had to make alliances with some progressive whites, who some of the more radical blacks felt were not really the kind of people that blacks should work with. But Young was pragmatic. He realised that he had to develop political power and this involves compromise and bargaining. So the alliance has to be dictated by practical politics. Rhetoric is so incredibly dangerous. For example, you talked about 'nationalism', but what does that mean in terms of what black people really need? This is what we in the United States learned in the 1960s and 1970s. It is so important to make sure that rhetoric does not get in the way of practical politics, and real black economic and social development.

The British experience of colonial paternalism

Paul Rich, University of Warwick: What strikes me from the historical angle is how different the United States is from Britain in terms of formation of interracial alliances. The point about Detroit is that it has a very strong local identity. Richard Thomas has told us about the formation of the Detroit Interracial Committee and how these alliances were able to be formed in a local and parochial way. The British experience is one of strong central control over race relations, combined with the imperial legacy. This colonial paternalism goes back to the 1950s when white liberals started intervening in race relations and much of the black radicalism of the last 10–15 years has to be seen historically as a reaction to these experiences.

You only have to read black autobiographies to understand the significance of the black experience of having to deal with, and to react against, this kind of colonial paternalism. The problems of alliance formation in Britain are profoundly affected by this context. Of course, Ann Dummett and her husband have written about the problems of the community relations councils and the whole grid of race relations apparatus in Britain, which coopted the black elite into the structure of race relations administration, and this makes the bitterness and the polarisation in race so much more complicated in the British situation compared with the US pattern.

Richard Thomas: In response, I would agree that there are certainly exceptional cases but it is so very important to realise that alliances are going to be the major way that minority groups achieve success in most multiracial societies. We are beginning to see this in every multiracial society in the world today. This does not mean that one should not build conditions into those alliances, but most certainly alliances should be pursued.

Race relations in Canada and Australia

Freda Hawkins, Emeritus Professor of Political Science, University of Toronto, now at Centre for Research in Ethnic Relations, University of Warwick: I would like to make what I hope is a positive point in relation to a very important comment made by Professor Thomas. He said that we must look at all multiracial societies, not just one of them, and I would like to make a specific recommendation in relation to that. Before I do, and I hope this is not out of order for an outsider, I would like to say a word about Lord Scarman. Lord Scarman, as many here know, is one of the most brilliant and liberal British jurists to turn up in many years. His effort in relation to the riots in Brixton is one of the last of a series of very fine reports which he has done on various issues of public policy including Northern Ireland. But much more than that, he has exercised a wonderfully liberalising influence on the British establishment. I will not say more than that, but I think that point ought to be made.

Now let me turn to the question of multiracial societies. I would like to urge that all those people in Britain who are concerned with race relations should not only look at the United States in race relations matters — even though that model is interesting and helpful — but they should also look at Canada and Australia. They are traditional countries of immigration in recent history, and Canada and Australia are much more comparable with Britain in population size and in terms of political traditions. Let me explain briefly why it is important to look at them. The two countries have doubled their populations in the postwar period without stress or strain: no riots, no political discontent, no alienation of groups. For 30 years I have lived in the Canadian city of Toronto, in which over 50 per cent of the inhabitants are foreign-born. It is a city with many faults, and Canada, in general, and Australia both have faults too. Racism and discrimination do persist, but on the whole they have achieved considerable success.

Let me explain quickly how this has happened. They have liberalised their immigration laws in the past 20 years. They have both got universal immigration policies, taking immigrants from all over the world, including large numbers of refugees. They have succeeded because their governments have given leadership, and their governments have changed people's attitudes. The governments in power, and politicians and prominent people in the community, have been liberal and universal in their thinking and are helping to build these two countries as multiracial societies. I suggest it is worth looking at them as well as the United States and elsewhere.

Black experiences and sociological paternalism

Chas Holmes, Camden Policing the Police: What I would like to say does not necessarily touch on what my organisation does, but more on me as a black person. To take the last comments first: for people to say that Australia — which has Queensland where they used to organise aborigine hunts in the 1930s — is a liberal democracy, then if that is liberal, I am unimpressed. Richard Thomas has made various points about us not talking rhetoric but getting on and making alliances; somebody else mentioned colonial paternalism. Maybe that is not prevalent now, but the trend seems to be towards sociological paternalism which involves not just white but also black professors and journalists and 'community leaders'.

Even the black speakers kept talking about 'they' when they are talking about racism. They did not talk about 'we' but 'they' as if they, being academics, were not affected by it: a very strange sort of phenomenon. I noticed that after Herman Ouseley criticised Lord Scarman people were a little tense, but when Richard Thomas came on and talked about alliances, and working together, people felt a lot better about that. Well, I do not think you should feel better, because what Herman Ouseley said applies to what is happening here in Britain in 1986.

Grace Haines, Industrial Language Service: I am sick to death of being researched as a black person. I am sick to death of coming to conferences like this and talking about people, when the people about whom we are talking are getting such a raw deal. Black people have been pushed so far against the wall that the only way is to move forward now, and if moving forward means carrying a brick in one hand, then so be it. Until this society realises that they cannot keep treading on black people it will burn.

Violence is the only action open to black people

Anon: Throughout the course of this conference it seems as though black people have been talked about as if we are in some way disabled. I am sick of that: it is the white people in this society that are disabled. They are the ones who have a cancer, a disabling cancer, called racism, and it is for them to deal with it. We will deal with our struggle in the way we know we can get progress. Go out anywhere in the inner city and ask the youth which way they feel is open to them to get change, other than to take to the streets. The white society of this country has placed us in a position that the only action that we have is violence; the *only* action that we can possibly take to make white people aware of what we are suffering is violence.

The political parties and the whole political structure of this country do not take into account — and unless they are *forced to* will never take into acount — the views of black people. That is an unfortunate situation. I am not saying that we should all be violent, but it is the only course of action that is open to us, and it is necessary for us to take that action if we are going to achieve any change. If the political parties in this country were really committed to black people, and were really prepared to reflect the views of black people, then yes, there might be an argument against violence.

As yet there is no argument whatsoever for us aligning ourselves with any political party in Parliament or sitting down listening to the words of Lord Scarman who, I must admit, has tried. What kind of change is going to come from the people in government who sit in big buildings and discuss us without black people even being represented?

This particular conference has also been guilty of that, in that we are discussing issues here that affect *all* black people in all inner cities. These are issues that affect all black people, not just academics, lawyers, sociologists, professors, university graduates, and people from the United

States who come and tell us, like Richard Thomas, that we should join this very police force that is shooting our people down. I fail to understand the ideology behind what he is saying. How do we join a police force whose whole mentality is violence, whose whole mentality is racism, whose whole aim is to eliminate black people, to commit genocide against black people, because that is what is happening, that is the reality. And it is not just in this country they are killing black people, and that is why we must carry this debate into much wider issues and I was glad to hear Professor Thomas say that it is a world issue.

When at a conference like this people say racism is something to talk about, and black people can learn to live with it, how can black people take it seriously? We have been existing for 500 years like that and nothing has happened. Too much talking has gone on, and anybody who tells me that I should be non-violent when I have a chance of being shot down by some arrogant police officer is joking. The law of survival is fight: kill or be killed.

What role for whites in the fight against racism?

Margaret Smith, Youth and Community Service, Leeds City Council: I live and work in an inner-city area and I have to admit that because I am white I can never understand the black experience as a black person can. I want to follow the route described by Professor Thomas, because some of the other comments have been so totally depressing. What is the point of trying to do anything if you are white, if black activists have the attitude that whites cannot contribute to the campaign? If we are unable to build any sort of alliances, what can whites do? I can never be black: I can live with black people, I can work alongside them, but I cannot change the fact that I am white, just as black people cannot change the fact that they are black. All I am asking for is some room to work together, but perhaps there are not very many of us who want this. If when we try to do it, we are just kicked down because we are white, then there is no chance of working together, is there?

Herman Ouseley: I am not going to say a great deal because I have said quite a lot already, and I would like to have said a lot more, but given the time constraints, that was not possible. I share a common view with Richard Thomas that we should not be too depressed, despite the picture which has been painted. This picture is one of daily oppression and depression for black people, and it is one that they have to face every day, and the things that have been said by black people today marks the reality.

My criticisms of Lord Scarman were not aimed at him personally, but at the process in which he was involved. Like many other black people, I did not attend the hearings in 1981 because I did not expect anything positive to come out of the inquiry. And 5 years on, in 1986, we can see what has happened: the police have more powers, the Government has introduced more cosmetics and more tokenism, and there have been more urban rebellions.

As the speaker from the floor said a few moments ago, young black people on the streets are expressing themselves in the only way open to them, and in the only way they know. It was quite visible that to the people who took to the streets in Brixton the events were the most exciting thing that happened in their lives. This was not because they wanted to go out there and burn the place down, or attack policemen and destroy their environment, but because their existence is so bloody awful. Just think that 9- and 10-year-old kids were seeing that as the most exciting thing in their lives: that is what people have to look forward to.

The last woman who spoke needs to consider the words said earlier. It is not about 'what can I do; I cannot do anything; black people are rejecting us'. We are not. Our criticism is of white people in positions of power: and the reality is that the way those institutions operate, no matter how you tinker with them, the outcome for black people is exactly the same. The evidence shows it; yet we keep forgetting it! What have you, a white person who cares, got to do? You cannot go on continuing to be part of those institutions that deliver nothing to black people but crumbs or second-class status. And so you have got something very positive to do in everyday terms, like the advice being given by the brother at the back about educating black children about the ways of the world: the reality. These are positive things, and as I said earlier, if every person in a position of power did their bit, even if it was just tokenism on the part of everyone, that would add up to a lot of progress. At the present time, all we have got is a few people doing a little bit of tokenism, which adds up to very little.

The final point is this whole issue about alliances. Yes, we need alliances, but over here in Britain we have been trying to build these for a long time. Black people have been knocking on the door and trying to get in: they have been saying 'we want to work with you'. The fact that black people are organising themselves now is because they have been rejected so much. Every time someone knocks down a brick, someone else puts up a wall. Unfortunately, that is the reality of the rejection, the non-inclusion, the lack of a social contract that Stuart Hall discusses in Chapter 3. These are things that need to be tackled. This is where black and white people together can play a vital part. The message is: 'Go out and do something about it!'.

Richard Thomas: Let me respond to the brother at the back. There is always the risk that any black person takes when he or she tries to share the experiences, individual and collective, outside their context. I had to take that risk, because I am very concerned about what is happening over here in Britain, but at the same time, I could not be so presumptuous as to dictate to you, or to suggest to you, how you should solve your problems. I can only talk about what happened in Detroit, and what is happening in the United States. The only thing that I can say is that as you were talking, and as some of the other young people were expressing their views, I could not help but think that in the States we went through this same period after the 1967 riots. I cannot presume that it is the same thing. In the United States black people are organised, and worked with other groups, to obtain political power. The political power has not solved the problem of economic disadvantage and deprivation, or for that matter the problem that we have had for the last 10 or 15 years because of the decline of the auto industry. These are the problems with which black political leaders are struggling. As part of their strategy they have worked with others, white union bosses and progressive groups. The major problem that Mayor Young faces is to keep the car plants from moving out: new problems may require new alliances, which may or may not work.

Anon: It therefore has to be an anti-capitalist alliance?

Richard Thomas: You had better convene another conference to discuss that!

Need for a Royal Commission on the Police

Anon: My question is directed towards Richard Wells, from the Metropolitan Police, who made his presentation this morning. I listened to him with some dismay, because he seemed to have missed the real issue which this conference is about, and that is the origin of the urban riots and especially race and policing. He did not refer to these issues in the sense that the conference was expecting. I listened to Professor Kilson outline an analysis of the process of politicising and deracialising policing which took place in America in the late 1960s and 1970s. I want to put to Richard Wells: do any of the models he put to us this morning help in any way to deracialise the British police — because that is a very big problem.

John Alderson: I was a policeman for 36 years, and perhaps I may make a comment in the temporary absence of Richard Wells? I feel that his talk this morning reflected much of the thinking among senior ranks in the police service, and it was an honest attempt to offer dialogue and conciliation. However, I think the pace of change and the speed of events is so fast that it has actually overtaken traditional police thinking.

If you are asking for ways forward, *it becomes ever more clear that the police will not be able to reform themselves from within*. The reform has to come from without, and this will only occur if political pressure, through the parties and other institutions, is brought to bear. One way — perhaps the only effective way — of bringing about constructive change in policing is the establishment of a Royal Commission on the Police. We ought to be aware of the dangers of further urban disorder, and one possible reaction which has not been mentioned today is that of a right-wing backlash. The extreme right-wing thrives on violence and there is a real possibility that further disorder, particularly in the light of newspaper reporting and comments, may lead to the growth of neofascist violence.

I think that implicit in the comments of Professor Thomas was the view that, beyond a certain point, violent protest results in a reaction. We may have reached that point and unless we pursue adequate and effective constitutional ways of bringing about police change and accountability, we shall have violence spreading from various directions. The only way to get fundamental change through the political system would be via a Royal Commission on the Police. I know the Labour Party is sympathetic to this, and I think the Alliance is as well. If we get the right sort of result at the next election we might have a Royal Commission in 1988.

The possibility of socialist alliances in contrast with 'black capitalism'

Errol Lawrence, Director, Runnymede Trust Housing Unit: There are a number of quick things I would like to say. The first point is that Stuart Hall made the point about the cycle of event, conference, nothing happens, event, another conference, and nothing happens. So here we are today in the perpetual cycle, and I am rather doubtful about the comparison between the British and the American experiences, and in any case we have had this debate before. I am also suspicious about the particular position that we are getting from the United States because I have heard other people from the US who would be very critical of the kinds of political developments that have taken place there, and I do not think that we are getting the full rounded picture of what is going on in the US.

There is one point that Professor Thomas made that I have some sympathy for, and that was that we need to beware of rhetoric. I assume he is talking about radical rhetoric, and I have some sympathy for that, but at the same time we also have to beware of what I would call 'pragmatic rhetoric'. Most of the black people here would certainly know that we have pragmatic rhetoric in Britain now. The assumption that seems to be coming from the United States is that somehow we in Britain are some way behind. It is not true; we have had the debate about 'oh well, there is all this rioting, and really we have to have some pragmatic solutions. There are people there and they need to be fed and they need to be housed.' We have had those arguments and we are still having those arguments.

One of the problems with the pragmatic rhetoric and approach is that it spawns a kind of black capitalism. I am not sure how much good black capitalism is going to do for my family who still live where I was born and grew up. I have been lucky: I got out, but my parents are still there, and my brothers and sisters are still living in those conditions. I am not sure black capitalism has anything to offer them, and I think there must be other kinds of solutions.

But on the whole question about alliances, it seems to me that the situation is very different here in Britain. There is actually a strong socialist tradition in this country. We all have our criticisms of the British Labour Movement, and even more so of the British Labour Party, but there is at least a tradition of socialism here, and there is actually the ground upon which alliances can be formed. Whether they will or not is another matter, but the grounds upon which they can be formed are there. There are the glimmerings of some kind of anti-racist movement within the socialist movement of this country, and there is a possibility of alliances being formed. I always get the impression of America, and I am willing to be corrected, that partly to do with the kind of Cold War struggle they see socialism as a dirty word. So the only options open are varieties of radical nationalism or a black capitalism, and I do think that the options for us here are quite different.

A last point, which has been made by a number of speakers, is that when black people speak, white people do not listen. I am certainly aware of a number of very trenchant criticisms that have been made of the Scarman Report by black writers, but I wonder how many white people have read them. Part of the problem of the way white people discuss these issues is the assumptions they make about black people. For example, black people's knowledge of policing is always described as their 'feelings' and 'perceptions' because (as you know) black people are highly emotional: this is all part of the stereotyping.

One of the things that came out of the Scarman Report is the consultative machinery, but this has produced nothing. I have no sympathy at all for black people who get involved in these mechanisms. A lot of people in the various communities are very critical of black people who take part in these cosmetic institutions which have no real power. These kind of mechanisms were never intended to allow black people, or indeed white people in the community, to have any say in policing. They are a way in which the police can sell what they want to do to so-called community leaders. It is just a public relations façade, without any real community control and involvement.

Political power and police accountability in Detroit

Mike Cummins, Race Policy Adviser, Haringey: I wonder whether John Alderson, the retired police officer, who is now supporting accountability, supported that philosophy when he was a senior police officer? My real question is to Professor Thomas and concerns black political power in Detroit. First, to what extent has trade unionism been a factor in the alliance, and in the growth of black people's involvement and power? Second, how have these developments affected policing: to what extent is police violence under control, and how accountable are they? Are the police now accountable to the local electorate?

Richard Thomas: If I understand it correctly, you are asking about political power in Detroit and whether or not the trade union movement has been involved. The trade union movement in Detroit goes back to the 1930s and Coleman Young has been very much involved in it. There was a lot of conflict within the UAWCIO in the 1940s as blacks became more and more concerned about political power within the union itself. But the UAWCIO played a very important role in developing political alliances with the emerging black community and the Democratic Party in the 1940s and the 1950s.

When Young finally was able to run for power many of the black caucuses played an important role in moving the UAW in the direction of supporting Mayor Young. The UAWCIO was obviously very important in that general coalition. I have to point out that blacks had incredible problems within the UAW from the 1940s — they were constantly fighting within the UAW to gain significant power, and it was not smooth sailing. One reason why they stuck with the UAW was because they realised how important it was to have that coalition. The power within the industrial unions, linked with the Democratic Party, helped to move Young into office.

On the question of police accountability, this was certainly a major grievance before black people secured a measure of political power. Young was elected to office on a platform that included, number one, firing the police chief and getting rid of STRESS, which was an incredible unit that in essence went around shooting people under all sorts of false pretexts. As soon as he got into office, Young was able to fire the chief, but the problems did not stop. He still had a number of difficulties, and one of his strategies was to enrol far more blacks into the police force, and he did some of that through affirmative action. The police are accountable now because 63 per cent of the police in Detroit are black and because most of the people who control city hall are black. Most of the officials in the Police Department are black, so there is now a black Police Commissioner and blacks throughout the command structures. They are able to monitor much of what is happening. For the first time in many years black people in Detroit can at least rest easy that a bunch of white cops will not indulge in the kind of white racist brutality that existed before Young.

Ann Dummett: On behalf of everyone present, I would like to thank Herman Ouseley and Richard Thomas most warmly. I think we have had a most enlightening discussion.

PART 7

The Roots of Urban Unrest

CHAPTER 19

Unrest and the political agenda

JOHN BENYON

A recurring hallmark of the reporting and assessment of British urban unrest in the 1980s has been the language of warfare. 'BLACK WAR ON POLICE' asserted the *Daily Mail* on 7 July 1981, even though the riots in Liverpool 8 were clearly multiracial; 'BLOODY BATTLE' was the view in the *Daily Star* the same day.[1] In *The Brixton Disorders* Lord Scarman drew attention to the analogy with war in his comments on the disturbances in Brixton in April 1981: 'the toll of human injury and property damage was such that one observer described the scene as comparable with the aftermath of an air raid'. This view was confirmed in *Time Magazine* of 20 July 1981, which quoted the comments of a 50-year-old Liverpudlian, as he surveyed the damage in Lodge Lane, Liverpool 8: 'I was in Liverpool during World War II. I suddenly thought it seemed just the same: buildings turned to rubble; shopkeepers sitting on their steps, crying, wondering what to do. And then I realised there *was* a war on.'

The language of warfare was again evident in 1985. After the disorder in Handsworth, the *Sun* headlined 'HATE OF A BLACK BOMBER' in its 'Blitz issue' of 11 September. On the same day the front page of the *Daily Mail* proclaimed 'BLOODLUST', and inside the headline was 'Flames of Wrath in the City of Fear'. The disorder in Tottenham prompted the *Daily Telegraph* (8 October 1985) to carry the headline 'Battlefield of Mob Violence', and the *Daily Mail* in its editorial on the same day described the events as 'urban warfare'. This newspaper was of the opinion that there was 'A daily war being waged against white families by the younger members of a burgeoning black community.'

This view was flatly contradicted by white residents, and indeed was palpably untrue, but that did not deter the *Mail* or other newspapers. The idea of an internal war being waged by a subversive 'enemy within' was common currency in the newspapers, and is illustrated by the following report in the *Daily Telegraph* on 9 October, 1985:

Trotskyites, socialist extremists, Revolutionary Communists, marxists and black militants from as far away as Toxteth descended

165

on Tottenham yesterday. . . . They cheered speakers who declared:
'This war is just beginning', and supported calls for the police to be
put under the control of the local community . . .

White, bearded men in sandals, many accompanied by girls,
rubbed shoulders with the local black people and supported calls for
more violence . . .

That an allegedly serious newspaper could print such a ludicrous piece of
writing perhaps indicates the extent to which the media and other opinion
leaders were seduced by their own bellicose language, and by their febrile
imaginings that an army of subversives was on the march.

Setting the terms of the debate

The interpretation that the urban unrest was an internal war waged by
conspirators and subversives was a dominant theme, and did much to
establish the terms of the debate which followed the disorder. The predominant message in the media was that increased force and coercion was
needed to fight the 'enemy within'. Many commentators for various, and
sometimes nefarious, reasons tended to exaggerate the scale of the disorders. They were *English* riots which involved relatively small numbers of
people. For example, in the case of Brixton, in 1981, during the worst night
of violence on Saturday 11 April it seems that a few hundred people were
involved: a tiny fraction of the Lambeth population of 246,000 and under 1
per cent of that in Brixton. This is not to seek to minimise the significance
of the disorders; rather to place them in perspective.

In July 1981 considerably more people took part in the disorders in
Liverpool, Manchester, London and elsewhere. During this period almost
4000 people were arrested for public order offences and of the 3704 for
whom data are available, 766 were described as West Indian/African, 180
as Asian, 292 as 'other' and 2466, or 67 per cent, were white. Some 66 per
cent of those arrested were under 21 (20 per cent were under 17) and about
half the total were unemployed.[2] These figures confirm the impressions of
observers that the riots were multiracial and broadly reflected the racial
composition of the areas in which they occurred. This is perhaps a rather
different interpretation from that put forward by the nation's media. The
figures also confirm that the participants were largely young.

Another view which was prevalent in 1981 and 1985 was that the riots
were unprecedented in recent British experience. Mr. John Stokes, MP for
Halesowen and Stourbridge and not noted for his reticence on such
matters, said in the House of Commons on 13 April 1981: 'Riots on this
scale have not happened for 200 years. Are not these riots something new
and sinister in our long national history?' Similar comments were made in
1985, and Sir Kenneth Newman described the rioting as 'alien to our

streets'. However, these views are clearly untenable and confirm the pre-valence of 'historical amnesia'. As outlined in Chapter 2, many serious disorders, which resulted in hangings and transportations, occurred in the nineteenth century. In 1908 a Select Committee on 'The Employment of Military in Cases of Disturbances' reported that the armed forces had been called out on 24 occasions since 1869 to suppress disorders. This century, too, many violent clashes have occurred, for example at Tonypandy in the Rhondda (1910); the East End of London (1911); Liverpool, Cardiff, Plymouth, London and elsewhere (1919), London, Belfast and Birkenhead (1932). Indeed, as the appendix to Chapter 2 details, contrary to popular impressions the 1930s appears to have been a period in which considerable disorder occurred.

The incidents of urban unrest were neither unique events nor interracial disturbances, but these were the ways in which they were portrayed by much of the media, and by many politicians. They were interpreted as exceptional threats to law and order which required exceptional responses, and this approach has considerably influenced subsequent government and police reactions. The riots *were* events which indicated serious social and political grievances and frustrations, and this view was put forward by opposition politicians, community leaders, trade unionists and others. Lord Scarman generally adopted this approach, but also included aspects of the 'exceptional threat' analysis. Despite his prescriptions on urban and racial disadvantage, youth unemployment and racial discrimination, it does seem that the law and order interpretations have predominated in in-fluencing the governmental agenda.

Political agendas and issue initiation

An agenda is a list of things to be done, and the political agenda is made up of matters which are considered to be in need of attention and action by government.[3] This notion raises a number of questions including 'con-sidered by whom?' and 'attention and action by what level of gov-ernment?'. Indeed, many agendas exist simultaneously, at different levels of government, within particular agencies and departments, within politi-cal parties and factions, and within other groups and institutions. For example the list of matters which are considered to require attention and action by Liverpool's Housing Committee may differ considerably from that of the Council itself, or those of the local parties, or of the regional and government agencies: to cite just a few institutions which may be involved. It can be suggested that the greater the differences between these institutional or formal agendas the greater the frequency and intensity of conflict within the political system.

These *institutional* or *formal* agendas are likely to be more specific than the other type of agenda — the *public* agenda. This consists of issues which have achieved public interest and visibility, and which a sizeable proportion of the public considers to be significant and in need of action. It is likely to be broader and more general than comparable institutional agendas, and distinguishable communities and groups (different 'publics') may have dissimilar agendas. It may be hypothesised that the greater the incongruence between the public agendas of different communities, the greater the likelihood of conflict. Furthermore, the greater the disparities between a public agenda and formal agendas, the greater the intensity and frequency of conflict within the political system.[4]

In the discussion which follows, the level of the agendas will be that of the national political system. The formal or governmental agenda refers to those matters considered to be in need of attention by the government, while the public agenda means the issues of concern to the British public. In practice this entails recognition by a significant portion of the public, not all of them or even necessarily a majority. A primary means of forming the national public agenda and of expressing it is the news media, a point which merits further attention later.

The *political* agenda is thus made up of two different agendas: the public and the governmental (sometimes called the formal). These may tend to differ and the extent of these differences will affect social and political conflict. In order to secure action by government, issues clearly need to be placed on the formal agenda. There is of course a limit to the number of issues with which any agenda can cope, and although at the level of government a large number of concerns can be handled, factors such as finance, legislative time and politicians' predilections constrain the agenda. Resources are finite, while the number of problems is almost unlimited, and proponents of particular problems must compete with others who are seeking to advance different demands.

It is possible to identify three ways in which issues may be initiated onto the governmental agenda.[5] The *insider* model involves the initiation of agenda items by those within government or close to it, who deliberately seek to keep them off the public agenda. Examples might include proposals to increase the provision of private health treatment within the National Health Service, or suggestions to ban trade union activity in certain occupations, or attempts to permit an increase in the maximum weight of heavy lorries. The originators of such agenda items seek to limit them to the formal agenda in order to minimise opposition and increase the chances of success. The *mobilisation* model entails a process of initiation by insiders, first onto the governmental agenda and then subsequently into the public arena. Policies initiated in this way require the support of the public for their implementation. Examples might include proposals for privatisation or aspects of race relations legislation.

The third model describes the process whereby issues are first placed on the public agenda and then forced onto the governmental agenda. This is the *outsider* model, and it requires first that the problem should be seen as such by the public at large and second that the government should be viewed as having a responsibility to tackle it. Examples of this form of agenda setting might include a number of environmental issues, such as air pollution and the disposal of poisonous waste. Perhaps an out-sider-initiated issue which has recently passed from the public agenda to the governmental agenda is the problem of acid rain.

The outsider process of initiation may encounter a number of problems, not least the difficulty of securing public interest and attention. Problems may exist in certain areas, and affecting various people, but may go unnoticed by the wider public. Government agencies may be aware of them but are unlikely to take positive action until the problems become issues with which they are forced to deal. Issues are problems or matters which are recognised as in need of resolution or improvement. Clearly, these may be subjects of dispute as resources are limited and interests affected. Differences may occur over whether problems are really unsatis-factory or whether anything can be done about them. It may be argued that the cost of improvements is too great, or that the matter is not one with which government should properly concern itself. Arguments may take place over the real causes of the problem, or over the best solutions.

It has been suggested that problems need to pass through three separate stages of the political agenda if they originate through the outsider process of initiation. First, they must *command attention*; second, they must be *seen as legitimate* matters for government action; and, finally, they need to *invoke action*.[6] At each stage proponents of the issues may encounter attempts to hinder their progress, such as redefinition of the problems and proposed solutions, and overt opposition. Problems may be highlighted and furthered by violent events such as riots, and proponents of issues can employ threats of violence as a strategy to advance their cause.[7] However, as pointed out earlier, riots may place other issues on the agenda, such as criminal activity, lack of police equipment, and insufficient police training and coercive powers. The issues which are placed on the public agenda, and on that of the government, will largely be determined by the pre-dominant interpretations of the disorders. Riots may be a means of focusing attention on urban deprivation and racial disadvantage, but the outcome of their impact on the political agenda may not be a significant improvement of conditions in the inner cities.

Political issues and urban unrest: gaining attention and legitimacy

The recent riots were clearly events which commanded considerable attention. In 1981 this lasted intermittently from April until the end of the year, with the publication of the Scarman Report on 25 November, and into 1982. Newspaper and television coverage was extensive and the riots were undoubtedly the topic of the year, entailing debates, ministerial statements and questions in Parliament. The urban unrest in September and October 1985 also attracted great attention, with prolonged television and press coverage. However, as described in Chapters 1 and 2, and by others in this book, opinion leaders interpreted the events differently. While some emphasised the problem of 'insensitive' policing, many invoked the idea of warfare waged by subversives and black youths, and others stressed the lack of discipline and self-control of the young rioters. Some blamed the problem of unemployment, others pinpointed racism, while many said the cause of the disorder was simply 'sheer criminality'. So while the events themselves commanded attention, there were considerable differences of opinion on the problems which lay behind them. In 1981 Lord Scarman's inquiry helped to sort out the gallimaufry of explanations, itemising and clarifying a number of problems in the inner-city areas, but there was no such authoritative official inquiry in 1985.

There are many ways whereby problems can gain attention and be placed on the political agenda. They may be highlighed in campaigns by political parties, pressure groups, trade unions or employers. The growth of professions means that many areas of public policy have institutions willing to champion alleged wrongs. Other channels may be less visible but more effective, such as civil servants, ministers and other parts of the government machinery.

Access to the political agenda is not equally available to all who seek it. Some groups and individuals have far greater power than others to place issues on the agenda. Indeed it has been argued that certain types of problems and many groups of people are systematically excluded from participation: there is a mobilisation of bias whereby some issues are organised into politics while others are organised out.[8] It has also been argued that prevailing social and political values, as well as institutional practices, limit the political agenda.[9] Those who can initiate issues through insider and mobilisation strategies are better-placed than groups which are forced to employ outsider processes, for even if an issue is successfully raised it may subsequently be redefined or excluded in the interests of the more powerful. Violent protests can be seen as the result of this exclusion, and indeed the remarks about the 1981 riots made by Sir David McNee in the *Sunday Mirror* on 31 October 1982 seem apposite: 'That is what it's all about. Power. Power to dictate. Power to shape lives.'

Although political attention is a necessary requirement for problems to reach the political agenda, it is not on its own sufficient to ensure that an issue will be successfully pursued. Problems must be seen as ones with which government can, and should, be concerned, and what is or is not a proper matter for public action is likely to be a subject for debate.

The aftermath of the riots in the 1980s included considerable argument over which issues were legitimate ones for government action. For example, many of the political reactions were to condemn the disorders as 'sheer criminality' and, viewed in this way, the proper response of society was to deal firmly with those involved and not to capitulate to their demands. In 1981 some politicians seemed to believe that even holding the Scarman inquiry was not a proper response; one view expressed in the Commons on 13 April 1981 was: 'does not the inquiry itself appear to make the violence worthwhile?'. A similar response was the frequent reference by politicians, police officers and particularly the press to 'conspirators' and 'agitators'. The implication appeared to be that problems raised by the rioting were smokescreens for subversion. The Prime Minister's repeated assertions that the disorders were 'inexcusable and unjustifiable' sometimes seemed to imply that since the riots were illegitimate, so too were suggested remedies.

One means whereby nascent issues can be legitimised is through an official inquiry.[10] Public inquiries can focus attention on particular problems and are able to make influential recommendations. Such pronouncements are likely to be seen as authoritative and 'objective', and issues so highlighed are thus successfully legitimised. Lord Scarman's inquiry can be seen in this way: his findings and recommendations, while not legally binding, had considerable political and moral force: they *ought* to be put into effect as they were sanctioned by an eminent authority after a lengthy investigation. This was the point of view put forward by the Labour Shadow Home Secretary when he urged the Government to implement the proposals in full. He said in the Commons on 25 November 1981 that Lord Scarman's repetition of the policy recommendations 'adds a dimension of authority and objectivity that elevates the whole question above the dispute of party politics'.

The 1981 and 1985 disorders focused attention on conditions in Britain's inner cities. The reactions to, and explanations of, the riots did much to determine the issues on the political agenda, which was in 1981 further defined by Lord Scarman. His inquiry identified matters which he considered were those the Government had a responsibility to tackle; these fell into three broad areas: policing policies and practices; inner-city deprivation and un-employment; racial disadvantage and discrimination. However, the interpre-tation of the disorders which was mentioned earlier — that they were ex-ceptional threats which required exceptional responses — was also implicit in Lord Scarman's findings, and this legitimised the issues of police training, and tactics and equipment for handling public disturbances in a certain way.

Outsider-initiated issues and political responses

Issues initiated through outside pressure, of which the utilisation of violence is one possibility, are the least likely to achieve successful outcomes. Political rules and institutions are biased against them, and they are likely to lack significant sponsorship. It is particularly in the third stage of the political agenda, once issues have gained attention and been legitimised and have moved from the public agenda to that of the government, that outsider-initiated issues are likely to encounter the greatest difficulties.

It is at this stage that delay and partial responses may occur, resulting in loss of public and political interest. At the time of its establishment many sceptics viewed the Scarman inquiry as a means of postponing action and appeasing critics. A frequent response to political problems is to set up an inquiry — often a Royal Commission — thereby appearing to investigate the matter seriously, but in fact delaying action until the problem fades away. As Lawrence Marks wrote in the *Observer* on 13 September 1981:

> The scenario was familiar. Both the law-and-order lobby and its liberal critics would be reassured that the outbreak was not being ignored, the politically weak black community would be divided, the media would soon lose interest — and in the autumn there would be judicious report on race relations in the inner city to place along side all the other judicious reports on the same subject in the Home Office library.

Some might argue that this is broadly what has happened, but it was not possible in November 1981 for the Government to be seen to be shelving the Report. Possibly this was because rioting recurred in July, keeping the problems in the public eye, or perhaps it was because Lord Scarman won the confidence of many Brixton people and ran his public inquiry in such a way as to encourage interesting and informed public debate. As the reactions to his Report show, not everyone by any means was pleased with the final outcome, but a number of issues were clarified and identified as in need of political action. This did not, though, ensure that action would be taken.

Action to tackle political problems can take a number of forms.[11] *First*, there can be a *serious attempt* to implement policies to solve the problems. However, the success of such an attempt will depend on accurate problem definition, reliable and comprehensive information, and whole-hearted commitment. The general issues of racial disadvantage and urban deprivation were raised in the aftermath of the riots, and by Lord Scarman who pointed out that over many years policies to improve the position have been characterised by half-heartedness and incrementalism. Political commitment and a full understanding of the problems are needed if success is to be achieved. To take one example, information on the employment of members of the ethnic minorities is needed if an equal opportunities policy is to be implemented successfully. However, this kind of monitoring has not been practised by most public and private employers. Proper monitoring reveals the type of position found in Liverpool where, in 1982, only 251 local authority employees out of 31,000 were black.

The more one examines policies in the areas of urban deprivation, racial discrimination and racial disadvantage, the more clear it becomes that many government policies have been ill-conceived, *ad hoc* and based on partial or inaccurate information. Since these issues were placed on the governmental agenda, and given added impetus in 1980, 1981, 1985 and 1986, there seems little evidence that those attempts to solve them, which can be regarded as serious, have proved effective. By contrast, apparently successful initiatives and developments have occurred in policing policies, especially in terms of training and equipment for handling disorders.

A *second* basis for political action may be *a search for agreement*. Rather than a serious attempt to solve the perceived problems, this approach is one of consensus-seeking, and as such it is likely to involve compromise and cosmetic changes. Policies based on this approach may well involve increased consultation, so that at least some critics are satisfied. This kind of action may also involve a partial implementation of proposals, in an attempt to avoid more fundamental changes. For example, the provisions in Section 106 of the Police and Criminal Evidence Act 1984 have been seen as being based on a strategy of mollifying police interests while incorporating some local people in consultative procedures. Cooptation of 'moderate' critics into parts of the process, some argue, may lessen the demands for further more radical changes. Similarly, it is claimed that allegedly cosmetic changes in the police complaints procedure, in Part IX of the Police and Criminal Evidence Act 1984, were intended to diminish the campaign for a wholly independent investigative machinery as suggested by Lord Scarman.[12]

This second approach may be motivated by an attempt to reconcile different groups, or by a desire to avoid committing additional resources. The responses of a number of governments to the problems of the cities seem to have been based on a strategy of appearing to act while in fact doing little. For example, frequent reference has been made, by government ministers and others, to Section 11 aid under the Local Government Act 1966, and to the Urban Programme and the Inner City Partnership schemes, thus giving the appearance of taking firm action upon which all can agree. But despite this apparent consensus, on examination it becomes clear that the resources involved, substantial in absolute terms, are really relatively small in comparison with the investment which is needed in jobs, housing and infrastructure.[13]

A *third* approach to issues entails *the management of evidence* which shows there is a problem.[14] A redefinition of the basis of statistics may lessen the pressure to tackle the matter. The new basis of collecting unemployment data, introduced by Mr. Norman Tebbit in 1982 and amended on several subsequent occasions, might be seen in this way. Others have viewed the Youth Training Scheme, introduced in 1983, as a means of removing from political visibility a large number of young unemployed people. Measures introduced in the budget on 16 March 1983 meant that some 152,000 fewer people registered as unemployed. Crime statistics, too, seem to have been used to justify particular policies and points of view on law and order questions in inner-city areas.

A *fourth* form of action has been termed *showcasing*, or *tokenism*.[15] This entails taking limited action, which suggests that the problem is being tackled and which gives a positive impression to those with a grievance, but then doing little more. In Brixton, since the 1981 riots, it is said that virtually everything that does not move has been painted — a clear example of showcasing — but meanwhile the unemployment rate amongst young people has doubled. As John Clare comments in Chapter 5, in many of the areas in which disorder occurred various environmental improvement schemes have been undertaken. These include clearing up derelict rubble-strewn sites, and extensive programmes of tree-planting, and although these schemes have brought a welcome improvement in the appearance of these areas they can be seen as further evidence of showcasing. The Garden Festival in Liverpool in 1984 was also seen by a number of critics as an example of showcasing or tokenism.

A *fifth* form of action involves defusing issues by *establishing new organisational structures*. These can create an impression of improvements under way, although in fact few if any additional resources are allocated. The creation of new units of administration can prove a cheap and effective means of dealing with an issue, such as urban decay, which has become salient. The City Action Teams (CATs) which have been established might be seen as examples, as might the Merseyside Task Force, although it has been suggested that despite its lack of funds the Task Force brought about a number of improvements.[16]

Finally, political action on an issue may involve *no action*. Besides outright rejection, there are several ways of *delaying* implementation of recommendations, even if they have been legitimised by an inquiry such as Lord Scarman's. A common strategy is to carry out further investigations, and this has been a frequent ploy by the Home Office. One example was the series of working parties to consider police complaints. One was established in 1971; a review was held in 1974; the position was monitored after the establishment of the Police Complaints Board; a Home Office working party reported in March 1981; and following the 1981 riots yet another internal investigation was started.

Another means of delay is for the government to accept proposals 'in principle', but to plead lack of funds or the need for consultation. This postponement frequently means abandonment or emasculation of the recommendations. As time elapses the urgency of action is likely to diminish as public interest switches to new concerns. Dr. David Owen, speaking in the House of Commons on 26 November 1981, was concerned that the Scarman Report was likely to suffer this fate: 'This country had become more expert than almost any other in suffocating a report and in embracing a report with general praise and generalised endorsement of its philosophy but not following it through with the most detailed implementation.' Over 5 years later, many people feel that these fears were well-founded.

Power and the political agenda

A study of issues and the political agenda tends to suggest that quite frequently problems invoke only partial responses or delay and procrastination. Pious statements by government ministers, however important, do not in themselves result in decisive action. Some issues are resolved, but many appear merely to fade away, perhaps to recur in the future. It has been said that for government, as for philosophy, old questions are not answered — they merely go out of fashion.[17] Interest in problems needs to be sustained if they are to pass successfully through the tortuous decision-making processes of government. Even powerful sponsorship, by such as ministers, political parties or peak pressure groups, cannot ensure that committed action will be taken, but this kind of support clearly increases the chances of problem resolution. Furthermore, if the costs of inaction appear too great, and public interest is sustained through continued debate or a recurrence of dramatic events, the likelihood of serious attempts to cure the problems will be enhanced.

Even when a problem has gained attention, and has been recognised as a legitimate matter for government involvement, there is no guarantee that a serious attempt will be made to solve it. This may be so for issues initiated by insider or mobilisation processes, but seems to be particularly likely for those initiated by outsider means. Political and economic resources are limited and there are many demands for them. The proponents of a particular issue are competing with those in favour of different concerns, and their success in ensuring action depends upon their political power. There are many power resources, such as money, knowledge, skills, status, possessions, access to the media, and it is clear that these are unequally distributed in society. People living in British inner-urban areas are likely to have less power resources than those in more affluent communities.

The exercise of political power is sometimes quite visible, such as, for example, a pressure group successfully campaigning on a particular issue. However, there is also another 'hidden face' of power, which is less overt and which involves enforcing social values and institutional practices that limit the scope of the political processes. On this view, some problems are prevented from becoming issues at all by the operation of non-decisions. It has been said that the power to prevent issues and conflict from surfacing may be one of the most insidious of all forms of political power.[18]

It is possible to identify a 'third dimension' of power which may be exercised through the bias in the socially structured and culturally patterned behaviour of groups and practices of institutions, and it is argued that power is exercised over another person or group when their interests are adversely affected.[19] Perhaps this form of power is illustrated by the figures announced in April 1983 which revealed that only those earning at least £29,567 a year were paying less direct taxes in 1983 than they were in 1979. Married couples with two children, earning the average income of £172 a week, were paying extra tax equivalent to 6.9 pence on the standard rate, while a poorer family on three-quarters of the average earnings had been even worse hit: their tax payments had risen from 1979 to 1983 in real terms by the equivalent of 7.9 pence on the standard rate of income tax. There was little evidence that the wealthy had been actively campaigning for these changes, but nevertheless political power was exercised to further their interests to the detriment of the less well off.

These covert and insidious forms of power can greatly affect the outcomes of issues which appear on the political agenda. The responses may be those of consensus-seeking and cosmetic change, or the management of evidence, or showcasing, or the establishment of new organisational structures, or delay and emasculation. Even serious attempts to tackle an issue can be thwarted by lack of commitment and inaccurate information. Unless the proponents of an issue have sufficient power to ensure that it continues to receive attention, it may fade from the political agenda.

Attention has been drawn to the difficulty of sustaining interest in an issue and a five-stage 'issue–attention cycle' has been suggested. Each stage may vary in duration, but the same sequence is usually followed:[20]

1. *The pre-problem stage*: some highly undesirable social condition exists, which may be of concern to experts and groups but has received little public attention; for example, racism and poverty in the United States in the early 1960s, and racism, urban deprivation and police malpractice in British cities in the 1980s.
2. *Alarmed discovery and euphoric enthusiasm*: the public suddenly become aware of and alarmed by the evils of a particular problem, often as the result of dramatic events — such as the five long hot summers of riots in the United States between 1964 and 1968 and the urban unrest in Britain between 1980 and 1986. Invariably, there is great enthusiasm about solving the problem within a relatively short time.
3. *Realising the cost of significant progress*: gradually there is a spreading realisation that the cost of solving the problem is very high and may require sacrifices by large numbers of people, as the most pressing social problems often involve either exploitation of one group in society by another, or the prevention of one group from enjoying something that others want to keep for themselves.
4. *Gradual decline of intense public interest*: the public become discouraged, or they feel threatened, or they get bored, and their desire to keep

attention focused on the issue wanes — particularly if another issue is entering stage two.

5. *The post-problem stage*: the issue moves into a prolonged limbo — a twilight realm of lesser interest or spasmodic recurrences of interest. But the public have become aware of the problem and it may resurface sporadically, and new institutions and policies may have been established which are likely to continue to have some impact on the problem.

The issues raised by the riots seem to have passed some way through the issue–attention cycle. The problems of police relations with the community, and associated questions such as recruitment, discipline, equipment, complaints and accountability, were highlighed by the disorders and passed into stage two of the cycle. There was also 'alarmed discovery' of inner-city deprivation, youth unemployment and racism and racial disadvantage. The costs of tackling these problems were stressed and other issues, such as the reported growth in crime in the cities, were highlighted. It seems that some members of the public — or at least the media — became bored by the issues, or discouraged; others may have felt threatened by the financial costs of taking action, or the costs of what has been portrayed as a 'softly-softly' approach to crime. Thus many of the issues to which attention was directed by the riots, and by Lord Scarman, seem to have passed through the issue – attention cycle to stage five, where they now exist in 'prolonged limbo'.

The news media play a crucial role in determining how long attention is focused on a problem. As soon as they realise that their emphasis on a problem is threatening many people, and boring even more, they are likely to shift their focus to 'new' issues. Hence, in many cases a government can delay action which it dislikes, because of cost or ideological aversion, until the issue disappears from the public agenda. Of course, it is usually necessary for the authorities to do something, particularly if an inquiry has made positive recommendations, and it is possible that unless the root causes of the problems are tackled, the issues may again be thrust on the agenda by dramatic events. But even such recurrences may fail to revitalise the issues if the news media do not report them, either as a matter of policy or because they believe the public's appetite for those topics has been sated.

Reports indicated that further rioting, on a reduced scale, occurred in some areas in 1982, 1983 and 1984. In 1982 the media's attention was riveted on the South Atlantic and very few accounts of any disorders appeared in the press. One researcher wrote in *The Sunday Times* on 4 July 1982:

> Many people in Toxteth believe that police and media are in a conspiracy of silence. 'Last summer's riots didn't stop', they say; 'they went on in different forms. It was the reporting that stopped'.

But Neil Lyndon did not himself feel there was a conspiracy of silence by the media; rather he considered that this failure to mention the events he had witnessed indicated something far worse:

> A 100-strong, stone-throwing mob, fighting riot police around a sealed-off major thoroughfare, has come to be seen as an unexceptional event in a section of major British city. It such a riot goes unreported to society at large once, it can happen again and again. By such means, among many others, is a ghetto created — when the events that occur within it are not judged by the normal standards which pertain without.

Of course, in 1985 and 1986 urban unrest again burst on to the front pages of the newspapers, refocusing attention on conditions in Britain's inner cities. But there seemed to be less surprise at the disorder and, as outlined earlier in this chapter, the predominant response in the media was a call for a 'get-tough policy', rather than a considered analysis of the root causes of the unrest, and an assessment of the lack of action since 1981.

The consequences of the failure to tackle the problems highlighted by the disorders may indeed be the development of ghettos, characterised by deprivation and neglect, tough policing and disintegrating political authority. The results of an increased repudiation of political authority are likely to affect the wider political system. Citizen indifference and open defiance may occur, as apathy and indignation succeed each other.

Both indifference and defiance are likely to prove costly to the government, and this point is further discussed in the next chapter. Indifference results in declining income through taxes, and lack of response to programmes which require citizen participation, such as those to tackle rising crime or voluntary schemes to administer the welfare system. Indignation and 'smouldering apathy' are likely to erupt occasionally as defiance and further violence, and although this can usually be contained it will sometimes spill out of the inner city into other areas. And, indeed, if this path is taken — if the governmental agenda does not deal seriously with racism, urban deprivation, political exclusion and police misconduct — it may become more and more appropriate to employ the language of warfare in discussions of Britain's inner cities.

Notes

This is a revised and amended version of an article which was entitled 'Going through the motions: the political agenda, the 1981 riots and the Scarman inquiry'. This was published in *Parliamentary Affairs*, Vol. 38, No. 4 (Autumn 1985), pp. 409–22.

1. For a discussion of the news media's coverage of the 1981 disorders see G. Murdock, 'Reporting the riots: images and impact', in J. Benyon (ed.), *Scarman and After*, Oxford: Pergamon Press, 1984, pp. 73–95.
2. Home Office, *Statistical Bulletin*, 20/82, 13 October 1982, pp. 1–2, and table 2, p. 9.
3. For discussion of the political agenda see: R. W. Cobb and C. D. Elder, *Participation in American Politics: The Dynamics of Agenda Building*, Baltimore: John Hopkins University Press, 1975; R. W. Cobb, J. Ross and M. H. Ross, 'Agenda building as a comparative process', *American Political Science Review*, 1976, pp. 126 *et seq.*; W. Solesbury, 'The environmental agenda', *Public Administration*, Vol. 54, Winter 1976; J. J. Richardson and A. G. Jordan, *Governing Under Pressure*, Oxford: Martin Robertson, 1979; J. T. Benyon, 'The riots, Lord Scarman and the political agenda', in Benyon, *Scarman and After*, *supra* note 1; D. T. Studlar, 'Non-white policy preferences, political participation and the political agenda in Britain', in Z. Layton-Henry and P. Rich (eds), *Race, Government and Politics in Britain*, Basingstoke: Macmillan, 1986; M. Crenson, *The Un-Politics of Air Pollution*, Baltimore: John Hopkins University Press, 1975.
4. Cobb and Elder, *Participation in American Politics*, *supra* note 3, pp. 12–16.
5. This scheme is based on that developed by Cobb, Ross and Ross, 'Agenda building as a comparative process', *supra* note 3, pp. 127–36, although they define the models slightly differently.
6. Solesbury, 'The environmental agenda', *supra* note 3, p. 384.
7. H. L. Nieburg, 'Violence, law and the informal polity', *Journal of Conflict Resolution*, 1969, pp. 192 *et seq.*; H. L. Nieburg, 'The threat of violence and social change', *American Political Science Review*, 1962, pp. 865 *et seq.*
8. E. E. Schattschneider, *The Semi-Sovereign People*, New York: Holt, Rinehart and Winston, 1960, p. 71.
9. P. Bachrach and M. Baratz, 'Decisions and nondecisions: an analytical framework', *American Political Science Review*, 1963, pp. 632 *et seq.*; P. Bachrach and M. Baratz, *Power and Poverty: Theory and Practice*, New York: Oxford University Press, 1970.
10. Solesbury, 'The environmental agenda', *supra* note 3, pp. 387–92; Richardson and Jordan, *Governing under Pressure*, *supra* note 3, pp. 70–3 and 77–91; R. Chapman (ed.), *The Role of Commissions in Policy Making*, London: Allen and Unwin, 1973; R. E. Wraith and G. B. Lamb, *Public Inquiries as an Instrument of Government*, London: Allen and Unwin, 1971.
11. For a discussion of a number of these points see J. K. Stringer and J. J. Richardson, 'Managing the political agenda: problem definition and policy making in Britain', *Parliamentary Affairs*, Vol. 33, Winter 1980.
12. For further discussion on current policing issues see J. Benyon and C. Bourn (eds), *The Police: Powers, Procedures and Proprieties*, Oxford: Pergamon Press, 1986.
13. See, for example, Department of the Environment, *The Urban Programme 1985*, London: DOE, June 1986.
14. Stringer and Richardson, 'Managing the political agenda', *supra* note 11, pp. 27–30.
15. Cobb and Elder, *Participation in American Politics*, *supra* note 3, p. 127.
16. M. Parkinson and J. Duffy, 'Government's response to inner-city riots: the minister for Merseyside and the Task Force', *Parliamentary Affairs*, Vol. 37, Winter 1984, pp. 76–96.
17. Solesbury, 'The environmental agenda', *supra* note 3, p. 396; or put another way: 'many a dusty committee report must be lying on the shelves of Whitehall departments labelled "problem gone away" (or at least "no-one of political importance interested in problem")', Richardson and Jordan, *Governing under Pressure*, *supra* note 3, p. 87.
18. T. Benton, 'Objective' interests and the sociology of power', *Sociology*, 1981, p. 163.
19. S. Lukes, *Power: A Radical View*, London: Macmillan 1974, p. 22.
20. A. Downs, 'Up and down with ecology — The "issue–attention cycle"', *The Public Interest*, Summer 1972. This account of the 'issue–attention cycle' is drawn from that given by Downs on pp. 39–41.

CHAPTER 20

The roots of urban unrest

JOHN BENYON and JOHN SOLOMOS

The authors of the essays in this book are drawn from a variety of backgrounds and experiences, but there seems to be a good deal of common ground in their views and analysis. There is agreement on the need to view violent disorders in the broader political, social, cultural and economic contexts in which they occur. The contributors tend to reject a number of the predominant explanations, mentioned in Chapters 1, 2 and 19, which were put forward after the recent disturbances. For example, the view that the riots were a conspiracy organised by agitators or drug dealers is not regarded as a satisfactory explanation, and there is little support for the theses that 'human wickedness' or greed and criminal gain were the causes of the disorder.

There is consensus that urban unrest arises under certain conditions. Five key characteristics of the areas in which the rioting has occurred are highlighted in Chapter 2, and these are high unemployment, widespread deprivation, manifest racial discrimination and disadvantage, political exclusion and powerlessness and common mistrust of, and hostility to, the police. These features are stressed, with varying degrees of emphasis, by nearly all the contributors to this book, and they were described by Lord Scarman in *The Brixton Disorders* as providing:

> a set of social *conditions*, which create a predisposition toward violent protest. Where deprivation and frustration exist on the scale to be found among the young black people of Brixton, the probability of disorder must, therefore, be strong.[1]

Social injustice: the central thread

These five characteristics indicate the roots of urban unrest, but how are they translated into disorder and violent action? Clearly, in Britain and in other countries people may experience one or more of these forms of disadvantage without taking part in riots and protest. The consensus among the contributors to this book is that unemployment, deprivation, racism, political exclusion and police malpractices are conditions under which unrest may occur, but it is necessary to look for other factors which help to explain the outbreak of disorder.

The central feature seems to be a sense of injustice by those suffering from racism, deprivation and police activity. Urban unrest is a violent reaction to events and experiences. It requires a stimulus to set it in motion. The tinder is created by the underlying conditions, but it is ignited by a particular event which provides the spark. Almost inevitably the immediate precipitant event which triggers unrest involves police officers. As described in Chapter 1, in 1980, 1981, 1985 and 1986 each major outbreak of disorder was triggered by an incident involving the police and black people. In each case the police action was seen as yet another example of unjust treatment, which then led to a violent reaction.

Social injustice is the central thread which runs through the contributions in this book, and it is closely linked to the issue of racism in British society. The chapters by Stuart Hall and Martin Kilson set the tone in this respect — a point emphasised in Lord Scarman's reflections in Chapter 15. Considering the contrasting experiences of Britain and the United States, both Hall and Kilson stress that the root cause of urban unrest can be found in the exclusion of specific groups from the processes of political, social and cultural incorporation, which enable societies to reproduce themselves in an orderly fashion. As this exclusion operates systematically over a long period, it produces a deep sense of injustice in the excluded groups. It is this sense of injustice which can be provoked into a violent form of protest.

It is clear that both in Britain and the United States specific groups of people are excluded. Evidence discussed in many of the chapters in this book shows that racism has systematically excluded Britain's black citizens from equal participation in society. The political, social and economic environments have increasingly put black people under pressure, and in such a context the lack of remedies through mainstream institutions makes violent outbursts likely. Experiences in the United States, described by Martin Kilson and Richard Thomas in Chapters 4 and 17, are salient to the British case. In the US the interrelationship between race and urban crisis has been at the centre of discussions of unrest for over 20 years. A huge volume of research conducted in the United States since the early 1960s supports the argument that the social and political marginalisation of black and other minority groups created tensions which on occasions resulted in outbreaks of violent protest against the injustices which were being experienced. Kilson and Thomas show that notable successes for the black community were achieved, and it is clear that the US riots tended to push some sections of the political establishment towards greater concern about urban problems. However, it is also evident that there is still a long way to go before black people in the United States are treated equally, and are able to share fully in the benefits of American society.

Injustice is thus the central root of urban unrest. It may arise from racism, high unemployment, poor housing, urban deprivation, political exclusion or police misconduct. There are, though, five other factors which may be associated with these issues and with urban unrest. These are ineffectiveness of government policies, a decrease in levels of identity with the polity, few opportunities for political participation, falling levels of voluntary consent and a decline in perceptions of the regime's legitimacy.

Ineffective government programmes

There seem to be three senses in which government ineffectiveness may occur: the machinery may not function effectively, the policies may not produce the intended results and the outcomes may fail to meet citizens' expectations. The inner-city policies of successive governments seem to have been ineffective in each of these ways. The agencies and institutions involved have functioned ineffectively and resources have not been allocated efficiently, the deterioration in urban conditions has continued, and consequently promises, and people's expectations, have not been met. Lord Scarman pointed this out in November 1981:

> The failure of the many attempts over the last three decades to tackle the problem of inner-city decline successfully is striking . . . it is noticeable that large sums have been spent to little apparent effect . . .
> The lack of an effective coordinated approach . . . conflicting policies and priorities . . . appear to have been a frequent source of confusion and reduced drive.[2]

Many of the contributors in this book comment on the ineffectiveness of inner-city policies in the 5 years since *The Brixton Disorders* was published. The lack of effective action has affected all those living in Britain's decaying urban areas, but black people in particular have suffered.

As Benyon points out in Chapter 2, poverty and hardship do not necessarily in themselves lead to protest. Discontent is likely to be strong when there is a gap between what people experience and that which they have been led to expect. Offe has pointed to 'the increasingly visible conflict between the promise and the experience, form and content, of state policies',[3] and this can lead to an increasing level of disenchantment. Millikan and Blackmer suggested that an outcome may be 'a revolution of rising frustrations'.[4] It has been claimed[5] that frustration can result in withdrawal and apathy, or in bitterness and anger which may result in an outburst of aggression, and this interpretation was applied by Davies, Gurr and others to the riots in the 1960s in the United States.[6]

The repeated failure of government policies to bring the promised material improvements seems likely to result in discontent and anger, and this may be particularly evident amongst young people. Ambitions and expectations tend to be greater when people are young, and their aspirations may be reinforced at school, and by advertising images of the affluent society. In short, young men and women living in disadvantaged circumstances in Britain's cities seem especially likely to resent the ineffectiveness of government programmes. This may affect their perceptions of identity with the polity, their view of the legitimacy of its rules and agents and their voluntary consent to its actions. As a recent Home Office study pointed out:

> Where any social group perceives government institutions as being indifferent to its needs, the authority and legitimacy of social controls ultimately promulgated by those same institutions will be increasingly questioned.[7]

Questions of identity

An important aspect of any society is the extent to which its members identify with the polity, the political system and prevailing values.[8] Central questions are whether people share a common identity in terms of shared norms and values, and whether their group identity is more salient than their identification with the polity. The integrity of the national political and social systems may be threatened if the primary identity of significant numbers of citizens is with values which conflict with those of the polity. The formation of national political identity involves the integration into the polity of disparate groups, and the acceptance of a common set of values and beliefs. This broad consensus, about goals and modes of pursuing them, relates to the perceived legitimacy of the regime and its agents, and to the level of consent, and also to institutional participation, and the effectiveness of the system's outputs.

If the attempts by governments to tackle unemployment, racial discrimination, and inner-city disadvantage are regarded as ineffective and lacking in commitment, the level of identification which people so affected have with the political system and its predominant values may diminish. Why should people who are excluded identify with the system which is excluding them? Lowenthal has argued that there is an 'underlying cultural crisis' which is visible in 'the increasingly defective functioning of the process of socialisation and of the formation of identity'.[9]

Identity with group norms may become pre-eminent if the integrity of society's rules, institutions and values becomes undermined. Some behaviour regarded as deviant elsewhere in society may become accepted within particular groups, leading for example to increased levels of crime or a willingness to participate in violent action. Evidence gathered in the aftermath of the US riots in the 1960s revealed considerable support for the rioters, particularly amongst other black Americans in large cities. McCord and Howard reported that 52 per cent of people surveyed in Oakland, and 30 per cent of those in Houston, considered the riots were 'helpful'. A study of the views of black people in 15 cities found that over half were in sympathy with the rioters.[10] Similar figures were reported after the riots in England in 1981. A poll of young people showed that 28 per cent considered the disorders were justified, and 44 per cent agreed with the statement 'violence to bring about political change can be justified' (41 per cent disagreed; 15 per cent did not know).[11] These findings were in marked contrast with polls of the whole population which showed strong disapproval of the riots.

Black people in Britain suffer from urban deprivation, compounded by racial discrimination. They experience high rates of unemployment, and those in work tend to earn low wages. Afro-Caribbean and Asian people also experience great disadvantage in housing, as a result of discriminatory practice.[12] Other measures of disadvantage similarly show how members of the ethnic minorities fare consistently badly, and this led Lord Scarman to state:

> Racial disadvantage is a fact of current British life. It was, I am equally sure, a significant factor in the causation of the Brixton disorders. Urgent action is needed if it is not to become an endemic ineradicable disease threatening the very survival of our society.[13]

Urban disadvantage in general, and racial disadvantage and discrimination in particular, may lead to a decrease in people's identity with the values and institutions of the political system. Such a lack of identity with the regime is likely to result in diminished consent and perhaps a repudiation of political authority, it may affect the effectiveness of government policies and it has implications for political participation.

Opportunities for participation

The importance of citizen participation in political systems is widely recognised. In democracies elections are a vital means of legitimising the government and the regime, and of ensuring voluntary obedience. Political participation, through institutions such as parties and pressure groups, is a principal method whereby demands are articulated, and it may facilitate the governmental process through the voicing of people's wants and expectations.

However political participation is not limited to formal channels, and indeed need not be legitimate. As discussed in Chapter 2, British history reveals many instances of popular disturbances and violent protest. Of course there were few opportunities for institutional participation for the vast majority of people, especially in the towns, and increasingly from 1790 onwards reform of the suffrage was a cause of great agitation. Many historians now regard much of the rioting during this period as 'collective bargaining by riot',[14] whereby workers could bring pressure to bear on their employers, or more generally as a means of political participation for those with no other opportunities of political voice.

The most obvious means for enabling, but also constraining, participation are elections, parties, trade unions and pressure groups. These tend to reinforce identification with the rules, procedures and values of the polity, they enable the articulation of demands, they facilitate consent and they strengthen acceptance of the legitimacy of the political system. Inner-city areas tend to have few institutions through which participation can be channelled and demands made. If branches of political parties exist at all they are often virtually moribund, and trade unions are not effective means of voicing protest at racism and urban decay — even if someone has a job and joins a union. Elections for the city or borough council may occur annually, but these are not effective means for people to voice specific grievances.

The absence of opportunities for institutional participation by local people has been commented on in many studies of inner-city areas. The Liverpool Inner Area Study reported in 1977:

> There is not sufficient delegation or public involvement to allow expression of the needs and values of the inner-city area in local authority services.[15]

And 4 years later, in the wake of serious disorder in part of the area, Lord Scarman made similar comments: 'Local communities should be more fully involved in the decisions which affect them. A "top-down" approach to regeneration does not seem to have worked.'[16] He called for full and effective involvement and greater consultation — in short, for more political voice for local residents.

As a result of the lack of opportunities for political participation, new modes of representation are developing in some areas. Examples include tenants' associations, community groups, squatters' organisations, unemployed workers' centres and legal advice offices. It has been reported that:

> Much of the action is sporadic, many of the associations ephemeral or schismatic. But the climate of doubt and criticism, the availability of ideologies stressing the need for participation . . . ensures easy regeneration of grass-roots political activity.[17]

The black communities in many inner-city areas have also founded organisations for mutual support and the articulation of grievances. Devon Thomas has described how the Brixton community is 'active and dynamic' and has been 'creating structures and institutions to cope with its members' needs'.[18] However, the extent to which these groups are able to influence local and national policies has still to be demonstrated, and a fundamental factor remains the low level of black political representation, to which attention was drawn by Lord Scarman.[19] So despite the establishment of pressure groups and self-help organisations, according to George Greaves, the Principal Community Relations Officer in Lambeth:

> Black people are hardly ever in a position to influence decisions made about them — decisions which sometimes alter the course of their lives in fundamental ways. They are hardly ever consulted about matters which affect them, and on the rare occasions when they are consulted they feel their advice goes unheeded.[20]

Layton-Henry has outlined four ways in which black political participation may develop.[21] First, there may be a gradual integration into the class structure and involvement in associated institutions such as the political parties, trade unions, chambers of trade and professional associations. There is evidence that this is occurring and, for example, the PSI survey reported that among male employees 64 per cent of West Indians and 59 per cent of Asians are trade union members, compared with 57 per cent of whites.[22] In terms of party support, those members of the ethnic minorities who express a view tend to support the Labour Party. In the General Election of 1983 the Gallup Poll reported the shares of the ethnic minority support as Conservative: 20.5 per cent; Labour: 64 per cent; Alliance: 14 per cent.[23] It should be noted, though, that the number of non-whites, especially Afro-Caribbeans, who did not vote was significant.

A second possibility is that continuing racial disadvantage and discrimination will encourage black unity, a separate identity and political action on this basis. A third view is that the racism and disadvantage will cause growing disenchantment and withdrawal from participation in the political system. There is some evidence to support both these possibilities, but in general Afro-Caribbeans and Asians seem to believe that they should participate in multiracial organisations and mainstream political processes. For example 80 per cent of West Indians and 94 per cent of Asians agreed with the statement in the PSI survey: 'People of Asian/West Indian origin should join in political organisations alongside white people.'

The fourth possibility is based on the influential work of Katznelson, which hypothesised that paternalistic buffer institutions had been established by governments to neutralise black demands and to keep race off the national political agenda.[24] However, Layton-Henry argues, the notion that these institutions prevent black people from exercising political influence is not convincing. Some may choose to participate in these organisations, others may form pressure and defensive groups, and yet others may join political parties and seek election to representative positions. But the number who become involved in any of these ways in inner-city areas is likely to be small while doubts remain about the likelihood of having any significant impact on government decisions. In general, opportunities for political participation through formal channels, such as parties and pressure groups, tend to be relatively infrequent in inner-city areas. And, as Huntingdon suggested,[25] unless the development of opportunities and institutions for participation keeps pace with the underlying pressure for the articulation of demands, problems for the political order may ensue.

Participation is important not only to legitimise the regime, and to aid the effectiveness of its performance, but also to enhance identification with the polity. The integration of groups may not be straightforward; it requires receptivity and flexibility in the system. There is a two-way relationship between identity and participation: the latter facilitates the former, and vice-versa. Institutional participation makes integration more likely and also lowers the probability of dramatic non-institutional participation, or voice, in the form of violent protest.

> In any institutionalised society the participation of new groups reduces tensions; through participation, new groups are assimilated into the political order.[26]

The implications of a lack of political institutions and procedures in inner-city areas may be serious; the results may be alienation, withdrawal, resentment or anger:

> Apathy and indignation succeed each other: the twin children of the absence of authoritative political symbols and institutions.[27]

Consent on the ebb

Opportunities for participation are related to the level of consent. Citizens are more likely to agree to comply with decisions about which they have formally voiced their opinions. Consent is also influenced by other considerations such as the legitimacy of the system, and identity with the polity, and institutional participation is likely to be important in establishing these factors. According to Almond and Verba their five-nation study revealed that:

The opportunity to participate in political decisions is associated with greater satisfaction with that system and with greater general loyalty . . . the sense of ability to participate in politics appears to increase the legitimacy of a system.[28]

Participation is a feature of the process of socialisation, or 'politicisation' as Easton terms it,[29] whereby identification with the prevailing values, rules and procedures is developed. It is a means of generating loyalty and allegiance to the political system, and so is important in determining consent and acquiescence. The low level of participation in institutionalised processes in Britain's inner cities may thus detrimentally affect the extent to which citizens voluntarily consent to government policies, to the state's agents, and to the rules and procedures of the regime.

The consent of citizens is also less likely to be forthcoming if the government or political system is perceived to be performing ineffectively.[30] Conversely, if consent is not voluntarily given this may adversely affect government effectiveness. If people do not voluntarily do what government wishes of them, the administration must seek to compel them, which may prove to be expensive or impractical.

The ineffectiveness of attempts to combat inner-city decay and disadvantage may tend to diminish the consent of citizens in these areas. A similar effect may be brought about by a low level of identity with the regime, its goals and prevailing values. Government policies which are felt to condone or perpetuate racial discrimination and disadvantage are likely to conflict with values of many citizens in inner-city areas, resulting in a decline in consent.

There is considerable evidence for the decrease in levels of voluntary consent in urban areas. Some commentators have highlighted the higher levels of crime, while others have cited the lack of cooperation with the police. Lord Scarman reported that in Brixton the police had 'not succeeded in achieving the degree of public approval and respect necessary for the effective fulfilment of their functions and duties',[31] and the PSI study of the Metropolitan Police found a 'disastrous' lack of confidence in the police among young black people.[32]

This lack of consent may be manifest as eruptions of violent disorder, and as a refusal to comply with directives and rules. This will adversely affect the way government can be carried out, for as Connolly points out:

In a highly structured order, the withdrawal of allegiance . . . will carry profound implications for the performance of the economy, the tax levels required by the state, the scope of the state's police functions, and the ability of the state to bear the burdens imposed upon it. It may, in short, impair the state's ability to play its legitimate role in the current order of things.[33]

If consent declines, the government and its agencies find it necessary to employ coercion. Since 1979 expenditure on policing and the criminal justice system has more than doubled — a rise in real terms of over 30 per cent — and the Home Office budget for 1987/88 is over £5.5 billion. But coercion is not only expensive, it may also be ineffective or even counterproductive. The use of coercion, such as well-equipped and highly paid police officers, may suppress urban unrest temporarily, but research suggests that these sorts of measures usually result in even greater frustration and feelings of injustice, leading to further outbreaks of violent disorders.[34] Furthermore, coercion may undermine the legitimacy of the regime.

Perceptions of legitimacy

Essentially, legitimacy is the quality of being lawful or right. A claim that something is legitimate rests upon the assertion that it is proper according to rules or principles, and a government and its behaviour can be evaluated in this way. However, although the Constitution provides a means for judgement on the legitimacy of an administration's actions, the rules and principles may be interpreted in different ways. Dahrendorf has offered the following view:

> A government is legitimate if what it does is right both in the sense of complying with certain fundamental principles, and in that of being in line with prevailing cultural values.[35]

The behaviour and actions of a government are important sources of its legitimacy. This seems to be true in two senses. If it conducts itself properly, that is according to accepted rules and principles, its legitimacy will be reinforced. And so too, if its performance is adjudged to be right, according to prevailing values and expectations, its legitimacy will be strengthened.[36]

Effective performance is a means whereby citizens will ascribe legitimacy to the government and to the system, and so too is identity with the polity and its values. Institutional participation is a means of realising identity, effectiveness and consent, but it is also directly a source of legitimacy, through elections, groups and other organisations. These relationships are described by Lowenthal:

> The legitimacy of a political order requires, in addition to the clarity, consistency, and effective functioning of the legally established procedures, two things: a value consensus between the governing . . . and the governed, and a confidence of the governed, rooted in their experience, that this procedure will normally promote successful action in the direction of those common values.[37]

From Lowenthal's description it can be seen how the legitimacy of the British political order is likely to be severely strained as a result of racial discrimination and disadvantage, urban decay and dereliction, unemployment, political exclusion and police misconduct. 'Effective functioning of the legally established procedures' is doubtful in a number of respects, such as racism, police malpractice, and lack of opportunities for institutional participation. The declining levels of identity, and the increasingly wide gulf between people's experiences and prospects in the inner cities and those elsewhere, undermine the 'value consensus' and 'the confidence of the governed'. The notion of 'a value consensus' implies reasonably high levels of consent and compliance, but there is evidence that these have declined in inner-city areas. Furthermore, Lowenthal's criterion of 'normally successful action' is unlikely to be judged favourably by those living in Britain's inner cities, and particularly by black people. As Keith Thomas reported, in England crises of legitimacy:

> Have only arisen when the regime fails to deliver other goods expected of it — law and order, religious toleration, political participation or social justice.[38]

If, indeed, the legitimacy of the political order requires a value consensus, the confidence of the governed, and effective functioning, it is clear that these conditions are unlikely to be found amongst people experiencing racism, unemployment, social deprivation, police malpractice and political exclusion in Britain's inner cities.

Five wasted years

The contributions in this book, like many other analyses which have appeared since 1981, indicate that the roots of urban unrest are to be found in the political, social and economic exclusion which operates in Britain's inner cities, and which above all affects black people. The central aspects of this exclusion are racial discrimination, high unemployment, social disadvantage (especially low incomes, high rates of crime and poor housing), lack of political representation, and police malpractice.

The effects of this racial and urban disadvantage have been considerable on the six interrelated political factors. It seems no exaggeration to point to crises of statecraft and government in terms of the effectiveness of government policies, and the identity, participation, consent and perceptions of legitimacy by many citizens in Britain's inner cities. Most significantly there is a crisis of injustice in the urban areas, and this is the fundamental root of the recent urban unrest.

If these views, and the analysis of the contributors to this volume, are right it becomes evident that only a vigorous assault on these root causes will remove the reasons for riots in Britain's cities. However, it is now over five years since Lord Scarman stated '*urgent action* is required if the social conditions which underlay the disorders in Brixton and elsewhere are to be corrected',[39] and during that period there has been little, if any, evidence of such 'urgent action'. Indeed, as many authors in this collection point out, in a number of respects the underlying social conditions in Britain's inner cities have deteriorated. Unemployment is higher, housing is worse, incomes have fallen, crime is higher, and black people continue to suffer from racism and exclusion. As Usha Prashar argues in Chapter 13, there has been 'too much talk and not enough positive action'.

The five wasted years since 1981 have resulted in even greater disillusionment and disenchantment. So much was promised and yet so little has happened. The five wasted years have exacerbated the crisis of government effectiveness and legitimacy, and of citizens' identity, participation and consent, and claims of social justice have been further shaken by the dashed promises and palpable unfairness. Only one consistent response has been evident in the past five years, and that has been the provision of more resources, more training and more equipment for the police. Instead of tackling the roots of urban unrest the Government has spent five years building up force to deal with the manifestation of those root conditions. But this is like the doctors of yore who applied their quack treatments to deal with the symptoms of an ailment rather its causes, and in so doing often made the fundamental condition worse. By failing to diagnose the roots of urban unrest the British Government's remedy of using tough policing and criminal justice sanctions is merely tackling the symptoms of the disorder, and is liable to exacerbate the underlying malaise.

The approach of the present Government should come as no surprise. History shows that the usual response to violent protest and riots was repression and coercion. History also reveals that this course was normally ineffective, and that disorder only diminished when movement was made in the direction of the reforms which were demanded. The current regime is merely adopting the myopic approach of so many of its predecessors, and it will take a great deal of campaigning and pressure to bring about the necessary changes.

At least since 1979, the political climate has not been conducive to calls for positive action to deal with racism and social injustice, or for measures to combat the other aspects of urban and racial disadvantage identified in this volume. As the predominant political ideas have shifted to the right, so the probability of the required political action to tackle the roots of urban unrest has diminished. The Thatcher Governments have sought to decrease public expenditure, to enable lower taxation and the growth of an 'enterprise culture'. But public expenditure has grown greatly in some areas, such as social security payments for the unemployed, and spending on the police and defence. The main brunt of the retrenchment has fallen in areas such as housing and local government services. As John Clare, Herman Ouseley and others outline in this volume, the paltry aid for the inner cities, through the Urban Programme and other initiatives, has been dwarfed by the financial cuts applied to inner-city local authorities.

A gloomy prognosis

The auguries for the immediate future are not good. There is little, if any, evidence that the British Government is prepared to conduct a vigorous campaign against racism, urban disadvantage and social injustice. The political will and commitment is absent, and the necessary increases in public expenditure and changes in policies and the law run directly counter to the Thatcher Government's avowed intentions.

The excluded black and white citizens in the urban areas will continue to suffer deprivation and injustice. New alliances will be formed, which will seek to force the issues onto the political agenda but, as the account in Chapter 19 shows, issues initiated through outsider processes face particular difficulties. The growth of the voluntary sector, with its successful self-help activities, is likely to continue in the inner cities, and an increasing number of black people will achieve economic and social success and begin to form a 'black middle class'. Black people will be elected as Members of Parliament and as local councillors, but will find it difficult to mobilise national support for inner-city problems. Even if the Labour Party is elected to office it is far from clear that the necessary concerted effort to fight urban deprivation will be forthcoming. Certainly the inner cities will receive far greater support than at present, but a Labour Government will have many other demands made on it which are likely to dilute a whole-hearted initiative to combat the roots of urban unrest. In any case the return of a Conservative Government seems most probable.

It is difficult to be optimistic about the short-term future. At the end of his study of urban disadvantage in Hackney, Harrison comes to a gloomy prognosis:

> The British system is not self-correcting. Thus the process of polarisation may continue in intensity. Unless its present course is quickly and radically reversed, Britain could become a country as deeply and destructively divided as many in Latin America. Revolution does not seem likely, rather a chaos of individual and sectional pathologies and disruptions. . . . Police methods will become the primary response to socio-economic grievances. As the threats to law and order grow, so will the pressure for stricter measures to contain them, reducing the civil liberties of everyone.[40]

As Harrison points out, this is already happening in our cities, and far-reaching reforms and committed action are needed to halt the trends. It has been argued in this chapter that six perceptible trends are evident: growing ineffectiveness of government programmes, a decrease in levels of identity with the polity, falling opportunities for political participation, declining voluntary consent, diminishing perceptions of the regime's legitimacy and growing experience of injustice. The conditions which have given rise to these factors are unemployment, social deprivation, racial discrimination and disadvantage, political exclusion and powerlessness and police malpractices.

Riots are cathartic — they result in the release of pressures and tension. But violent outbursts are bound to recur unless the underlying roots of urban unrest are removed, and so far there is little evidence that this is happening. The war against racism, deprivation and injustice in the cities, and against unemployment, crime and police misconduct, is a daunting one. Such a crusade will entail material sacrifices by the more affluent members of society, and will threaten some entrenched interests. But if urban violence is not to become endemic, and if British society is to profess liberty, compassion and civilised values, a committed campaign against the roots of urban unrest must be implemented. Unfortunately, as yet, there is little sign of any such commitment.

Notes

1. *The Brixton Disorders 10–12 April 1981: Report of an Inquiry by the Rt. Hon. the Lord Scarman, OBE*, London: HMSO, 1981 (Cmnd. 8427), para. 2.38.
2. *The Brixton Disorders*, *supra* note 1, paras 6.5–6.6.
3. C. Offe, *Contradictions of the Welfare State*, London: Hutchinson, 1984, p. 144; see also J. Habermas, *Legitimation Crisis*, Boston: Beacon Press, 1975.
4. M. Millikan and D. Blackmer (eds), *The Emerging Nations*, Boston: Little, Brown and Co., 1961, p. 41.
5. For example see A. Yates, *Frustration and Conflict*, New York: Wiley, 1962; K. Lewin, *A Dynamic Theory of Personality*, New York: McGraw-Hill, 1935; J. Dollard, *et al.*, *Frustration and Aggression*, New Haven: Yale University Press, 1974; see also contributions in L. Masotti and D. Bowen (eds), *Riots and Rebellion*, California: Sage, 1968.
6. T. Gurr, *Why Men Rebel*, New Jersey: Princeton University Press, 1970; J. Davies, 'The J-curve of rising and declining satisfactions as a cause of revolution and rebellion', in H. Graham and T. Gurr (eds), *Violence in America*, London: Sage, 1979.
7. S. Field, 'Urban disorders in Britain and America', in S. Field and P. Southgate (eds), *Public Disorder*, London: HMSO, 1982 (Home Office Research Study No. 72), p. 33.
8. For a discussion of the significance of identity, and consideration of crises of identity, legitimacy, participation, distribution and penetration in the development of Western States, see L. Binder *et al.*, *Crises and Sequences in Political Development*, New Jersey: Princeton University Press, 1971; R. Grew (ed.), *Crises of Political Development in Europe and the United States*, New Jersey: Princeton University Press, 1978.
9. R. Lowenthal, *Social Change and Cultural Crisis*, New York: Columbia University Press, 1984, p. 34.
10. W. McCord and J. Howard, 'Negro opinions in three riot cities', *American Behavioural Scientist*, Vol. 11, No. 4, 1968, pp. 24–27; A. Campbell and H. Schuman, *Racial Attitudes in Fifteen American Cities*, supplementary studies for the Kerner Commission, Washington: US Government, 1968; D. Sears and J. McConahay, *The Politics of Violence: the New Urban Blacks and the Watts Riot*, Boston: Houghton Mifflin, 1973.

11. MORI poll for Granada Television, reported in *The Sunday Times*, 6 September 1981; see also MORI poll in the *Daily Star*, 31 August 1981 and NOP poll in the *Observer*, 15 November 1981.
12. See for example C. Brown, *Black and White Britain: The Third PSI Study*, London: Heinemann, 1984; J. Rex, 'Disadvantage and discrimination in cities', in J. Benyon (ed.), *Scarman and After*, Oxford: Pergamon Press, 1984, pp. 191–9.
13. *The Brixton Disorders*, supra note 1, para 9.1.
14. E. Hobsbawm, *Primitive Rebels: Studies in Archaic Forms of Social Movement in the 19th and 20th Centuries*, Manchester: Manchester University Press, 1959; G. Rude, *The Crowd in History*, London: Wiley, 1964; E. Thompson, *The Making of the English Working Class*, Harmondsworth: Penguin, 1968.
15. Department of the Environment, *Change or Decay: Final Report of the Liverpool Inner Area Study*, London: HMSO, 1977.
16. *The Brixton Disorders*, supra note 1, para 6.7.
17. B. Elliot and D. McCrone, *The City: Patterns of Domination and Conflict*, London: Macmillan, 1982, p. 133.
18. D. Thomas, 'Black initiatives in Brixton', in Benyon (ed.), *Scarman and After*, supra note 12, p. 188.
19. *The Brixton Disorders*, supra note 1, para 2.36; see also comments by K. Young, 'The challenge to local government', in Benyon (ed.), *Scarman and After*, supra note 12, pp. 223–4.
20. G. Greaves, 'The Brixton disorders', in Benyon (ed.), *Scarman and After*, supra note 12, p. 71.
21. Z. Layton-Henry, *The Politics of Race in Britain*, London: Allen and Unwin, 1984, pp. 167–78.
22. Brown, *Black and White Britain*, supra note 12, pp. 169–70 and 217.
23. Layton-Henry, *The Politics of Race in Britain*, supra note 21, pp. 171–2.
24. I. Katznelson, *Black Men, White Cities*, London: Oxford University Press, 1973.
25. S. Huntingdon, *Political Order in Changing Societies*, New Haven: Yale University Press, 1968.
26. *Ibid.*, p. 198.
27. *Ibid.*, p. 88.
28. G. Almond and S. Verba, *The Civic Culture: Political Attitudes and Democracy in Five Nations*, New Jersey: Princeton University Press, 1963, p. 253.
29. D. Easton, 'An approach to the analysis of political systems', *World Politics*, Vol. 9, 1957, pp. 383–400.
30. R. Rose, 'Ungovernability: is there fire behind the smoke?' *Political Studies*, Vol. 27, No. 3, 1979, pp. 351–70, pursues these points in detail.
31. *The Brixton Disorders*, supra note 1, para. 4.70.
32. *Police and People in London*, Vol. 1: D. J. Smith, *A Survey of Londoners*, London: Policy Studies Institute, 1983 (PSI No. 618), pp. 325–7; see also S. Field, *The Attitudes of Ethnic Minorities*, London: HMSO, 1984 (Home Office Research study No. 80), pp. 29–31; P. Stevens and C. Willis, *Ethnic Minorities and Complaints Against the Police*, London: Home Office, 1981 (Research and Planning Unit Paper 5).
33. W. Connolly, 'The dilemma of legitimacy', in W. Connolly (ed.), *Legitimacy and the State*, Oxford: Blackwell, 1984, p. 225.
34. See for example, A. Buss, *The Psychology of Aggression*, New York: Wiley, 1961; National Advisory Committee on Criminal Justice Standards and Goals, *Disorders and Terrorism*, Washington: US Government, 1976; C. Johnson, *Revolutionary Change*, London: University of London Press, 1968; see also supra note 5.
35. R. Dahrendorf, 'Effectiveness and legitimacy: on the "governability" of democracies', *The Political Quarterly*, Vol. 51, No. 4, 1980, p. 397.
36. Grew (ed.), *Crises of Political Development in Europe and the United States*, supra note 8, p. 20.
37. Lowenthal, *Social Change and Cultural Crisis*, supra note 9, pp. 88–9.
38. K. Thomas, 'The United Kingdom', in Grew (ed.), *Crises of Political Development in Europe and the United States*, supra note 8, p. 64.
39. *The Brixton Disorders*, supra note 1, para. 6.42; emphasis added.
40. P. Harrison, *Inside the Inner City*, Harmondsworth: Penguin, 1983, p. 435.

Select Bibliography

There is a large literature on topics such as policing, race relations, urban disadvantage and inner-city problems, and for a selection of books and articles in these areas readers are referred to bibliographies such as those on pages 263–74 of *Scarman and After* (Pergamon Press, 1984) and on pages 299–312 of *The Police: Powers, Procedures and Proprieties* (Pergamon Press, 1986). There is also a great deal of literature on the riots in the 1960s in the United States, and the following selection includes a number of important US books. There is much less written on recent urban unrest in Britain, and most of that which has appeared is in magazines and journals. The attention of readers is drawn to sources referenced at the end of many of the chapters in this book.

Alderson, J., *Policing Freedom*, Plymouth: Macdonald and Evans, 1979.
Alderson, J., *Law and Disorder*, London: Hamish Hamilton, 1984.
Banfield, E. C., 'Rioting mainly for fun and profit', in J. Q. Wilson (ed.), *The Metropolitan Enigma*, Cambridge, Mass.: Harvard University Press, 1968.
Banton, M., *Police–Community Relations*, London: Collins, 1973.
Banton, M., *Racial and Ethnic Competition*, Cambridge: Cambridge University Press, 1983.
Benyon, J. T. (ed.), *Scarman and After: Essays Reflecting on Lord Scarman's Report, the 1981 Riots and their Aftermath*, Oxford: Pergamon Press, 1984.
Benyon, J. T., 'Going through the motions: the political agenda, the 1981 riots and the Scarman inquiry', *Parliamentary Affairs*, **38**, 4, 409–22 (1985).
Benyon, J. T., *Legitimacy, Conflict, Order: Urban Disadvantage and Political Stability in Britain*, Colchester: European Consortium for Political Research, 1985.
Benyon, J. T., *A Tale of Failure: Race and Policing*, Policy Papers in Ethnic Relations No. 3, Warwick: Centre for Research in Ethnic Relations, 1986.
Benyon, J. T., 'Turmoil in the cities', *Social Studies Review*, **1**, 3, 3–8 (January 1986).
Benyon, J. T. and Bourn, C. (eds), *The Police: Powers, Procedures and Proprieties*, Oxford: Pergamon Press, 1986.
Bridges, L., 'Policing the urban wasteland', *Race and Class*, **XXV**, 2, 31–47 (1983).
Bristol TUC, *Slumbering Volcano? Report of an Inquiry into the Origins of the Eruption in St. Paul's, Bristol on 2 April 1980*, Bristol: TUC, 1981.
Brogden, M., *The Police: Autonomy and Consent*, London: Academic Press, 1982.
Brown, C., *Black and White Britain: The Third PSI Survey*, London: Heinemann, 1984.
Burgess, J. R., 'News from Nowhere: the press, the riots and the myth of the inner city', in J. R. Burgess and J. R. Gold (eds), *Geography, the Media and Popular Culture*, London: Croom Helm, 1985.
Button, J., *Black Violence*, Princeton: Princeton University Press, 1978.
Cain, M., *Society and the Policeman's Role*, London: Routledge and Kegan Paul, 1973.
Castells, M., *City, Class and Power*, London: Macmillan, 1978.
Cloward, R. A. and Piven, F. F., *The Politics of Turmoil: Essays on Poverty, Race and the Urban Crisis*, New York: Pantheon, 1974.
Clutterbuck, R., *Britain in Agony*, Harmondsworth: Penguin, 1980.
Clutterbuck, R., *The Media and Political Violence*, London: Macmillan, 1983.
Cowell, D. *et al.*, (eds), *Policing the Riots*, London: Junction Books, 1982.

Dahrendorf, R., *Law and Order*, London: Stevens, 1986.

Daniel, W. W., *Racial Discrimination in England*, Harmondsworth: Penguin, 1968.

Davis, T., 'The forms of collective racial violence', *Political Studies*, **34**, 1, 40–60 (1986).

Dear, G., *Report of the Chief Constable, West Midlands Police, on Handsworth/Lozells Disturbances — September 1985*, Birmingham: West Midlands Police, 1985.

Dummett, A., *A Portrait of English Racism*, Harmondsworth: Penguin, 1973.

Edelman, M., *Politics as Symbolic Action: Mass Arousal and Quiescence*, Chicago: Markham, 1971.

Edwards, J. and Batley, R., *The Politics of Positive Discrimination*, London: Tavistock, 1978.

Feagin, J. R. and Hahn, H., *Ghetto Revolts: The Politics of Violence in America's Cities*, New York: Macmillan, 1973.

Field, S. and Southgate, P., *Public Disorder*, Home Office Research Study No. 72, London: HMSO, 1982.

Fogelson, R. M., *Violence as Protest: a Study of Riots and Ghettos*, Garden City, New York: Doubleday, 1971.

Fowler, N., *After the Riots*, London: Davis-Poynter, 1979.

Freeman, M. D. A., 'Law and Order in 1984', *Current Legal Problems*, **37**, 175–231 (1984).

Gifford, Lord *et al.*, *The Broadwater Farm Inquiry Report*, London: Broadwater Farm Inquiry, 1986.

Glazer, N. and Young, K. (eds), *Ethnic Pluralism and Public Policy*, London: Heinemann, 1983.

Gordon, P., 'Police and black people in Britain: a bibliographic essay', *Sage Race Relations Abstracts*, **10**, 2, 3–33 (1985).

Graham, H. D. and Gurr, T. R. (eds), *Violence in America*, London: Sage, 1979.

Grew, R. (ed.), *Crises of Political Development in Europe and the United States*, Princeton: Princeton University Press, 1978.

Gurr, T., *Why Men Rebel*, New Jersey: Princeton University Press, 1970.

Hall, S., *Drifting into a Law and Order Society*, London: Cobden Trust, 1979.

Hall, S., 'Summer in the city', *New Socialist* (September/October 1981).

Hall, S., Critcher, C., Jefferson, T., Clarke, J. and Roberts, B., *Policing the Crisis: Mugging, the State and Law and Order*, London: Macmillan, 1978.

Hamnett, C., 'The conditions in England's inner cities on the eve of the 1981 riots', *Area*, **15**, 1, 7–13, (1983).

Hirschman, A. O., *Exit, Voice and Loyalty*, Cambridge, Mass.: Harvard University Press, 1970.

Home Office, *Racial Attacks: Report of a Home Office Study*, London: Home Office, November 1981.

Honderich, T., *Violence for Equality*, Harmondsworth: Penguin, 1980.

House of Commons, *Racial Disadvantage: Fifth Report from the Home Affairs Committee, Session 1980–81*, HC 424, London: HMSO, 1981.

Humphry, D., *Police Power and Black People*, London: Panther, 1970.

Husband, C. (ed.), *'Race' in Britain*, London: Hutchinson, 1982.

Hytner, B. *et al.*, *Report of the Moss Side Inquiry Panel to the Leader of the Greater Manchester Council*, Manchester: GMC, 30 September 1981.

Institute of Race Relations, *Police Against Black People*, London: IRR, 1979.

Jackson, P. M., Meadows, J. and Taylor, A. P., 'Urban fiscal decay in UK cities', *Local Government Studies*, **8**, 5 (September/October 1982).

Jacobs, B. D., *Black Politics and the Urban Crisis in Britain*, Cambridge: Cambridge University Press, 1986.

Joshua, H. and Wallace, T., *To Ride the Storm: The 1980 Bristol 'Riot' and the State*, London: Heinemann, 1983.

Kerner, O. *et al.*, *Report of the National Advisory Commission on Civil Disorders*, New York: Bantam Books, 1968.

Kettle, M. and Hodges, L., *Uprising!: The Police, the People and the Riots in Britain's Cities*, London: Pan, 1982.

Knapf, T. A., *Rumors, Race and Riots*, New Brunswick, N.J.: Transaction Books, 1975.

Layton-Henry, Z., *The Politics of Race in Britain*, London: Allen and Unwin, 1984.

Lea, J. and Young, J., *What is to be Done about Law and Order?*, Harmondsworth: Penguin, 1984.

Lipsky, M. and Olson, D., *Commission Politics: The Processing of Racial Crisis in America*, New Brunswick, N.J.: Transaction Books, 1977.

Masotti, L. and Bowen, D. (eds), *Riots and Rebellion*, California: Sage, 1968.

McClure, J., *Spike Island: Portrait of a Police Division*, London: Macmillan, 1980.

McCone, J. A. *et al.*, *Report of the Governor's Commission on the Los Angeles Riots*, Los Angeles: State of California, 1965.

Merseyside Police Authority, *The Merseyside Disturbances: the Role and Responsibility of the Police Authority*, Liverpool: Merseyside Police Authority, December, 1981.

Miles, R., 'The riots of 1958: notes on the ideological construction of "race relations" as a political issue in Britain', *Immigrants and Minorities*, **3**, 3, 252–75 (1984).

Miles, R. and Phizacklea, A., *White Man's Country*, London: Pluto Press, 1984.

Murdock, G., 'Reporting the riots: images and impact', in J. Benyon (ed.), *Scarman and After*, Oxford: Pergamon Press, 1984.

National Advisory Committee on Criminal Justice Standards and Goals, *Disorders and Terrorism: Report of the Task Force*, Washington: US Government Printing Office, 1976.

Newman, Sir K., *Public Order Review: Civil Disturbances 1981–85*, London: Metropolitan Police, 1986.

O'Connor, J., *The Fiscal Crisis of the State*, London: St. James, 1973.

Ouseley, H. *et al.*, *The System*, London: Runnymede Trust, 1981.

Ouseley, H. *et al.*, *A Different Reality: Report of the Review Panel*, Birmingham: West Midlands County Council, 1986.

Parkinson, M. and Duffy, J., 'Government's response to inner-city riots: the Minister for Merseyside and the Task Force', *Parliamentary Affairs*, 37, 76–96 (1984).

Peach, C., 'A geographical perspective on the 1981 urban riots in England', *Ethnic and Racial Studies*, **9**, 3, 396–411 (1986).

Policy Studies Institute, *Police and People in London*, 4 volumes, London: Policy Studies Institute, 1983.

Pryce, K., *Endless Pressure*, Harmondsworth: Penguin, 1979.

Race and Class, Special Double Issue, *Rebellion and Repression*, **XXIII**, 2/3 (Autumn 1981/Winter 1982).

Reicher, S. D., 'The St. Paul's riot: an explanation of the limits of crowd in terms of a social identity model', *European Journal of Social Psychology*, **14**, 1–21 (1983).

Reiner, R., *The Politics of the Police*, Brighton: Wheatsheaf, 1985.

Rex, J., *Race, Colonialism and the City*, London: Routledge and Kegan Paul, 1973.

Rex, J., 'The 1981 urban riots in Britain', *International Journal of Urban and Regional Research*, **6**, 1, 99–113 (1982).

Rex, J. and Moore, R., *Race, Community and Conflict*, London: Oxford University Press, 1967.

Rex, J. and Tomlinson, S., *Colonial Immigrants in a British City*, London: Routledge and Kegan Paul, 1979.

Rossi, P., Best, R. and Eidson, B., *The Roots of Urban Discontent*, New York: Wiley, 1974.

Scarman, Lord, *The British Disorders 10–12 April 1981: Report of an Inquiry by the Rt. Hon. the Lord Scarman, OBE*, London: HMSO, November 1981 (Cmnd. 8427).

Sears, D. O. and McConahay, J. B., *The Politics of Violence*, Boston: Houghton Mifflin, 1973.

Sherman, L., 'After the riots: police and minorities in the US 1970–1980', in N. Glazer and K. Young (eds), *Ethnic Pluralism and Public Policy*, London: Heinemann, 1983.

Silverman, J., *The Handsworth/Lozells Riots, 9–11 September 1985: Report of an Inquiry by Mr Julius Silverman*, Birmingham: Birmingham City Council, 1986.

Sivanandan, A., *A Different Hunger: Writings on Black Resistance*, London: Pluto Press, 1982.

Skolnick, J., *The Politics of Protest*, New York: Ballantine Books, 1969.

Smith, D. J., *Racial Disadvantage in Britain*, Harmondsworth: Penguin, 1977.

Solomos, J., 'Political language and violent protest: ideological and policy responses to the 1981 and 1985 riots', *Youth and Policy*, **18**, 12–24 (1986).

Tabb, W., *The Political Economy of the Black Ghetto*, New York: Norton, 1970.

Taylor, S., 'The Scarman Report and explanations of riots', in J. Benyon (ed.), *Scarman and After*, Oxford: Pergamon Press, 1984.

Tilly, C., *From Mobilisation to Revolution*, Reading, Mass.: Addison-Wesley, 1978.

Tilly, L. and Tilly, C. (eds), *Class Conflict and Collective Action*, London: Sage, 1981.

Tumber, H., *Television and the Riots*, London: British Film Institute, 1982.

United States Department of Justice, *Prevention and Control of Urban Disorders: Issues for the 1980s*, Washington: US Government Printing Office, 1980.

Unsworth, C., 'The riots of 1981: popular violence and the politics of law and order', *Journal of Law and Society*, **9**, 1, 63–85 (1982).

Young, K. and Connelly, N., *Policy and Practice in the Multiracial City*, London: Policy Studies Institute, 1981.

Index